THE PHILOSOPHY OF CLINT EASTWOOD

THE PHILOSOPHY OF CLINT EASTWOOD

Edited by

RICHARD T. MCCLELLAND

AND

BRIAN B. CLAYTON

UNIVERSITY PRESS OF KENTUCKY

Scholarly publisher for the Commonwealth,
serving Bellarmine University, Berea College, Centre College of Kentucky, Eastern Kentucky University, The Filson Historical Society, Georgetown College, Kentucky Historical Society, Kentucky State University, Morehead State University, Murray State University, Northern Kentucky University, Transylvania University, University of Kentucky, University of Louisville, and Western Kentucky University.

Editorial and Sales Offices: The University Press of Kentucky
663 South Limestone Street, Lexington, Kentucky 40508-4008
www.kentuckypress.com

18 17 16 15 14   5 4 3 2 1

Library of Congress Cataloging-in-Publication Data

The philosophy of Clint Eastwood / edited by Richard T. McClelland and Brian B. Clayton.
pages cm. — (The philosophy of popular culture)
Includes bibliographical references and index.
ISBN 978-0-8131-4263-0 (hardcover : alk. paper) — ISBN 978-0-8131-4264-7 (pdf) — ISBN 978-0-8131-4265-4 (epub)
1. Eastwood, Clint, 1930—Criticism and interpretation. I. McClelland, Richard T., 1947- editor of compilation.
PN2287.E37P48 2014
792.02'8092—dc23   2013039727

This book is printed on acid-free paper meeting the requirements of the American National Standard for Permanence in Paper for Printed Library Materials.

Manufactured in the United States of America.

Member of the Association of American University Presses

To Roger Ebert (1942–2013),
film critic par excellence

Contents

Introduction

Eastwood as Philosopher

Richard T. McClelland and Brian B. Clayton

It is easy to forget that philosophy has not always been practiced as it commonly is today. Most philosophers working today (and over the last couple of centuries) have been academics, usually in universities. There they teach, do research, write for publication, gather to present at professional meetings, and the like. Professional journals and monograph series are often sponsored by university departments, and conferences of all kinds commonly convene on university campuses worldwide. Most philosophers these days possess advanced degrees from universities (though increasingly such degrees do not ensure employment in academic positions). Considered in terms of these traditions of professional formation and deployment, there is ample reason to doubt that Clint Eastwood could plausibly be taken to be a philosopher or to be doing the work of a philosopher in his filmmaking (as actor, director, producer, and/or musician). After all, he does not possess an advanced degree in philosophy (or any closely related discipline), he does not work in an academic institution, he does not present his own creative work in the usual venues that philosophers use. Nevertheless, it is our view that Eastwood is doing substantial philosophical work in and by means of his films. It is the purpose of this introduction to say what we mean by this claim. In doing so we also wish to direct our readers toward the specific essays that make up this volume and some of their distinctive themes. It may be, also, that our notion of practical philosophy (which is what we think Eastwood is doing) will have application elsewhere in the arts and sciences.

One reason for thinking that Eastwood might be philosophizing in his creative work is almost purely negative. Philosophy has not always been practiced as it is today. Indeed, throughout most of its long history it was not. In the ancient world most philosophers (including the few women philosophers known to us) were persons of independent means, members of the wealthy social elites of their societies. Later on, when learning and education were dominated by religious institutions, especially in Europe, most philosophers were priests or monks (what the medieval world would have known as "clerks"), and some (such as Augustine) rose very high in the clerical orders of the medieval church. Later still, John Locke made his living as a professional civil servant working for the British Crown. Rousseau supported himself as a secretary and tutor to wealthy clients. Only in modern times have philosophers characteristically (indeed, almost exclusively) been found working as professors in universities (and related institutions).[1] We have no wish to introduce a spurious "demarcation problem" for philosophy. But we point out that our present institutional dispositions are entirely contingent and leave room for other approaches. Our view is that Clint Eastwood, notably as a director but also as an actor and a musician, carries out in his creative work substantive philosophical inquiry. Indeed, it has been the work done on this volume which has primarily persuaded its editors of this view. However, his philosophical work has a distinctive character, one that is often in sharp contrast with what ordinarily passes for "philosophy."

Philosophy as Craftsmanship

Eastwood is above all else a craftsman, an artisan, a maker of cultural artifacts.[2] Many of his films fall into readily recognizable genres. Several of our authors point to ways in which Eastwood either moves from one genre to another or calls a genre into question and offers even a radical revision of the tradition that belongs with the genre. Thus, Deborah Knight and George McKnight, in their essay, argue that over the course of his career Eastwood has shifted primarily from the genre of romance to that of tragedy. Such a shift, in their view, was needed to explore more deeply the responses of individual characters to injustice and other forms of suffering, especially injustice committed against innocent persons. Several of our authors have found Eastwood's *Unforgiven* (1992) an arresting critique and revision of the tradition of the Western. Erin Flynn argues that this revision draws out a view of the traditional Western that is implicit in the history of that genre. Richard Gilmore argues that revision of this genre/tradition was needed in order to construct narratives of redemption. Karen Hoffman looks widely at Eastwood's attitudes toward violence and in particular violence by gun, as well as to the vision of masculinity that underlies such violence. In her view

Eastwood has undergone a development that constitutes a vital critique of both gun violence (especially in terms of its social and psychological consequences to the gunman) and of the associated conception of masculinity, a development that stretches from the *Dirty Harry* movies (starting in 1971) to *Gran Torino* (2008), with *Unforgiven* as a pivotal moment in that development. David Calhoun also casts his revisionist net very widely, finding evidence for a shift in Eastwood's thinking about the value of so-called rugged individualism, an element of many of Eastwood's early films, already put to the question in *Play Misty for Me* (1971) and decisively rejected in *Million Dollar Baby* (2004) and *Gran Torino.*

These essays show Eastwood to be deeply embedded in his artistic consciousness and in the traditions of his craft, and possessed of a deep understanding of those traditions. But he is also a revisionist, someone who calls these traditions into question and offers alternatives to them.[3] As such, in our view he does the work of a philosopher, someone who can rise above the stream of practices that constitute a tradition and achieve a view of it that assesses its strengths and weaknesses. None of this work is explicit, verbally articulated by the artist. Rather, it is implicit in the work he produces, and especially in the set of multiple artifacts that constitute the revision itself.[4] But we may go further, for Eastwood himself insists that a primary purpose of his filmmaking is to tell stories. And these stories engage characters in moments of decision that affect the overall shape of their narrative contexts. And this adds further dimensions to the notion of practical philosophizing.

Characters, Decisions, and Narratives

Eastwood has said almost innumerable times that "the story is king." Moreover, he understands stories in a very traditional kind of way: as having beginnings, middles, and ends, all of which need to be presented if the story is to be told. This very traditional kind of narrative structure thus has an intelligible unity to it, the unity of structure both partially constituting the intelligibility of the story and determining how the story will unfold in the course of the film. The characters that he portrays, as an actor, and those whose actions he orders as director, only make sense in the context of the stories they inhabit and contribute to.[5] Of particular interest to him are stories in which characters make decisions that decisively alter the whole shape of their lives and thus the meaning of their stories. In *A Perfect World* (1993), for example, the story of Butch Haynes (Kevin Costner) is given to us in terms of just such decisions and their tragic effects on his own life. More easily overlooked but just as decisive for the shape of his life, are the decisions made by the boy Phillip "Buzz" Perry (T. J. Lowther), whom Haynes kidnaps. This film could also be easily fitted into the development concerning gun violence noted by Hoffman in her essay. And it has captured the sustained attention of Calhoun in his discussion of community and transcendence. Several of our authors have also noted how often Eastwood displays his stories in terms of their entanglement with the stories of other characters, the stories of Butch and Buzz being almost paradigmatic of this process. Knight and McKnight have gone so far as to argue that "the inexorable convergence of storylines" is an essential feature of Eastwood's aesthetics. The consequences of violence tracked in the films considered by Karen Hoffman also often depend on such intertwining of story lines. The recent film *Hereafter* (2010) has captured the attention of several of our authors, and one reason for this is the obvious care with which the plot gradually draws together three otherwise independent narratives, and the main characters that inhabit them. Indeed, here we see just how important decisions made by those main characters cause their lives to intertwine all the more strongly (although Marcus's narrative also disentangles from the others by the film's end). Doug McFarland, in his study of *Hereafter,* notes that solutions to the main life-problems of the characters only emerge as their lives intersect. And Calhoun's thesis about the ascendency of community in the later films of Eastwood also emphasizes human connectedness and the moral obligations that arise from it. These studies, and Eastwood's practices in this regard, underscore a point made by Alasdair MacIntyre: "we are never more (and sometimes less) than the co-authors of our own narratives. . . . We enter upon a stage which we did not design and we find ourselves part of an action that was not of our making. . . . An action is a moment in a possible or actual history or in a number of such histories. . . . The narrative of any one life is part of an interlocking set of narratives."[6] Something Eastwood does very skillfully in his capacity as director is to show (not just tell) how multiple lives might come to intersect in this way. As such, his style of direction (aided powerfully, of course, by the writing) constitutes not only an aesthetic but also a meta-story. If we are right to argue that Eastwood's oeuvre shows marked signs of coherent development across decades, then that body of work also constitutes a kind of meta-narrative on many of the major themes that preoccupy him.

Not surprising, given the demands of fitting such meta-stories into the confines of a two-hour film, and given the dramaturgical demands of such meta-stories, Eastwood focuses much of his storytelling on moments of decision. Here Calhoun's analysis of *The Bridges of Madison County* (1995) is very much a case in point. The very heart of this film is the decision made by Francesca Johnson (Meryl Streep) *not* to run away with Robert Kincaid (Eastwood). The consequences of this decision (itself counter to the much more commonly portrayed alternative) for all the other characters in the film are displayed with consummate skill and emotional force. Our view is that a further mark of the practical character of Eastwood's philosophizing is this focus on characters in moments of great decision-making. These are the kinds of decisions, as we see again and again in Eastwood's films, that alter the whole meaning of the characters' lives. In this way, his films constitute a kind of laboratory of moral psychology, exploring the labyrinthine paths of human desire and its frequently problematic outworking in narrative terms. Aristotle argued long ago that "choice discriminates character more than action does," and Eastwood follows a similar rule in his practice.[7] Richard Gilmore discovers a further dimension of such practices, exploring how desires may be hidden from us or disguised to us, and similarly finds Eastwood philosophizing about desires by means of images rather than words—in other words, implicitly rather than explicitly.[8] (Compare this to Clayton's notion of "visual argumentation.") Eastwood joins hands with Socrates and many other philosophers with this emphasis on self-knowledge and self-discovery, in keeping with the ancient Delphic prescription to "know thyself." (There is room for a further study of this theme in Eastwood's oeuvre, as also of the associated suffering and effort that such knowledge requires.) Gilmore also adds a very valuable insight regarding the moral complexity of Eastwood's characters (both acted and directed) as the very ground for the narrative surprises that often appear in his films. These dynamics of decision-making, together with their consequences for the meanings of whole lives, are not the only Aristotelian moments in Eastwood's work. And these further moments reveal yet other dimensions of the practical and implicit character of his philosophizing.

Flourishing, Law, and the Meaning of Loss

There are probably a host of ethical issues implicit in Eastwood's films.[9] Among them are concerns with justice, or more properly, with injustice, as we have already noted. Injustice, especially against innocent persons, characteristically brings with it some kind of loss or harm. And Eastwood is clearly preoccupied with the problem of how individual characters (and their relevant communities) cope with such harms and losses. We return to the matter of loss below. But Eastwood is also preoccupied with a more traditional philosophical problem: What is the nature of justice? How is it to be understood in relationship to morality and to institutional life? Knight/McKnight and Flynn take up this matter and explore it in some detail. Flynn argues, in particular, that Eastwood attempts to establish some kind of transcendence of the moral law over civil law, but that this attempt is problematic precisely because it lacks an explicit verbally formulated justification and explanation. Calhoun also explores this matter of the relative transcendence of morality over law and civil institutions associated with the laws of communities, finding in *Pale Rider* (1985) a particularly pivotal moment in the development of Eastwood's thinking on the issues. A closely associated matter (conceptually) is the nature of honor, which enters into Hoffman's essay on gun violence. Part of Eastwood's work on alternatives to such violence (and also on alternative conceptions of masculinity), according to Hoffman's argument, is a conception of honor alternative to what is commonly found in our culture. The whole issue of transcendence and of giving a transcendental (or even a supernatural) basis for morality (and thus a basis for criticism of laws and civil institutions) is also treated by Clayton in a very illuminating analysis of Eastwood's camera work which should also be compared to remarks on camera work by McFarland and Calhoun.[10]

The wider issue of how individuals (and groups) cope with loss is treated extensively by McFarland in terms of *Hereafter*. Part of the problem is to establish the meaning of various kinds of losses, and McFarland finds help in two texts that bracket much of the history of the ancient world (Augustine's *Confessions* and Plato's *Phaedo*). It is notable here that McFarland conceives some of the losses in this film in terms of a "fall from grace," a concept richly expounded by Augustine and proprietary to the traditions of classical theism. McClelland, in his second essay, finds two inductions in Eastwood's filmography concerning the meaning of losses and especially of the greatest of all losses, death. One such induction is positive, the other negative, though the effect of having both is rather surprising in his view. Where many of our authors have found it profitable to bring Eastwood's films into dialogue with major primary texts from the history of philosophy, McClelland has sought to establish a similarly creative dialogue between the films and contemporary empirical psychology and neuroscience. (We leave it to our readers to judge how successful all these attempts may be.) McClelland and Knight/McKnight have also picked up a more particular kind of loss that Eastwood has become increasingly sensitive to in recent decades: the losses attendant upon aging. Such an interest is perhaps not surprising in a man who has entered his ninth decade.[11] Whether it is the deaths of those we love, the loss of physical vigor due to aging, the curtailment of life-hopes and dreams due to our own bad decisions or the injustices of others, all are subject to a similar scrutiny: Can losses be remedied? Can we respond resiliently to them? What is required for a resilient response (as opposed to a vulnerable response)? Does resilience extend even to death? We hope that some of our essays will help to open up a wider discussion of these issues in contemporary film studies. Meanwhile, their handling by Eastwood marks another dimension of his practical realism. It also marks his broad concern with the theme of human flourishing, its ingredients and conditions.

Aristotle thought that human friendships (of various kinds) were vital ingredients in a flourishing life, and wrote extensively about them. In his essay on *Million Dollar Baby* and *Gran Torino*, Jason Grinnell has drawn upon Aristotle's essay on friendship to help us understand Eastwood's approach to human flourishing. He is particularly concerned to draw out the standards of excellence internal to such flourishing, especially where friendship is concerned. Of particular interest for readers may be his point that in *Million Dollar Baby* the main character, Frankie Dunn (Eastwood), is caught in a dilemma between the demands of friendship and the demands of his religious and moral tradition. The "disappearance" of Dunn at the film's end may suggest to many readers that the resolution of this dilemma leaves the filmmaker himself in moral terra incognita, unsure (as of yet, perhaps) how to explore it further. Finally, it is worth underlining significant discussions by Jennifer McMahon and David Calhoun especially of the point that individuals in Eastwood's ethical universe do not flourish apart from the flourishing of their communities and vice versa. Aristotle himself moves from consideration of the psychological and relational conditions of flourishing (in his *Ethics*) to consideration of social and political conditions of flourishing (in his *Politics*). So here is yet another way in which the Stagirite finds an epigone in a modern artist, albeit only implicitly and never explicitly. This latter quality of Eastwood's philosophizing requires further comment.

Implicit Philosophy

Clint Eastwood is a man of few words. Indeed, he is almost infamous for his laconic acting style.[12] He depends upon facial expressions, gestures, and whole-body language to communicate with his audience, perhaps as much as any other actor working today. Moreover, the same spare, nonverbal style spills over into his directing and even into his music. James Couch has done much in his essay to explore two iconic gestures or nonverbal behaviors common to Eastwood's acting personae: smiling and spitting. McClelland, in his first essay, explores the relevance of this spare style for Eastwood's use of silence in *Hereafter.* We add here that this is not merely the result of Eastwood's personality. It is also something he learned, in his exposure to the Stanislavsky method of acting taught by Michael Chekhov (1891–1955, nephew of the great Russian playwright) in the Actors Lab that Morris Carnovsky (1897–1992) and his wife, Phoebe Brand (1907–2004), helped to establish in Los Angeles in 1941.[13] We point in particular to Stanislavsky's emphasis on nonverbal communication and Chekhov's theory of "the psychological gesture," which is both a communicative device and a tool for preparing actors to enter into their roles. Chekhov's theory, derived from Stanislavsky, was embodied in his books *On the Technique of Acting* (1912, reissued in 1991) and its abridgement in *To the Actor* (1953, reissued in 2002). Eastwood is known to recommend the latter book to aspiring young actors even today.[14] The entire bent of Eastwood's early life is toward practical matters rather than intellectual ones, toward doing rather than saying, and the Stanislavsky emphasis on nonverbal communication must have suited him like a glove to a hand. We also think that this choice of style (driven howsoever it may be by personality and educational history) virtually requires that philosophical conclusions be represented in Eastwood's work only implicitly and not explicitly.[15]

Clayton's essay contributes to our understanding of the implicit character of Eastwood's philosophizing, by means of his close analysis of Eastwood's camera work, that camera work being construed as a kind of "visual argumentation." Calhoun and Gilmore have considered similar effects in their essays. We hope hereby to open up a conversation about not only Eastwood's work, but that of other filmmakers, writers, and actors whose conceptual creativity is conveyed by similarly implicit methods. Of course, there is another side to this, as we have already noted: Erin Flynn argues that Eastwood's preference for nonverbal approaches to abstract subjects has its limitations and can be faulted for its inability to offer an explicit, verbally formulated explanation and defense for the views of justice that Eastwood embodies in some of his films. Every manner of artistic creativity has its limitations (we consider some of the limitations of our own collection below). But further exploration of implicit philosophizing should keep Flynn's critique in mind. Before passing on to consider the limitations of our own work, however, one further ramification of implicitness should be noted.

We have tried in our own writing about films and in the editorial strategy pursued in the present volume to follow one major rule. That rule says that one does not use a film or a group of films merely as a hat rack upon which to hang one's favored philosophical theses. Rather, one tries to let philosophical theses emerge from the details of films themselves, to be fixed by those films, considered as artifacts of the creative processes of their makers. Many of the essays in this volume draw films into dialogue with important texts from the history of philosophy, as we have already noted. McClelland draws films into dialogue with contemporary science. The danger of such dialogues is, of course, that preconceived positions may be merely foisted onto the films, thus violating our fundamental rule. We think that this would result in poor film criticism, but we can only assure our readers that we have made every effort to forestall such effects. Rather, we have drawn upon other sources only because the films themselves seemed not only to invite such dialogues but to demand them in order to uncover multiple layers of their meaning. It will be for our readers to judge how well or poorly we have done so. And this brings us, finally, to the issue of our limitations.

Limitations and Future Extensions

There are plenty of issues that we have not considered in this volume, but that are highly relevant to critical interpretation and evaluation of the work of Clint Eastwood. We had originally hoped to have several people write on his music, and some comments about his music have been made in a few of our essays. Eastwood himself is a gifted jazz pianist (a role he reprises with soft irony in his 1993 film *In the Line of Fire*), has composed music for his own films, and has found music, especially jazz, to be a central element of his own life (as it is also for his son, Kyle Eastwood, who has composed music for some of his father's films, notably *Hereafter*). However, we were unable to get a more full treatment of Eastwood's music than those few brief comments allow. Eastwood as musician, then, performer, arranger, composer, lies over the horizon of our essays. Even further over that horizon lies due consideration of the philosophical significance of his music and its various functions in his films. We regard this as one of the most urgent missing elements in writing about Eastwood's work.

Similarly, though the issue of images and conceptions of masculinity figures significantly in Karen Hoffman's essay, we do not feel that gender has come in for anything like the treatment that it deserves. And this applies where conceptions of both masculinity and femininity are concerned (as well as any other form of gender that may be present in Eastwood's work). In particular, images of wounded women appear very often in Eastwood's films, women who have been abused, attacked, insulted, degraded, or even murdered in a variety of ways (and see Knight/McKnight for women as among the innocents who are the subjects of injustice in Eastwood's films). There are repeated explorations of the forms of relationship that are possible between men and women that also should be explored further. We regret that we have not had opportunity to do so more than we have. The whole issue of what is possible in intimate adult relationships, what constitutes flourishing in this arena, and the like can be taken further than it has so far been in the literature.[16] There is likewise room for continued discussion of the extent to which Eastwood himself does or does not succeed in critically responding to cultural stereotypes of gender roles.

We have also tried to include some work on specific techniques of filmmaking that Eastwood makes use of, but realize that there is much more to be explored here than the essays by Clayton, Calhoun, and McFarland have been able to do. McClelland's "neurocinematic" study is also intended to open up areas of investigation that could be taken much further. The application of empirical scientific methods of investigation to filmmaking and film-viewing is in its infancy. We hope there will come a time in the not distant future when philosophers and scientists can be present on film sets to closely study and analyze techniques of filmmaking in situ.

Several of our authors have commented on religious themes in Eastwood's work, including use of religious imagery (the cruciform position of Walt Kowalski's dead body at the end of *Gran Torino,* for example), religious doctrines (such as in *Hereafter*), and religious institutions (especially in the form of priests or other clerical figures). But the whole subject deserves a much fuller exposition than we have been able to give it.

We find Eastwood to be something of a natural moral psychologist, but there is much more to be said about motivations for actions and decisions, as these appear in his films. And many epistemological issues (not least about what it is that we can know about the conditions of human flourishing) are similarly underdeveloped in our essays.

There is thus ample room for more work, and we hope that we may be able to contribute to it on future occasions and we hope to invite many others to join us in that effort. It remains for us, the editors, to thank all of our contributors for their good work and for their sacrifice of time and effort to make this volume possible. We hope that it will enrich our readers' enjoyment of one of the icons of American filmmaking.

Notes

1. In North America, at least, the organization of philosophy departments is closely associated with the rise of the research university in the mid- to late nineteenth century. Even Immanual Kant, often taken to be the paradigmatic earliest academic philosopher in the modern mold, was appointed Professor of Logic at the University of Königsberg only in 1770.

2. It is true that Eastwood has never written a filmscript, but rather chooses scripts written by others. But our view is that his work with those scripts is nonetheless creative and a form of quasi-authorship. Even as an actor in Sergio Leone's Western films, he was known to alter scripts freely.

3. For a much more jaundiced view of how far Eastwood is prepared to call traditional film genres into question, see Tania Modleski, "Clint Eastwood and Male Weepies," *American Literary History* 22 (2009): 136–158. The editors of this volume do not find her interpretations of Eastwood's films very convincing.

4. For a similar view of the philosopher as practitioner of a craft, as embedded in the corresponding tradition of his or her craft, and as potential reviser of that tradition, see Alasdair MacIntyre, *Three Rival Versions of Moral Inquiry* (Notre Dame, Ind.: Univ. of Notre Dame Press, 1990), chapter 6.

5. For a similar view of the intelligibility of narratives, their unity, and the persons who occupy them, see Alasdair MacIntyre, *After Virtue* (Notre Dame, Ind.: Univ. of Notre Dame Press, 1984), chapter 15.

6. MacIntyre, *After Virtue,* 213, 214, 218.

7. Aristotle, *Nicomachean Ethics* III.2, 1111b 5–6, trans. David Ross, ed. Leslie Brown (Oxford, U.K.: Oxford Univ. Press, 2009).

8. Gilmore's analysis is consonant with much recent scientific work on the unconscious mind, for which see Ran Hassin, James Uleman, and John Bargh, eds., *The New Unconscious* (New York: Oxford Univ. Press, 2005).

9. We regret that Sarah Vaux's *The Ethical Vision of Clint Eastwood* (Grand Rapids, Mich.: Eerdmans, 2012) reached us too late to be taken fully into account.

It is notable that she is attracted to many of the same films that our contributors have been drawn to.

10. Modleski, "Weepies," is deeply skeptical of Eastwood's capacity seriously to question or undermine traditional views of social institutions and conventions, but we think the hermeneutical strategy she pursues proves too much, virtually ruling out such a view of Eastwood's work a priori.

11. However, Eastwood is by no means the oldest active director. That honor falls to Manoel de Oliveira (born 1908), who continues to write, produce, and direct films past the age of one hundred. George F. Abbott (1887–1995) was active in filmmaking for eighty years (starting in 1915).

12. It is sent up hilariously in the figure of the Spirit of the West in the animated film *Rango* (directed by Gore Verbinski and written by John Logan, 2011).

13. The Lab existed until 1952, and was an extension to the west coast of the New York Group Theater. It should not be confused with the Acting Lab that exists today in Los Angeles.

14. This whole subject is illuminated by Richard Schickel, *Clint Eastwood: A Biography* (New York: Knopf, 1996), 59–64.

15. There is a further study to be made of the connection between implicit knowledge and gesture in Eastwood's work in the light of contemporary developmental studies of preverbal communicative dispositions in young children prior to the learning of language: see Susan Goldin-Meadow et al., "Young Children Use Their Hands to Tell Their Mothers What to Say," *Developmental Science* 20 (2007): 778–785; Raedy Ping and Susan Goldin-Meadow, "Gesturing Saves Cognitive Resources When Talking about Nonpresent Objects," *Cognitive Science* 34 (2010): 602–619; and Susan Cook et al., "Gesturing Makes Learning Fast," *Cognition* 106 (2008): 1047–1058. The whole subject of implicit knowledge as it is understood in empirical psychology and contemporary neuroscience has yet to make its full appropriate impact on philosophical epistemology.

16. However, see Drucilla Cornell, *Clint Eastwood and the Issues of American Masculinity* (New York: Fordham Univ. Press, 2009). A further notable contribution is Richard Letteri, "Dirty Baby: The Gender Politics of *Million Dollar Baby*," *Quarterly Review of Film and Video* 28 (2011): 204–217. The works of Sarah Vaux and Tania Modleski mentioned earlier in this introduction should also be counted here.

From Solitary Individualism to Post-Christian Stoic Existentialism

Quests for Community, Moral Agency, and Transcendence in the Films of Clint Eastwood

David H. Calhoun

The characters in Clint Eastwood's films are famously associated with rugged individualism and violent directness. The films early in Eastwood's popular success, such as the spaghetti Westerns directed by Sergio Leone, the *Dirty Harry* series, and films such as *Hang 'Em High* (1968) and *Kelly's Heroes* (1970)—notably, films that Eastwood did not himself direct—highlight characters that are solitary, brutal, and resourceful. These Eastwood characters are loners, even when they team up with others, as when Eastwood's Schaffer is the sole American in a British special-ops team in *Where Eagles Dare* (1968); masters of their circumstances, even when facing challenges and temporary setbacks, as in *Coogan's Bluff* (1968); subject to no law other than that which they impose on themselves in order to survive in a hostile environment. The stories set tasks before these figures, the characters resourcefully tackle the tasks, and viewers enjoy the vicarious pleasure of seeing the task successfully completed.[1]

Even after Eastwood began producing and directing films in the early 1970s, memorable characters carried forward the theme of violent and solitary individualism, in the continuation of the *Dirty Harry* franchise and films such as *High Plains Drifter* (1973), *The Eiger Sanction* (1975), and *The Gauntlet* (1977). The characters of these films, along with those of Eastwood's earlier work, are those that largely define Eastwood's public and cinematic persona. The *American Film Institute Desk Reference* biography of Eastwood finds continuity in Eastwood's screen character: "His persona, then and now, is tough, laconic, and towering."[2] Even where critics discern different phases of Eastwood's character, they typically find them variations on a single theme, emphasizing solitude, action, and cynicism.[3]

Given the canonical status of Eastwoodian solitary individualism, Eastwood's directorial debut, *Play Misty for Me* (1971), offers a striking contrast. The dramatic energy of the story is driven by the increasing perplexity and helplessness of radio host David Garver (Eastwood) in the face of stalking by an unhinged admirer, Evelyn (Jessica Walter). Garver is no isolated loner; the film explores his faltering attempts to build a relationship with his girlfriend, Tobie (Donna Mills), and it is his appetite for one-night stands that exposes him to Evelyn's stalking. Indeed, the film assigns partial responsibility for Evelyn's actions to Garver, to the extent that he willingly initiates a relationship with her, hesitates in acting to end it, and deceives others to evade responsibility as events spin out of control. This is clearly a different moral universe than that inhabited by Dirty Harry.

While his films are multidimensional in plot, setting, and affect, *Misty* marks the introduction of a set of themes that characterize the stories Eastwood has brought to the screen as a director and producer. First, Eastwood has shown a persistent interest in exposing the limitations of isolated individualism and tentatively exploring themes of community and human connection. Concomitantly with attention to community, Eastwood's stories highlight the moral complexity of human situations. Romantic pairings, families, surrogate family associations, and friendships form the nexus within which moral choices are made concrete. In different ways, *The Outlaw Josey Wales* (1976) and *Bronco Billy* (1980) herald the emergence of this theme, as both stories depict the voluntary gathering of groups that function as surrogate families. Even when the characters portrayed in the films are deeply flawed, the films themselves create a moral framework that highlights both their humanness and the implications of their choices and actions. As I will argue, this linkage of community and moral agency is evocative of classical Stoicism, with its emphasis on deliberate moral agency within a wider moral community.

Second, Eastwood's films confront characters not with discrete plot problems to solve, but with crises that demand deliberate moral agency. Often the stakes of the crisis are amplified by some mortal threat, such as the quarry who becomes the stalker in *Tightrope* (1984) or the twin dangers of urban violence and diseased old age in *Gran Torino* (2008). In all cases, however, the common factor is the existential quest for a meaningful vocation, the challenge to answer the question "How do I live?" Thus Eastwood's characters find themselves in what Catholic novelist Walker Percy has called "the search," which is "what anyone would undertake if he were not sunk in the everydayness of his own life. . . . To become aware of the possibility of the search is to be onto something. Not to be onto something is to be in despair."[4] The contrast to the search is everydayness, the condition that Kierkegaard called "despair" and Nietzsche called "herd thinking," zombie-like immersion in self-alienated identification with established social practices and beliefs in such a way that obscures human agency and the most pressing human concerns.[5]

Third, Eastwood's characters find themselves in a world where religious and spiritual symbols are at best ambiguous in their import and at worst drained of meaning. Characters pray and attend church, priests and pastors appear in the plots, and biblical stories and themes are referenced, but in the end these resources provide little guidance or comfort. Josey Wales recites words of scripture as a prayer over the grave of his murdered family, but the wooden cross with which he marks their grave cannot bear the weight of his grief or vengeful anger. The existential crises of Eastwood's characters thus occur in the shadow of what Nietzsche called "the death of God," the cataclysmic collapse of traditional Christianity.[6]

Eastwood's films reflect the post-Christian milieu of late modernity, but they also offer hints of transcendence, a sense that the quest for community and exercise of moral agency cannot be rooted in or exhausted by the immediate goals and choices of a solitary individual. Sometimes the intimations of transcendence are religious or supernatural, sometimes not, but they widen the moral context of the choices and actions the characters pursue.

I propose to explore this set of themes in Eastwood's films. I will begin by sketching out the stereotypical individualist Eastwood persona, in order to provide a foil for the richer view of the human condition that emerges in his later films. Next, I will argue that there is a coherent structure to the themes of community, moral agency, cultural collapse, and transcendence, which I will refer to as post-Christian Stoic existentialism, appealing to *A Perfect World* (1993) to exhibit how these themes are treated by Eastwood. After constructing a general interpretive frame, I will explore how these themes concretely appear in five representative Eastwood films: *Pale Rider* (1985), where the themes emerge clearly, albeit ambivalently, for the first time; *Unforgiven* (1992), which juxtaposes justice denied with the faint hope of grace;

Bridges of Madison County (1995), in which passionate impulse is contrasted to lifelong relational commitment; *Million Dollar Baby* (2004), which explores the potential discontinuity between love and theological-ethical principles; and *Gran Torino* (2008), where the decay of a Detroit neighborhood forms the backdrop for the possibility of re-created community.

The "Eastwood Persona": Violent Solitary Immediacy

The essential atmosphere of Eastwood's early films is anonymity. Director Sergio Leone especially uses the Western landscape to depict the lonely brutality of the human contexts and characters of the films. In the opening sequence of *For a Few Dollars More* (1965), for example, the wide shot of the empty Western landscape sets the stage for faceless violence. The wide camera shot allows us to see from a great distance the approach of a lone horseman, and then to witness his apparent killing by an offscreen rifleman.[7] We do not know the shooter—is it Monco (Eastwood), Colonel Mortimer (Lee Van Cleef), or someone else? In a way, it doesn't matter, because the point is that in a hostile environment such as this, death can come suddenly, unexpectedly, in ways that seem arbitrary, even pointless. *The Good, the Bad, and the Ugly* (1966) likewise begins with a desolate Western landscape, but after a split second the face of a killer swivels into view, with the ensuing murderous mayhem punctuated only by coyote howls and the whistling wind of the high desert.

The lonely anonymity of the landscape heralds the sterility of the characters that inhabit it. Blondie (Eastwood) and Tuco (Eli Wallach), the eponymous Good and Ugly, alternate in employing the harsh desert landscape as a weapon against one another. When an unexpected turn of events gives a barely alive Blondie a clue to the location of hidden gold, Tuco, who has nearly murdered Blondie by exposure, tries to wheedle the location of the gold with a grotesque parody of sympathy: "You're very lucky to have me so close when it happened. Think if you'd been on your own. Look, I mean when one is ill, it's good to have somebody close by—friends or relations. . . . I have you, you have me. Only for a little while, I mean." Blondie's reply drips with sarcasm: "I'll sleep better knowing my good friend is by my side to protect me."[8]

As this episode illustrates, the sole community established by Eastwoodian loners is temporarily alliance between suspicious enemies, or at best indifferent acquaintances. This is true not only of the roles Eastwood plays under direction by others, but those roles that carry forward the isolated individualism of his early work.[9] As bail bond enforcer Tommy Nowak (Eastwood) says in *Pink Cadillac* (1989), "I'm not much of a joiner."

While the landscapes these characters inhabit are expansive and anonymous, the moral context for their actions is governed by a narrowly cramped horizon. Nothing stands beyond the payoff for serving as a hired gun, finding the gold treasure, catching the bad guy, or delivering the witness alive to the courthouse. There is little character development. There is sufficient plot to drive the action of the narrative, but no more. Put another way, *stories* are offered, but those stories insufficiently reflect the true complexity of human community and human agency. Rugged individualism is a perennially appealing American theme, but as we will see, it is one that Eastwood has increasingly left behind.

From Solitary Individualism to Post-Christian Stoic Existentialism: *A Perfect World* (1993)

The loner characters of Eastwood's early film success can reasonably be described as "stoic" in the colloquial sense: solitary, emotionless, unaffected by hardships. But the trajectory of Eastwood's films evokes the far richer form of autonomy and moral rigor found in classical Stoicism, with its synthesis of austere self-governance and recognition of the demands of a wider moral community. To be sure, the Victorian homage to Stoicism by William Ernest Henley that provides the film title and personal inspiration for Nelson Mandela (Morgan Freeman) in *Invictus* (2009) is perhaps the only explicit Stoic reference in Eastwood's work. Even here, however, we see individual responsibility and obligation to a community placed in a rich dialectic. While the poem celebrates autonomy and self-mastery, and provided bracing inspiration for Mandela to survive his harsh imprisonment, Eastwood uses the poem (in a voice-over by Freeman) to illustrate the effect that understanding Mandela's experience has on South African rugby team captain Francois Pienaar (Matt Damon). This reframes the individualism of the poem in a way that reflects the classical Stoic notion that self-control does not enclose one in individual solitude but draws one into the community formed by all human beings. Emotional reserve does not imply indifference to others, even if it does involve a deep sense of the fragility of human life.[10] This is the path of engaged, autonomous, cosmopolitan moral rigor, living by the code articulated by Marcus Aurelius: "Hour by hour resolve firmly, like a Roman and a man, to do what comes to hand with correct and natural dignity, and with humanity, independence, and justice."[11]

Closely related to the notion of a moral community is the idea of a transcending moral order. Consider the famous dramatic analogy of the Stoic Epictetus: "Remember that you are an actor in a play, which is as the playwright wants it to be: short if he wants it short, long if he wants it long. If he wants you to play a beggar, play even this part skillfully, or a cripple, or a public official, or a private citizen. What is yours is to play the assigned part well. But to choose it belongs to someone else."[12] The notion of "playing a role" has obvious application to the film context, but Epictetus's outlook is even more directly relevant to Eastwood. The Stoics famously balanced the idea of a broadly deterministic universe with severe demands of self-control.[13] While the Stoics worked out with technical precision those things that were subject to human agency and those that were not, Eastwood's films offer a less technical variant of fixed circumstances and free choices.

Consider Eastwood's character study *A Perfect World* (1993). We gradually come to understand that prison escapee Butch Haynes (Kevin Costner) is trapped by the circumstances of his birth to a prostitute and a convict, his upbringing in a New Orleans brothel, and his juvenile incarceration in a strict Texas penal farm for joyriding in a stolen car.[14] Many of Haynes's actions, and the trajectory of his escape, seem preordained consequences of his past. But the task set before Haynes is to "play the assigned part well," and he does this by surprising us repeatedly throughout his flight, treating the young boy who initially is his hostage but soon becomes his traveling companion, Phillip "Buzz" Perry (T. J. Lowther), with sweetness, gentleness, and humor. Haynes breaks the law as he must to facilitate his flight, but he operates by a clear moral code—for example, affirming to Phillip the wrongness of stealing after Phillip shoplifts a ghost costume. We find that he is capable of violence, even frighteningly explosive violence, as when he erupts against the farmworker who has offered him hospitality, Mack (Wayne Dehart), when Mack cuffs his grandson one too many times.[15] Despite all of this, Haynes is not simply a slave of his circumstances, but chooses his path with independence and equanimity. The Stoics captured this view of human existence with another metaphor: "man is like a dog tied to a cart; if he does not walk along, he will be pulled along; but if he is pulled along, he is a bad man."[16]

On the other side of the manhunt, Texas Ranger Red Garnett (Eastwood) is sharply constrained by his role and circumstances, serving the will of the governor and bound by the law enforcement conventions that guide a manhunt. Even he has the opportunity to play his part, however, as when he, with essentially impotent but righteous anger, punches the FBI sniper who needlessly and fatally shoots Haynes near the end of the film. His action does not change events, but choosing and doing it reflect the nobility of moral self-assertion.

The relative helplessness of both Haynes and Garnett illustrates a modification of the classical Stoic view in Eastwood's films. The classical Stoics identified the "authorship" of the cosmos, its transcending moral structure, with the immanent divine rational principle, and regarded it as providential.[17] This notion of a benevolent cosmic moral order was adopted and adapted by Christian thinkers, who saw human action as occurring within the context of providential divine care. By contrast, the Stoic framework of Eastwood's films is post-Christian, where God is absent, silent, or at best hidden, and human beings are largely left to their own devices to determine how to act. Fragments and vestiges of Christianity still dot the landscape, as for example, in *A Perfect World,* the strict commitment of Phillip's mother, Gladys Perry (Jennifer Griffin), to her identity as a Jehovah's Witness, or the desperate intoning of the Lord's Prayer by Lottie (Mary Alice) in the face of Haynes's anger. Haynes himself shows familiarity with stories and principles of Christianity (as would any person living in the American South in the 1960s), but they offer him little guidance. The wider moral framework is there, but like the bewildered denizens of the marketplace witnessing Nietzsche's Madman, Haynes is on his own. As *A Perfect World* demonstrates, Stoic moral rigor in the modern context leads to existentialist anguish.

Stoicism and existentialism admittedly make odd conceptual partners. Nevertheless, both begin from a notion of self-responsibility, and both emphasize deliberate action in the face of moral crisis. They mark, therefore, alternative responses to the modern human condition. The juxtaposition of these traditions as responses to the crisis of modernity is a recurring and central feature of the works of Catholic novelist Walker Percy.[18] While Percy often presents Stoicism and the existential search as alternative means to escape everydayness, he has acknowledged that they are in principle complementary.[19] Austere self-governance, effected with deep awareness of the fragility of human life, and pursued in heroic defiance of the collapse of traditional ethical absolutes, provides a reasonable way to live in the wreckage of Western culture.

Despite this milieu of existentialist anxiety, there are hints of transcendence, intimations that the wider cosmic context of human choices and actions is real. The title of *A Perfect World* is clearly ironic: as criminal psychologist Sally Gerber (Laura Dern) notes, things like murders and prison breaks would not take place in a perfect world. But perhaps the perfect world does exist somewhere.[20] The opening sequence of *A Perfect World* begins the story at the end, with a head and upper chest view of Haynes lying in the grass of the meadow where the film concludes, with paper money blowing across him and Phillip's ghost mask beside him, ethereal music playing in the background. He cracks open his eyes, sees the sun above him and a helicopter that we come to find out is ferrying Phillip and his mother away, and he smiles. But we find out at the end of the film that Haynes is almost certainly dead by the time the helicopter passes overhead. If not in this world, perhaps perfection is found in some other world.

A Perfect World illustrates the outlook of post-Christian Stoic existentialism. It depicts appealing characters carried along by a rushing tide of circumstances who nevertheless choose and act freely and deliberately. Their lives are shaped by their choices with respect to the ultimate inescapable feature of human life, namely death, whether as a result of increasing age or accumulated transgressions against society. In facing their circumstances, characters like Garnett and Haynes do not passively succumb to convention, but heroically and defiantly press on, even in the absence of moral guarantees. They embrace the inescapable obligation to play the role assigned them.

Hints of Community, Justice, and Transcendence: *Pale Rider*

On one level, *Pale Rider* is a retelling of the classic Western *Shane* (1953), which unfolds against the backdrop of the conflict between homesteaders, who represent the new and civilized division of the land, and cattlemen, who violently agitate for the older, open West.[21] The opening sequence of *Pale Rider* dramatically establishes a *Shane*-style conflict—this time between tin-pan hand miners and the large-scale hydrologic mining of local boss Coy LaHood (Richard Dysart) and his men.[22] A series of beautifully executed crosscuts contrasts the calm, quiet community of the miner camp and the thundering horses of the LaHood gang as they ride to the camp to inflict harm and mayhem to discourage and drive out the miners.

Although the LaHood gang terrorizes the miners and destroys and damages property, at this point in the story they confine serious harm to killing a few animals. One of those animals is a dog belonging to a young woman in the camp, Megan (Sydney Penny). That killing sets up the second sequence of the film, which leads us beyond *Shane.* Megan goes into the woods to bury her dog, and after doing so she prays the Lord's Prayer interlaced with her own entreaties: "The Lord is my shepherd, I shall not want. But I *do* want. He leadeth me beside still waters. He restoreth my soul. But they killed my dog. Yea, though I walk through the valley of the shadow of death, I shall fear no evil. But I am afraid." As Megan continues to pray, ethereal orchestration and choral voices provide background for a series of long shots of the mountains and valleys, underlaid by the rumble of distant thunder. "Thy loving-kindness and mercy shall follow me all the days of my life. If you exist."[23] With that interrogative challenge, a dissolve momentarily superimposes on the scene of Megan a view of a lone horseman, accompanied by menacing brass notes, a move repeated when Megan ends her prayer: "If you don't help us, we're all going to die. Please. Just one miracle. Amen." Then, with the end of her prayer, the scene cuts fully to the horseman, now revealed in a close shot to be the mysterious Preacher (Eastwood).

The result is a repetition of the good-evil confrontation of *Shane,* but with an added supernatural dimension. Who is the Pale Rider? We never know him by name, only by the sobriquet "Preacher." But he is not the anonymous Man with No Name. He appears in response to the desperate prayer of a young woman, and eerily, prophetically, he rides into the camp as Megan and her mother, Sarah Wheeler (Carrie Snodgrass), are reading the narrative of the seals from Revelation 6. The Preacher rides a speckled gray horse, matching the description they read: "Come and see. . . . and behold a pale horse, and the one that sat on him was Death. And hell followed with him."[24]

A number of clues suggest that he is not just a friendly stranger. Tin-pan miner Hull Barret (Michael Moriarty) sees six bullet wounds in the Preacher's back, all circling his heart, in a pattern that looks to be necessarily fatal. When LaHood tells his hired gun Marshall Stockburn (John Russell) about the Preacher, he mentions that the Preacher recognized Stockburn's name. Stockburn admits that he once knew a man matching the Preacher's description, but the Preacher could not be that man, because he is dead. In the final gunfight of the film, the Preacher is inexplicably able to cross the street to confront individual deputies and pick them off, even though Marshall Stockburn stands at the head of the street supervising the search of the town. Just before the Preacher administers the coup de grâce to Stockburn, we see a flicker of recognition cross Stockburn's face. The Preacher is the supposedly dead man, somehow miraculously still alive or even resurrected.

While viewers do want to know who the Preacher is, in the narrative his identity is less important than the role he plays encouraging and binding together the tin-pan miners. When LaHood returns from Sacramento and is told that a Preacher has moved into the Carbon Canyon mining camp, he sees disastrous consequences for his plans to drive out the miners: "a preacher—he could give 'em faith. Shit. One ounce of faith they'll be dug in deeper than ticks on a hound." We see the effect of the Preacher's encouragement on the group when they vote against accepting LaHood's offer to buy out their stakes. Significantly, Hull's argument for staying in Carbon Canyon goes beyond a vague faith, appealing to family, to dreams, to the debt the miners owe to those who they have now buried, and to dignity. As he notes, loyalty to these values cannot be traded for LaHood's offer of money. After the miner Spider (Doug McGrath) is murdered by Stockburn and his deputies, the Preacher counsels: "Spider made a mistake—went into town alone. A man alone is easy prey. Only by standing together are you going to be able to beat the LaHoods of the world."[25]

The dramatic hinge of the film occurs when Preacher removes his pistols from his Wells Fargo safe-deposit box and drops in his ministerial collar. This event concretely poses a set of significant questions: What is the relationship between revenge and justice? Is religion tainted or discredited by resorting to violence, even to accomplish a just end? Must a religious individual—or an avenging angel—shed his pastoral persona to use force to effect the righting of wrong?

All of these elements demonstrate that *Pale Rider* represents something qualitatively different from the anonymous self-governance of the Eastwood persona. It's true that the closing gunfight (all thirteen or so minutes of it) is "classic" Eastwood. But the supernatural elements and the suggestion that both local and cosmic justice are somehow at work subverts interpreting the gunfight as a celebration of amoral violence. The Preacher rides off, again accompanied by the menacing brass soundtrack, but with Megan's affirmation of love.

Intimations of Redemption: *Unforgiven*

Eastwood's Oscar-winning *Unforgiven* is widely acknowledged as a revolutionary reimagining of the Western. On first glance, it seems a thoroughly postmodern take on the Western genre, with antiheroes on every side: the washed-up killer William Munny (Eastwood), his reluctant sidekick Ned

Logan (Morgan Freeman), the myopic would-be killer for hire the Schofield Kid (Jaimz Woolvett), cruel and despotic town sheriff Little Bill Daggett (Gene Hackman), and truth-stretching celebrity gunman English Bob (Richard Harris). *Unforgiven* is so rich on so many levels that it has attracted a great deal of comment, and will continue to do so. I'll confine myself to noting how the film exemplifies the trajectory I've identified here, which in my view undercuts reading it as a postmodern tale.

The first thing to note is that the plot of the film revolves around justice denied. After a couple of cowboys cut the face of prostitute Delilah Fitzgerald (Anna Thomson) at Greely's Beer Garden, Sheriff Little Bill Daggett punishes them with a property fine—horses, which they must pay come spring. Delilah and her friends judge the penalty to be offensively inadequate, and they collect money to pay a hired gun to exact revenge.[26] Their bounty offer activates the story's plot, with a variety of gunslingers coming to Big Whiskey in hopes of collecting the payoff. Little Bill's encounter with English Bob shows that he is more vicious toward hopefuls who come to town hoping to collect than he was toward the offending cowboys, revealing a fundamental shortcoming in his administration of justice and civilization in Big Whiskey.[27]

Eastwood's character, William Munny, is an unlikely candidate for righting wrongs. He is a former killer who almost inexplicably went straight, married a young woman, started a family, and turned to farming. One could find this narrative simply unbelievable.[28] I find, by contrast, that it illustrates what Ralph Wood, describing the path of novelist Walker Percy's heroes, calls "an uncanny transformation of grace," with Munny's wife as the agent of this grace.[29] As the film begins, however, Munny's redemption has collapsed: his wife has died of smallpox, raising the kids alone is difficult, and Munny is wrestling sick pigs in the mud of a hardscrabble farm. While Munny honors the memory of his wife, and attributes his current moral rectitude dutifully to her, a visit by the Schofield Kid with the story of the doings in Big Whiskey is enough to convince him that one more episode of gunslinging will give him the capital to escape his current travails.

The plot repeatedly gestures toward the question of justice and desert. Ned, the Schofield Kid, and Strawberry Alice (Frances Fisher) each at one point affirm the cosmic justice of killing the cowboys: "they got it comin'." Lying on the floor dying at the end of the final gunfight, Little Bill moans, "I don't . . . deserve this . . . to die this way." By contrast, Munny understands that all declarations of innocence are transparently false. As he notes to the Kid: "We all have it coming, Kid."[30] The ultimate horizon of this vengeful conception of justice is the finality of death. As Munny notes, "It's a hell of a thing, killing a man. You take away all he's got, and all he's ever gonna have."

Beyond the universality of guilt is the suggestion that attempts to justify acts of violence as serving the cause of justice are hollow. If the cowboy who cut Delilah's face had it coming, then everyone else in the sordid story will have to pay as well: the Kid's triumph in committing his first murder quickly turns to horror at the finality of the death he has caused; Ned's attempt to back out after the first murder leads to his being captured and then tortured and killed by Little Bill; Munny survives, but at the cost of reverting to the violent self he abandoned for the sake of his beloved wife. Eastwood recognized how the moral gravity of the story of *Unforgiven* differed from his prior Westerns: "In the past, there were a lot of people killed gratuitously in my pictures, and what I liked about this story was that people aren't killed, and acts of violence aren't perpetrated, without there being certain consequences."[31] The inevitability of those consequences suggests in turn a Stoic framework within which the apparently chaotic events of the film must be embedded, both fatalistic and providential.[32] As Munny rides out of Big Whiskey for the final time, Delilah's mouth curls into the slightest trace of a smile.[33] Perhaps she is recalling Munny's kindnesses to her, perhaps she is celebrating a sense that amid the violence justice was satisfied.

Despite the harsh moral equilibrium of the film, there are hints of friendship and fidelity. Munny tries to stay faithful to his departed wife, and, as the references to his family at the beginning and end of the film show, takes his responsibility for his children seriously. He tries to be kind to Delilah, who sees herself as worthless as a result of her facial scars. Neither the prospect of money, nor danger, nor illness can induce Munny to revert to the drinking that he gave up for his wife and continued to avoid to honor her after her death; it takes the news that his friend Ned has been captured and tortured to death to transform him atavistically to a whiskey-fueled killer. We do not know the details of the friendship between Munny and Logan, only that it has survived a long time and a transition from crime to anonymous respectability. But the friendship is sufficient to weigh against Munny's obedience to the wishes and principles of his dead wife.

The film's conclusion is ambiguous. We are told only in a text crawl that Munny disappeared from the farm with the children, perhaps to San Francisco. And years later when Munny's mother-in-law visited her daughter's grave, "there was nothing on the marker to explain to Mrs. Feathers why her only daughter had married a known thief and murderer, a man of notoriously vicious and intemperate disposition." Presumably Mrs. Feathers knew nothing of the terrible events in Big Whiskey. She never accepted Munny's initial conversion by grace, much less his apostasy and reconversion.

The puzzle of the film's conclusion is related to its title. The title of *Unforgiven* is significant, because it was chosen by Eastwood to replace the screenplay author's title.[34] Who is unforgiven, and by whom? Certainly the unforgiveness of Strawberry Alice and the other prostitutes at Greely's saloon propels the story forward. But the unforgiveness in the film is bigger than any one character, and raises a series of questions. Is the condition of being unforgiven permanent, or is grace possible? Certainly Munny's mother-in-law was not inclined to forgive Munny, even though Munny's wife's death was the result of smallpox, not any violence from Munny's own hand. Nor is forgiveness or grace evident in the harsh and rough justice meted out by the characters to one another. This suggests that the title is ironic: Munny in fact *was* forgiven by his wife for his years of violence and crime, and the grace she extended to him redeemed him. The Big Whiskey episode was a violation of her grace to him, but the only hint we are given—that he took his children with him and was never again heard from—suggests that grace nevertheless remained open to him as he returned to a law-abiding and civilized life.[35] The violent man who deeply understood his guilt was not unforgiven after all.

Consequently, *Unforgiven* illustrates the themes of post-Christian Stoic existentialism. Christian principles such as fidelity, mercy, and justice are, just like their divine author, present only by absence, as silent as the dead Mrs. Munny. The story draws the characters into an inexorable motion, a near-inevitable progression in which they must nevertheless chart their own pathways. And through it all, the faintest hope of redemption still flickers.

The Transformational Power of Devoted Family Love: *The Bridges of Madison County*

It is true that Eastwood receives top billing in *The Bridges of Madison County*, but Eastwood's Robert Kincaid is neither the narrative center nor the hero of the film. That role falls to Francesca Johnson (Meryl Streep), and the reason it does is central to my claim about the trajectory of Eastwood's films.[36] Kincaid is, in a sense, a variation on the stereotypical Eastwood loner. But he is more than a loner: he is disconnected from the routine and stability of family life, and consequently is detached from ordinary rhythms of place and custom, the sort of rhythms we see in Francesca's cooking, cleaning, and caring for her family. As Kincaid tells Francesca, his favorite place is Africa, not only for aesthetic reasons, the colors in the air, but also because it is a place beyond morality. Kincaid is beyond morality in a way that allows him to drop into human life like Zeus descending from Olympus, unconcerned about the implications and consequences of his actions. He is not a bad man, but his habitual detachment exemplifies the personality Walker Percy calls a "transcending self." Percy identifies scientists and artists as paradigm cases of these transcendent selves, persons whose self-conception places them outside of the world of everydayness—largely because their professions require that they objectify the world and treat it as god-like observers—and thereby gives them distance from ordinary human concerns and entanglements. Surely a photographer is such a transcending self, and Kincaid thinks of himself as one.[37]

While Kincaid is a transcending self, the good, solid people of Madison County exist at the opposite extreme, mired in conventionality, routine, and unreflectiveness. Their everydayness normally manifests itself as blind adherence to custom and social expectation, but we also see it in the gentle cruelty that enforces social norms through reputation and gossip. They therefore represent the everydayness that is a horror for Percy's Binx Bolling, and that Francesca Johnson also recognizes as a threat. It is the suffocation of that everydayness that pushes Francesca toward Kincaid in the first place. We see small hints of this in the family's patterns of interaction: Francesca's daughter, Carolyn (Sarah Kathryn Schmitt), brusquely ignores Francesca's choice of music on the family radio, she mocks Francesca's pious wish to have the family join together in saying grace before their meals (she literally says the word "grace" and the family tucks into dinner). We see a more ominous variation of this everydayness in the way the townspeople treat the marriage problems and affairs of those in the community. Even Francesca's husband, Richard (Jim Haynie), who loves her in his simple, unreflective way, exhibits immersion in everydayness at the end of the film when he and Francesca are waiting at the traffic light behind Kincaid's truck, in what Francesca knows will be the last time she will see Kincaid. Francesca's desperate anguish is palpable. Richard is perceptive enough to ask what is wrong, but when her answers are repeatedly evasive, he gives up and turns on the farm report on the radio rather than exploring further. An opportunity to push beyond everydayness is lost.

What is the upshot? Francesca has a torrid and passionate affair with

Kincaid, he leaves, and they never again see one another. The details of their affair are revealed only after both Francesca and Kincaid have died, at which time they request to be cremated and to have their ashes scattered together. So passion and eros conquer all, and *Bridges of Madison County* is affirmed as a romantic film.[38]

No, because Francesca decides to subordinate her romantic passion for the concrete reality of what she calls the "details" of the lives of her husband and children. It is something Francesca can barely do, as we see when she holds the door of the truck with a death-grip as they wait for the light to change behind Kincaid's truck.[39] But as she testifies, the concrete details of family life provide the anchors that allow her to stay rooted in and committed to her family. A conventional romantic version of the story would have Francesca stick it out with her family for some finite time (perhaps until the children have left the home), and then flee to Kincaid. That is not the direction the film takes. Francesca notes the fragility of her love for Kincaid, and sees it as inseparable from her love for her husband: "What Robert and I had could not continue if we were together. What Richard and I shared would vanish if we were apart." Just as the classical Stoics recognized, Francesca understands that the success and meaning of her life is rooted in the proper governance of impulse.[40] The subordination of what she wants to what she knows is right is precisely the sort of transcending ethical nobility praised by the Stoics.

Francesca's deliberate, painful, and nearly impossible choice to stay with her quiet, ordinary, and good husband, to "give her life to her family," and to raise her children accomplishes something much deeper and more significant. The rhythms of Francesca's life together with Richard have none of the thrill and ecstasy of her four days with Kincaid, but they share years that are sweet, tender, and solid, as the scene of Francesca gently caring for an ailing and elderly Richard makes evident. Francesca chooses to follow the path of the Stoic and rightly to govern her impulses based on her sense of obligation to her family. For his part, Richard knows that he has not been able to fulfill Francesca's dreams, and that awareness colors and intensifies his love for her as their shared life comes to an end. Perhaps he cannot generate even a fraction of the passionate fire of Kincaid, but he is a good man.

Something similar happens with Francesca's children. Her devoted care for them is, in a sense, unremarkable among the good people of Madison County. However, placed in the wider context of her deep desire to flee with Kincaid, which is disclosed to her children after her death, her love for her family and for Kincaid has the effect of giving her children a renewed sense of the possibilities of their own lives, including with their families. Carolyn, now an adult (Annie Corley), feels free to stay in Madison County for a while and reevaluate how her own damaged marriage will proceed. Son Michael (Victor Slezak) experiences a sense of the possible emergence of his own marriage from everyday routine.

Strangely enough, Francesca's fidelity to her family also roots the rootless Kincaid. Of course, his sense of loss is no less than hers, as we see when he stands forlorn in the pouring rain across the street from her, knowing it is the last time he will see her. His life continues to be one of wandering, but Francesca becomes for him such a reference point that he maintains a kind of fidelity to her for the rest of his life. She finds out only after his death, via a package from his attorney, that he had followed her advice to publish a photography book. More tellingly, the package Kincaid arranged to bequeath to Francesca includes key "details" of his own life, including the cameras that were his livelihood and his means of creating art.

Francesca's act of fidelity to her family and her self-disclosure to those she loved has the effect of redeeming them from the everydayness that propelled her to Kincaid. We do not know what long-term effects her revelation had for her children, but Francesca's choices and actions, at the very least, spurred awareness of the possibilities of the moral life and the transcending frame of obligations that can serve to contextualize one's difficult choices. In the end, therefore, this love story is a synthesis of romance and family fidelity that celebrates not the isolated value of self-centered happiness and autonomy, but the concrete details of family life and the transcending value of properly governed eros.[41]

The Inviolable Bonds of Adoptive Family: *Million Dollar Baby*

Like *Unforgiven, Million Dollar Baby* is a film that speaks on a number of levels. Most critical for our purposes here is that it explores broken and damaged relationships, and the costs of maintaining, reestablishing, or replacing them. The main character, boxing gym owner and trainer Frankie Dunn (Eastwood), is a man with dark shadows of guilt. Some unknown offense has estranged him from his absent daughter, Katy, and though he writes her faithfully every week, the letters are unerringly returned to him undelivered. His close friendship with ex-boxer Eddie "Scrap-Iron" Dupris (Morgan Freeman) is tainted by Frankie's guilt over Scrap's loss of sight in one of his eyes, for which Frankie—perhaps unreasonably—feels responsible. Frankie's priest, Father Horvak (Brían O'Byrne), who Frankie makes a practice of baiting and annoying with mock-serious theological questions, sees that Frankie's ironic attitude and persistent faithful church attendance mask a deep sense of guilt.

Aspiring boxer Maggie Fitzgerald (Hilary Swank) seems to have it even worse: she is poor and is past the reasonable age to begin a boxing career. What Maggie calls the "simple truth" of her background is that it is a trap of white-trash degradation. She needs Frankie to train her because it is her only way out of that trap, the only way for her to do—and possibly succeed at—the one thing she really loves.[42]

The over-the-top dysfunctionality of Maggie's family and the irrevocable estrangement of Frankie from his daughter perhaps make it inevitable that Frankie and Maggie will become close. Frankie initially resists the idea of training Maggie, then reluctantly trains her, and then takes her on fully after another trainer uses her as a pawn to arrange fights for other boxers. After their reconciliation, Maggie asks, somewhat accusingly, "You gave me away. How was that protecting me?" Frankie's promise that he will never leave her again confirms that although souls adrift, they have found adoptive family with one another. As Maggie notes, "I got nobody but you, Frankie." To which Frankie replies, "Well, you've got me."

It is easy to see the conclusion of the film as an ethical-political statement on assisted suicide. The bioethics controversy conceals a deeper theme, however: the demands and limits of loyalty and commitment that are the result of love.[43] Abandoned by their biological families, Frankie and Maggie have formed an adoptive family. After Maggie's crippling injury, Frankie's genuine affection makes it easy for him to stay with Maggie, to arrange her care, and even to protect her from her money-grubbing, lawyered-up family. The final crisis for Frankie is not that Maggie demands of Frankie something that he personally finds morally objectionable. That is too facile. It is rather that Frankie is in the impossible place of loving Maggie so deeply that he wants what is best for her and at the same time knowing that it is wrong to help her in the way she wants. Sin melds with love, which blends with Frankie's selfish reluctance to let Maggie go despite her broken condition.[44]

Maggie's condition, and Frankie's response to it, highlights another key value in the Stoic moral universe: autonomy. Even though her condition is not fatal, and she can live a meaningful and productive life (which Frankie urges her to do), her capacity to choose her own death becomes the acid test for her of her remaining power to act.[45] Of course, Frankie's desperate need to help her is complicated by his wish to preserve her autonomy even as he, choosing autonomously for himself, wants nothing more than to live out his days with her. As Frankie puts it to his priest: "But now she wants to die, and I just want to keep her with me. And I swear to God, Father, it's committing a sin to do it. By keeping her alive, I'm killing her. How do I get around that? . . . She's not asking for God's help, she's asking for mine." In adjudicating a conflict between obedience to theological principle and the obligation of love, Frankie is willing to risk estrangement from the unseen God to meet his concrete obligation to Maggie.[46] Frankie's revelation of the meaning of his Gaelic nickname for Maggie, *mo cuishle*—my darling, my blood—is his final affirmation of love and family commitment to Maggie before he injects the adrenaline that will kill her.

In a parallel to the conclusion of *Unforgiven,* Frankie disappears after Maggie's death. He never returns to the gym. Viewers of the film realize that Scrap has been telling the entire story in the form of a letter to Frankie's still-estranged daughter. He closes with a note of hope for grace: "Frankie didn't leave a note, and nobody knew where he went. I hoped he'd gone to find you, to ask you one more time to forgive him, but maybe he didn't have anything left in his heart." It's only a wisp of hope, one in conflict with the enormity of what Frankie has done, but entirely in keeping with Scrap's final attempt to reveal Frankie to his daughter, and in keeping with the sort of grace that redeemed William Munny.

Again, we have a set of related themes: the halting struggle for community in the wreckage of broken and dysfunctional existing relationships; the ebbing influence of traditional culture and religion; individuals playing out a role assigned to them by circumstances beyond their own choices and actions. The only transcendence on the horizon is the Kierkegaardian suggestion that a suspension of universal ethical norms might be legitimized by the particular needs of a concrete individual.[47] But neither Frankie nor Maggie is Abraham, and neither is responding to the command of God. Beyond that is only the barest hope for redemption.

Re-creating Community in the Ruins: *Gran Torino*

The suburban Detroit neighborhood inhabited by retired autoworker Walt Kowalski (Eastwood) is a riot of battling gangs, peeling paint, ill-kept yards, impolite kids, and weeds sprouting through the pavement.[48] As such, it can be taken as a metaphor for the crisis of modern nihilism, the challenge of finding meaning and purpose in the midst of cultural decay. Walt's well-maintained house and yard provide a kind of oasis of assertive autonomy in the midst of the collapse, but Walt knows that individual assertiveness is inadequate for meaning. This is the lesson of his experience in the Korean War, which revealed that war breeds horror and guilt, not camaraderie, courage, and heroic sacrifice. Walt's recently deceased wife found comfort in the church, but Walt rejects that consolation. While the church stands solid among the ruins of his neighborhood, in Walt's view it is corrupted from the inside out: it is the haunt of immature and inexperienced priests, such as Father Janovich (Christopher Carley), who prey on old ladies who are near to death (such as his own recently deceased wife). It is, as Nietzsche put it, the grave of gods.[49]

Walt's family is a disaster as well. He is estranged from his sons, one of whom, Mitch (Brian Haley), sells Japanese cars in what amounts to an assault on Walt's entire career defending America in war and building America by assembling Ford cars in a Michigan plant. (Eastwood accentuates Walt's *American* identity by camera angles of his house and front porch that emphasize his proudly displayed American flag.) His grandchildren are even more alien, with clothes, habits, and attitudes that Walt categorizes on a range from annoying to offensive.

Part of Walt's disgust with the church and his family, and his general misanthropy, is his understanding that all are sunk into banal everydayness. Father Janovich's knowledge of life and death is "pathetic" and trite nonsense learned at "priest school," especially in comparison to the reality of death that Walt experienced in Korea, hacking seventeen-year-olds to death with shovels. The notion of consumer religion is likewise ridiculously hollow. When Father Janovich asks why Walt confronted the Hmong gang members rather than calling the police, Walt deadpans, "Well, you know, I prayed that they would show up, but nobody answered." Walt sarcastically reads his birthday horoscope from the newspaper to his dog, Daisy: "This year, you have to make a choice between two life paths. Second chances come your way. Extraordinary events culminate in what might seem to be an anticlimax." Sometimes, however, there is a message amid the banal drivel, if only one has ears to hear.[50]

Where Frankie and Maggie created an adoptive family in *Million Dollar Baby,* the unfolding of events in *Gran Torino* leads to the construction of a community in the ruins of an old neighborhood as Walt, the putative patriarch, is himself gradually adopted into an alternate family. Walt's racist rudeness to the Hmong who now populate his old eastern European neighborhood (of course, he's rude and racist to everyone, not just to the Hmong, though his rudeness to his friends always has a playful edge) has the inadvertent effect of making him a hero when he drives away Hmong gang members who threaten the neighborhood and have targeted the young man living next door, Thao (Bee Vang). A friendly overture by Thao's assertive sister, Sue (Ahney Her), leads to a surprise for Walt: he actually likes his neighbors, perhaps better than his own kids and grandkids. Ultimately Walt reciprocally "adopts" Thao, toward whom he takes a kind of mentor role, teaching him how to "be a man," to work, to ask girls out.[51] The proof of Walt's affection for Sue and Thao is initially when he enjoys a backyard barbecue with them, much as one might expect him to do with his own family. Still more we see his affection when the Hmong gang shoots up Sue and Thao's house and then assaults and rapes Sue as retaliation for Walt's attack on one of the gang members. The angry tear on Walt's face as he storms back to his house manifests not only his sense of responsibility for instigating the war with the gang that led to their attack, but also his genuine affection for Sue. The commitment is evident to Sue and Thao, to such an extent that Thao expects Walt to live up to it: "Don't let me down, Walt. Not you." The final concrete affirmation of Walt's integration into his adoptive family comes near the end of the film, when Walt entrusts the care of his dog, Daisy, to the curmudgeonly grandmother of the Hmong clan next door (Chee Thao).

As with *Million Dollar Baby,* there is a central dramatic point of *Gran Torino*: Walt's decision to sacrifice himself to secure the safety of Sue and Thao. Walt's sacrifice is saturated in religious significance and symbolism. Before setting his plan into motion, Walt makes an initial confession to Father Janovich. On one level, it is a superficial ritual, done to honor his wife's dying wish that he submit to the sacrament of confession. So Walt begins with decades-old peccadillos that are hardly worth mentioning, such as a stolen kiss from a woman other than his wife at an office party. However, Walt understands the significance of admitting wrongs, turning at the end to admit a key failure of his life: his inability to develop closeness with his sons. This is an important admission, but Walt's deepest confession is not to Father Janovich, it is to Thao, whom Walt locks in the basement to prevent him from accompanying Walt to the gang house for the final confrontation. Eastwood visually replicates the confession booth screen with a security screen door separating Walt and Thao as Walt admits the central guilt of his life, the one from which he wants to save Thao: the abortive exercise of autonomy via violence.[52] As he told Father Janovich at one point, "The thing that haunts a man the most is what he isn't ordered to do." No commanding officer ordered Walt to shoot in the face the Korean who tried to surrender to him, but that killing bred guilt for his entire life. When, in the closing climactic sequence, Walt allows the gang members to conclude mistakenly that he has a gun, their killing of Walt in full view of the neighbors guarantees that they will be put away for a long time, and hence protects Sue and Thao. Everyone who views the film notices that Walt falls on the ground in a cruciform position. But while his sacrifice is a salvific protection for his new Hmong family, it is also a kind of salvation for Walt himself, insofar as it expresses Walt's own choice about his fate in the face of his serious illness. In the end, Walt's action accomplishes multiple objectives: it protects people for whom he has come to have deep affection, it solves his problem of facing his own illness with autonomy, and, by an act of sacrificial nonviolence, it potentially atones for the murder of the young enemy soldier in the Korean War.[53] On a deeper level, by genuinely caring for someone else, particularly someone as different as his Hmong neighbors, he shows that he understands the possibility of the search: community with others, and deliberate action in service of a transcending goal. Sue's affirmation to Walt—"You're a good man"—becomes not only an assuring assessment, but a criterion for living and for dying.

Movies That Get It: Successful Imaging of the Search

The narrative horizon of Eastwood's heroic loner films is almost suffocatingly narrow: steal the money, kill the target, find the bad guy, solve the mystery. Harmless entertainment, pleasingly resolved in finite time. By contrast, in the films we have considered here, those characterized by post-Christian Stoic existentialism, there are expansive horizons framed in terms of enduring questions: Is help coming for me, from God or from my neighbor? Must I in some way succor my neighbor? What is the meaning of love and family? How do I live in the face of an impossible choice? Is life possible in the ruins of the world I have spent my life building? The stories address these questions with nuance and complexity, and open up pathways that are difficult to trace neatly. We see intimations of transcendence as well: the value of seeking justice, the costs that justice requires, the easy shift from justice to hungry violence. We see the impulse to act beyond immediate desires and needs. We see the possibility of making real connections with particular people in all of their concrete complexity.

There is a link here back to Walker Percy. Significantly, Percy realizes that movies can play a role in the search. After all, Percy's observations about the search occur in a novel titled *The Moviegoer,* the main character of which is a movie addict who tends to reflect his experience through the lens of movie narratives and characters. The connections go deeper than accidental plotting, however; as Binx notes, movies are "onto the search" insofar as they explore the experiences and actions of characters who face the existential question of how to live. But while movies are "onto" the search, Binx concludes that "they screw it up." As movies depict the search, "the search always ends in despair. They like to show a fellow coming to himself in a strange place—but what does he do? He takes up with the local librarian, sets about proving to the local children what a nice fellow he is, and settles down with a vengeance. In two weeks time he is so sunk in everydayness that he might just as well be dead."[54]

Percy has in mind here the countless movies that arrange the plot details such that all is neatly packaged up by the end of the story. But to neatly package up the details is to betray the messiness of human existence and to subvert the search. Hegel famously argued for the difficulty of making a beginning. Percy's argument is that the difficulty of films (and, more broadly, stories of all forms) is in crafting the right ending, one that will open up human possibilities rather than foreclose them.

Understood this way, the themes of community, moral agency, and transcendence in the films of Clint Eastwood invite the cultivation of autonomous moral agency, and clear space for reflection on the human condition. They follow characters in messy situations, and offer tentative and partial resolutions that mimic the tentative and partial resolutions of our own lives. They explore the possibilities of relationships that go beyond the everyday, and explore moments of guilt, forgiveness, redemption, hope, and love.

Notes

1. Even in the comedic films such as *Two Mules for Sister Sara* (1970) and *Any Which Way You Can* (1980) the Eastwood persona is recognizable. In many comedic Eastwood films, such as *Pink Cadillac* (1989), the comedy arises from placing a tough loner into incongruous situations.

2. Melinda Corey and George Ochoa, ed., *American Film Institute Desk Reference* (New York: Dorling Kindersley, 2002), 242.

3. See, for example, Marc Eliot, *American Rebel: The Life of Clint Eastwood* (New York: Harmony, 2009), 4–5.

4. Walker Percy, *The Moviegoer* (New York: Knopf, 1961), 13.

5. Søren Kierkegaard, *The Sickness unto Death: A Christian Psychological Exposition for Upbuilding and Awakening,* Kierkegaard's Writings, vol. 19, ed. and trans. Howard V. Hong and Edna H. Hong (Princeton: Princeton Univ. Press, 1980), 14–27; for Nietzsche on the herd see, for example, *Beyond Good and Evil,* trans. Walter Kaufmann (New York: Vintage, 1966), section 199. Everydayness is articulated as a technical concept by Heidegger (see *Being and Time,* trans. John Macquarrie and Edward Robinson [New York: Harper and Row, 1962], 163–168, 296–304).

6. Friedrich Nietzsche, *The Gay Science,* section 125 (in *The Portable Nietzsche,* trans. Walter Kaufman [New York: Penguin, 1959], 95–96). In Eastwood's third full-length directorial feature, *Breezy* (1973), Edith Alice "Breezy" Breezerman (Kay Lenz) raises the question of the death of God in her first conversation with Frank Harmon (William Holden). Her comment is part of a con to convince Frank to feed her, but there is no doubt that the absence of God and concomitant decline of traditional religion are persistent themes in Eastwood's films.

7. The soundtrack includes what seem to be the sounds of the unseen killer whistling, loading, and then firing, but the sounds are insufficient to identify the shooter.

8. Film quotations in this essay are cited directly from the film soundtracks.

9. A rare exception to this is the conclusion of *A Fistful of Dollars* (1964), where Eastwood's character, Joe, generously offers money to help an abused family escape to find peace. Why he does this remains a mystery.

10. See Rist, *Stoic Philosophy* (Cambridge: Cambridge Univ. Press, 1969), 61; Epictetus, *The Handbook of Epictetus,* trans. Nicholas White (Indianapolis: Hackett, 1983), sections 3 and 11. Here the Stoic notion, developed from the Cynics, that human beings belong to the "cosmic city," plays a key role (see, for example, Cicero, *The Nature of the Gods,* trans. P. G. Walsh [Oxford: Clarendon Press, 1997], 75).

11. Marcus Aurelius, *Meditations,* trans. Maxwell Staniforth (New York: Penguin, 1964), 46 (2.5).

12. Epictetus, *Handbook,* section 17.

13. See Epictetus, *Handbook,* section 1; J. M. Rist, *Stoic Philosophy,* 126–132.

14. We find out as the film unfolds that Texas Ranger Red Garnett (Eastwood), who is leading the manhunt for Haynes, played a critical role in Haynes's assignment to the penal farm.

15. Haynes is hypersensitive about mistreatment of children, and committed to promoting what he takes to be their welfare. He decides to kill his fellow prison escapee, Terry Pugh (Keith Szarabajka), only in response to Pugh's threats toward Phillip. He is friendly and appreciative of the hospitality of Mack and his wife, and does not resort to

violence even when Mack accidentally discovers his identity, until Mack's frightened lashing out at his grandson causes something in Haynes to break. At the end of the film, as Haynes is bleeding profusely from a gunshot to the gut, and is surrounded by dozens of armed officers, he bizarrely negotiates with Phillip's mother to ensure that as a condition of his surrender of Phillip, Phillip will be allowed to trick-or-treat and enjoy visits to the fair.

16. Rist, *Stoic Philosophy,* 127.

17. Ibid., 126–127; Marcus Aurelius, *Meditations,* 45–46 (2.3).

18. Percy, *The Moviegoer,* 13; see also Ralph C. Wood, *The Comedy of Redemption: Christian Faith and Comic Vision in Four American Novelists* (Notre Dame, Ind.: Notre Dame Univ. Press, 2000), 158; Jan Nordby Gretlund, "On the Porch with Marcus Aurelius: Walker Percy's Stoicism," in *Walker Percy: Novelist and Philosopher* (Jackson: Univ. Press of Mississippi, 1991), 74–84.

19. Stoicism and existentialism represent the twin legacies of Percy's intellectual formation; see Jan Nordby Gretlund interview with Walker Percy, "Difficult Times," in Walker Percy, Lewis A. Lawson, and Victor A. Kramer, *More Conversations with Walker Percy* (Jackson: Univ. Press of Mississippi, 1993), 105–106.

20. Eastwood's continuing preoccupation with the "perfect world" is a key feature of the analysis of Sara Anson Vaux, *The Ethical Vision of Clint Eastwood* (Grand Rapids, Mich.: Eerdmans, 2012), xiv–xv, 123.

21. Numerous story elements of *Pale Rider* echo episodes in *Shane.* For example, the scene in which Shane (Alan Ladd) establishes his willingness to work for and with the homesteaders by chopping away at a stump with Joe Starett (Van Heflin) is replicated in *Pale Rider* with the Preacher (Eastwood) and miner Hull Barret (Michael Moriarty) alternating sledgehammer blows on a large stone. For links between *Shane, Pale Rider,* and other Eastwood films, see "Subverting *Shane*: Ambiguities in Eastwood's Politics in *Fistful of Dollars, High Plains Drifter,* and *Pale Rider,*" in *Clint Eastwood, Actor and Director: New Perspectives,* ed. Leonard Engel (Salt Lake City: Univ. of Utah Press, 2007), 129–156.

22. The opening sequence of *Shane* is visually similar to *For a Few Dollars More,* with a wide scenery shot marked by a lone rider. However, *Shane*'s swelling orchestral score creates a very different atmosphere than that of *Dollars*—one of anticipation and promise.

23. While Megan's prayer quotes the King James Version of Psalm 23 with minor variants, the final line uses wording closer to the Book of Common Prayer (Psalm 23:6).

24. The quote from Revelation 6:7–8 in the screenplay does not precisely match any standard English translation of the Bible, but its rhythms echo those of the King James Version.

25. The murder of Spider in town by Stockburn and his deputies copies the murder of Torrey (Elisha Cook Jr.) by gunslinger Wilson (Jack Palance) in *Shane,* just as the argument by Hull and the Preacher for the miners to stay replicates the Cemetery Hill speeches of Starett and Shane for the homesteaders to remain resolute.

26. Strictly speaking, Daggett charges the cowboys to compensate saloon owner Skinny Dubois (Anthony James) for the damage to his "property," namely, Delilah. One cowboy offers to give Delilah a horse, but Strawberry Alice (Frances Fisher) refuses to allow her to accept it and drives him away. Thus one act of unforgiveness begins the chain of events that brings William Munny to Big Whiskey (see Carl Plantinga, "Spectacles of Death," *Cinema Journal* 37, no. 2 [1998]: 68).

27. Plantinga, "Spectacles of Death," 69.

28. Claims made in *Unforgiven,* both by characters and the text-crawl narrator at the beginning and the end of the film, must all be taken cautiously. After all, the entire subplot with English Bob and his erstwhile chronicler, W. W. Beauchamp (Saul Rubinek), dramatically illustrates the imagination, invention, and outright fabrication of traditional Western narratives. Further, the Schofield Kid can't resist embroidering his tale of killing Quick Mike (David Mucci), initially claiming that he went for his gun, when he actually was helplessly sitting in the outhouse (on Western mythmaking, see Plantinga, "Spectacles of Death," 70, 75–76). However, the undeniable contrast of Munny's domesticity and frustrated pig-farming on the one hand and his coldness and gunfighting prowess on the other shows that some very dramatic transformation happened to him at some point. Even if the stories the Schofield Kid heard about William Munny were wildly embellished exaggerations, surely he was, at one time, a very violent and unpleasant man.

29. Wood, *The Comedy of Redemption,* 155. One might regard Munny's dead wife as an imagined ideal that is punctured by reality. This is of course a possibility. Whether one reads her this way or not has to do with whether one sees Munny's redemption as ultimately illusory.

30. Mario Sesti admires the "wonderment and wisdom" of Munny's comments in this sequence, and finds them a voice for Eastwood's own outlook, which he says sketches "an impossible notion of something like a contemporary theology" ("Unforgiven," in *The Hidden God: Film and Faith,* ed. Mary Lea Bandy and Antonio Monda [New York: Museum of Modern Art, 2003], 205). As I see it, however, the "theology" of *Unforgiven* is not found in the austere Stoicism of Munny's comments to the Schofield Kid in this admittedly transcendent scene, but in the intimations of grace and forgiveness that are mediated by the absent presence of Munny's dead wife, who is herself something of an absent incarnation of God (see Paul Wallace, "Love, Fear, and Insincerity in Clint Eastwood's *Unforgiven,*" http://psnt.net/blog/essays/love-fear-and-insincerity-in-clint-eastwoods-unforgiven/ [accessed August 8, 2012]).

31. Eliot, *American Rebel,* 263.

32. "The very narrative structure of the film—in which not one character refrains from committing ruthless abuses when pushed toward them by his or her nature or idea of justice—points to a higher form of consciousness, both tragic and calm, inexorable and perfect" (Sesti, "Unforgiven," 200).

33. The screenplay for *Unforgiven* gives no direction for a view of Delilah as Munny

leaves Big Whiskey. By contrast, it does specify that as he rides out of town "there are tears running down Munny's cheeks" (see David Webb Peoples, *The William Munny Killings: Original Screenplay,* production draft, April 23, 1984, http://www.imsdb.com/scripts/Unforgiven.html [accessed October 6, 2010]). Such a scene would establish repentance on the part of Munny, but Eastwood omits it from the film.

34. Earlier titles were *Whore's Gold, The Cut-Whore Killings,* and *The William Munny Killings* (see Eastwood's introduction to the film at the AFI's 40th Anniversary Night at the Movies, http://www.youtube.com/watch?v=n3WzeAz1nPE [accessed October 6, 2010]; Eliot, *American Rebel,* 263–264).

35. The original screenplay includes a scene with Munny and his children at home after his return from Big Whiskey that provides further evidence for Munny's genuine affection for and commitment to his children. He is depicted as genuinely happy to see his children, and proud that they carried on the work of the farm while he was away. He conceals the events that occurred in Big Whiskey from them, assuring his son that thanks to the loving redemption of his wife, "I ain't like I was no more" (Peoples, *The William Munny Killings*). This could be viewed as a self-protecting lie, or it could be understood as a deception to protect his children, given the fact that he has in fact become something different from what he was before he met his wife, despite the temporary resurrection of that self in Big Whiskey.

36. See Raymond Foery, "Narrative Pacing and the Eye of the Other," in *Clint Eastwood, Actor and Director: New Perspectives,* ed. Leonard Engel (Salt Lake City: Univ. of Utah Press, 2007), 196.

37. See Walker Percy, *Lost in the Cosmos: The Last Self-Help Book* (New York: Farrar, Straus and Giroux, 1983), 114–159.

38. A romantic vision of the film might have left the wistful lovers with their last fleeting view of one another in the rain (see Foery, "Narrative Pacing and the Eye of the Other," 202). However, this would miss what I take to be the central suggestion of the film, that the ecstasies of romance must take their proper place in the overall context of a well-lived life.

39. Meryl Streep noted that a significant element of the power of this scene in the film is the fact that in the midst of a movie focused on verbal content, this scene is almost entirely visual (*Bridges of Madison County* DVD release Special Features, "An Old-Fashioned Love Story: Making *The Bridges of Madison County*"). The sparseness of the film score also contributes to the scene's emotional affect. (For a further discussion of Eastwood's use of silence in his films, see Richard McClelland's first essay in this volume.)

40. Rist, *Stoic Philosophy,* 32–33.

41. The thematic decentering of the self is mirrored by the architecture of the film: while Francesca is the hero and main character of *Bridges,* viewers of the film discover her story vicariously as her children discover it. The multiple perspectives of the story reflect the way that one's story is woven with the stories of others in a family.

42. Walter Metz notes that Maggie's family ranks as "the worst poor-white-trash ste-

reotyping in any recent Hollywood film" ("The Old Man and the C: Masculinity and Age in the Films of Clint Eastwood," in *Clint Eastwood, Actor and Director: New Perspectives,* ed. Leonard Engel [Salt Lake City: Univ. of Utah Press, 2007], 215).

43. See John M. Gourlie, "*Million Dollar Baby*: The Deep Heart's Core," in *Clint Eastwood, Actor and Director: New Perspectives,* ed. Leonard Engel (Salt Lake City: Univ. of Utah Press, 2007), 249. For a Stoic account of the dynamic of individual virtue and affection for another, see Cicero, *On Friendship,* in *Other Selves: Philosophers on Friendship,* ed. Michael Pakaluk (Indianapolis, Ind.: Hackett, 1991), 79–116.

44. Another facile—and in my view false—reading is the claim that "Frankie sacrifices his [effectively adopted] daughter [Maggie] to the heavenly father (unless she is indeed damned), in the process possibly sacrificing his immortal soul" (Tania Modleski, "Clint Eastwood and Male Weepies," *American Literary History* 22, no. 1 [2009]: 139). Frankie's conflicted Catholicism plays a role in his dilemma, but he does not see his action in any way as serving the demands of God, or promoting his own redemption.

45. Some critics have attacked the movie on this count, precisely because Maggie, who is such a fighter, gives up so easily, and because Frankie, who supposedly loves Maggie so deeply, has ensconced her in a facility that does little to provide rehabilitative care. See Tim Gilmer, "Frankie's Lemon Meringue Afterlife," *New Mobility* (July 2005), http://www.newmobility.com/articleView.cfm?id=1039 (accessed August 25, 2012).

46. See Gourlie, "*Million Dollar Baby*: The Deep Heart's Core," 247–248.

47. Søren Kierkegaard, *Fear and Trembling,* in *Fear and Trembling* and *Repetition,* Kierkegaard's Writings, vol. 6, ed. and trans. Howard V. Hong and Edna H. Hong (Princeton: Princeton Univ. Press, 1983), esp. 54–67.

48. The physical setting of *Gran Torino* in this way parallels the narrative environment of another of Walker Percy's novels, *Love in the Ruins* (New York: Farrar, Straus and Giroux, 1971).

49. The casting of Carley as Father Janovich is a great example of how a director can shape the effect of a script. While Carley was thirty years old at the time *Gran Torino* was filmed, he looked much younger, perhaps early twenties. That casting choice emphasized Walt's view of the juvenile irrelevance of the church.

50. The possibility of genuine and compelling messages amid the static of popular culture is a Kierkegaardian theme brilliantly taken up by Walker Percy, perhaps most notably exemplified by his "The Last Donahue Show" (Percy, *Lost in the Cosmos,* 45–56).

51. Walt should have done all of these things for his own sons. Perhaps he did, but for some reason—perhaps because of the guilt Walt feels over killing the surrendering Korean—he finds it easier to relate to Thao than to his biological family.

52. It is difficult not to notice the contrast between *Pale Rider* and *Gran Torino* on this score. *Pale Rider* places the use of violence into a moral-theological context, while *Gran Torino* ultimately rejects it altogether. (Karen Hoffman reaches a similar conclusion in her essay in this volume.)

53. It is easy to read Walt's development in the movie as a move from being brusquely

self-centered to becoming "completely selfless" (Ed Gonzales, "Eastwood Critics Roundtable Pt. 2: Gran Torino," http://www.youtube.com/watch?v=gWun9zSQYvg [accessed 28 August 2012]). But this misunderstands goodness as a move away from the self, rather than the self's choice to affirm what is good and right no matter where it is found (see Aristotle, *Nicomachean Ethics,* 2nd ed., trans. Terence Irwin [Indianapolis, Ind.: Hackett, 1999], 9.8.1168b1–1169a34).

54. *The Moviegoer,* 13.

Hereafter and the Problems of Evil

Clint Eastwood as Practical Philosopher

Brian B. Clayton

> Talk to me about the truth of religion and I'll listen gladly. Talk to me about the duty of religion and I'll listen submissively. But don't come talking to me about the consolations of religion or I shall suspect that you don't understand.
>
> —C. S. Lewis, *A Grief Observed*

Clint Eastwood's *Hereafter* (2010) begins peacefully enough: we hear Bruce Forman playing on acoustic guitar the film's simple musical theme, composed by Clint Eastwood—a theme that is then joined by the sound of waves gently washing up on a shoreline. The sights are equally peaceful and tranquil: the camera first pans to show us a beautiful tropical beach filled with families and vacationers before it moves to the interior of a suite in a luxury seaside hotel. There we first see Marie Lelay (Cécile de France) as she gets out of bed and awakens her companion Didier (Thierry Neuvic) to remind him, in French, that they must go buy gifts for his children back home in Paris. Didier leaves the errand to Marie, who emerges from the hotel to cross the beach and visit the street vendors who cater to the tourists. The first sign that something is wrong is a low rumbling sound and the cries of alarm we hear from the perspective of Didier's room. Didier rises and goes to the balcony in time to see the ocean waters rapidly receding as an immense wave begins to rush toward the shore. The tsunami overwhelms children, adults, buildings, and trees and carries with it the debris created by its impact. Back in the street market, Marie and others seem at first to be puzzled by the roaring sound and by the sight of trees toppling at the far end of the street. As the waters roar up the street, pushing cars, bodies, telephone poles and other debris with them, Marie and the others realize the danger and try futilely to escape. Marie is eventually knocked unconscious and we see her beneath the waters and hear what seems to be the beating of her heart slow down and eventually cease. Eastwood shows us Marie's experience of a white light that backlights the figures of various people and then shows us two men who are attempting, apparently without success, to revive her. She is not breathing and has no pulse, while all around her the destructive work of the tsunami continues. Eastwood again shows us her vision of the white light and indistinct shapes and muffled sounds. The vision comes to include a helicopter overhead and then Eastwood returns to a shot of Marie as she vomits up the seawater, coughs, and returns to consciousness and to life. We next see Didier wandering through the devastation left after the floodwaters receded and running to take Marie in his arms when he spots her stumbling through the debris. All of this takes place within the first ten minutes of the film and sets out the general concern of the film with the "hereafter." However, the possible reality and nature of a "hereafter" is not the only theme that the film raises and explores. The same tsunami that leads to Marie's fascination with the "hereafter" is also responsible for the deaths of tens of thousands of people and the loss of homes, businesses, and property. Thus, the film also provides examples of the kinds of data that raise the perennial philosophical problems of evil. These data I will call instances of suffering, in a sense to be explained below. It is with the philosophical and pastoral problems of evil raised by suffering and with Clint Eastwood's treatment of these problems that the present essay will concern itself.

As both actor and director, Eastwood has dealt in many of his films with the kinds of suffering that generate the problems of evil. One has only to look at a partial list of the films since 2001 that Eastwood has directed or in which he has acted to get a sense of the various contexts in which he has addressed these experiences. One encounters suffering in the forms of a serial killer (*Blood Work*, 2002), child abuse and the murder of a child (*Mystic River*, 2003), severe physical injury (*Million Dollar Baby*, 2004), the horrors of war (*Flags of Our Fathers* and *Letters from Iwo Jima*, both 2006), the kidnapping of a child (*Changeling*, 2008), racism and gang violence (*Gran Torino*, 2008), apartheid and political oppression (*Invictus*, 2009), and natural disaster (*Hereafter*, 2010). In his choice of these scripts to direct and in his direction itself, we see an ongoing focus on the personal and practical dimensions of suffering that give rise to the problems of evil.

This essay will begin with a brief summary of what philosophers generally call "the problem of evil," but which I think is better thought of as the *problems* of evil. Of particular interest to us will be a distinction between what we can call the philosophical and pastoral dimensions of these problems. I will then briefly consider Eastwood's *Mystic River* as an example not only of his awareness of the philosophical dimension of the problems, but also of his relative lack of interest in this dimension and his more practical concern with the pastoral dimension. The remainder of the essay will then treat various versions of the pastoral problems of evil that arise in *Hereafter* and note how Eastwood treats these problems in the film. Just as his directorial and acting style is workmanlike and practical, he has been concerned to portray the problems of evil in very practical and concrete ways and to explore practical and concrete responses to the pastoral dimension of the problems. Eastwood argues visually that no matter what one has to say about the philosophical and cosmic dimensions of the problems of evil, one must still confront in a practical way the pastoral and personal dimensions of these problems. In this way, we will see Eastwood at work as practical philosopher.

The Problems of Evil

The data that give rise to the problems of evil I categorize as suffering. Suffering here includes those experiences of unwanted physical or mental pain that can cause a moral agent to seek the purpose or meaning of those experiences. The moral agent wants to understand these experiences and to understand why they occur. The moral agent may experience suffering either directly or vicariously. An example of a direct experience of suffering would be my experience of pain if my Achilles tendon were suddenly to rupture. An example of a vicarious experience of suffering would be my experience of seeing a cat struck by a car, yet still alive and in obvious pain. There are many degrees of directness and vicariousness, of course. These data give rise to both the philosophical and pastoral problems of evil.

The philosophical problems of evil are a challenge to religious belief. In *The Problem of Pain,* C. S. Lewis's popular treatment of this problem as it relates to traditional Christian theism, he puts the point this way: "In a sense, [Christian theism] creates, rather than solves, the problem of pain, for pain would be no problem unless, side by side with our daily experience of this painful world, we had received what we think a good assurance that ultimate reality is righteous and loving." What Lewis here calls "pain" is what I have called "suffering." As Richard McClelland has noted, "No amount or type of adversity is enough to pose a problem of evil. Only adversity seen in the light of the God hypothesis constitutes such a problem." Thus, the philosophical problems of evil are problems only for those who acknowledge the reality of suffering and who wish to consider the possibility that a God exists who is perfectly benevolent, powerful, and knowing.[1]

In his *Summa Theologica,* St. Thomas Aquinas considers two arguments against the existence of God. The second of these arguments relies upon a version of Ockham's razor to conclude that belief in God's existence is unnecessary and therefore unreasonable because we can account for all of reality without appeal to the existence of God as the source of reality. The first argument, however, is an attempt to prove that God does not exist. St. Thomas writes: "It seems that God does not exist; because if one of two contraries be infinite, the other would be altogether destroyed. But the word 'God' means that He is infinite goodness. If, therefore, God existed, there would be no evil discoverable; but there is evil in the world. Therefore God does not exist."[2] This is a simple version of the philosophical deductive argument from evil. There are more complicated versions of the argument, but this one will suffice for our purposes as allowing us to note a number of distinctions that philosophers have made over the years.

First, note that St. Thomas uses the word "evil" without telling us what he means by this term. Subsequent philosophers have generally distinguished between two types of evil, moral evil and natural evil. By "moral evil" philosophers refer to those wrongs that result from finite moral agency, especially human agency. For example, someone who murders another would be a moral agent who has wronged another and murder would fall into the category of moral evil. By "natural evil" philosophers intend to refer to harms that do not result directly or primarily from moral agency. For example, the tsunami with which *Hereafter* begins harms many people, but the tsunami itself is generally thought not to be the result of moral agency. Instead, the tsunami is the result of the regular operations of natural processes and any harm that results from it is not intended.

Both moral and natural evil can be used by the philosophical deductive argument from evil. For example, in *Mystic River,* when Jimmy Markum (Sean Penn) learns that his daughter Katie (Emmy Rossum) has been murdered, he might ask, "How can there be a God who lets my daughter be murdered?" Implicit in this question would be an argument we could summarize like this:

1. If God exists, then there should be no moral evil.
2. But there is moral evil (for example, murders of daughters).
3. So, God does not exist.

A natural evil, such as the tsunami, could provide a parallel version of the argument:

1. If God exists, then there should be no natural evil.
2. But there is natural evil (for example, death and destruction caused by tsunamis).
3. So, God does not exist.

The idea behind both of these arguments is that if God exists, then God would be ultimately morally responsible for the existence both of the moral agents who bring about moral evil and of the natural systems whose operations bring about natural evil. It is the existence of either of these kinds of evil that is taken to be incompatible with the existence of God, especially the God of theism.

The second thing we may note in connection with St. Thomas's version of the argument is that it is conceived of as a valid deductive argument such that if the premises of the argument are true, then the conclusion must also be true. In recent years, inductive versions of the argument have gained more attention among philosophers. In part, the growing interest in inductive versions is a result of the perception that deductive versions have been satisfactorily answered. The most famous such answer to the deductive versions of the argument is probably the "free will defense" that the American philosopher Alvin Plantinga set out in his book *God, Freedom, and Evil* (1974). In general terms, Plantinga argued that the first premises of the deductive arguments were not obviously true, that those premises relied on certain other assumptions, and that those assumptions were questionable. Plantinga's free will defense generated a great deal of discussion and debate among philosophers, but in the words of Michael L. Peterson, "The outcomes of these and other debates have been so favorable to theists that it is reasonable to say that the [deductive] problem has been laid to rest."[3]

In the wake of Plantinga's work, the resulting discussion has come increasingly to focus on inductive versions of the argument from evil, more generally known as the evidential argument from evil. In general, there are two types of evidential arguments. One type we can call the quantitative inductive argument from evil. It argues that there is simply too much evil for it to be reasonable for one to believe that God exists. One could formalize the argument as follows:

1. If God exists, then it is unlikely that there would be a great deal of evil.
2. But there is a great deal of evil.
3. So, it is unlikely that God exists.

In a world after Hitler, Stalin, and Pol Pot, it certainly seems reasonable to think that there is a great deal of evil, even a great deal too much evil.

The other type of evidential argument we can call the qualitative inductive argument from evil and it could be formalized in the following way:

1. If God exists, then it is unlikely that there would be purposeless evil.
2. But it appears that there is purposeless evil.
3. So, it is unlikely that God exists.

Instances of apparently purposeless evil and suffering abound. One has only to consider the suffering that occurs in nature as creatures engage in the Darwinian "struggle for existence," the existence of anencephalic human newborns, children born with Tay-Sachs disease, etc. One may reasonably ask, What is the point or purpose of all of the suffering caused by these conditions? Of course, the quantitative and qualitative versions of the arguments can be combined, too.

The third thing to note about St. Thomas's version of the argument from evil is his reply to the objection. He writes: "As Augustine says (*Enchiridion,* xi): 'Since God is the highest good, He would not allow any evil to exist in His works, unless His omnipotence and goodness were such as to bring good even out of evil.' This is part of the infinite goodness of God, that He should allow evil to exist, and out of it produce good." This reply is a very general theodicy, an attempt to justify to humans the ways of God. It is a general theodicy in that it doesn't give a specific reason for God allowing evil, but instead gives as a general reason that we can expect an all-powerful and perfectly good God to bring good even out of the evil that He allows. More specific theodicies point to some particular purpose that God might have in allowing for evil. For example, a common theodicy offered in response to moral evil is that such evil is the result of moral agency, which presupposes significant moral freedom, and that such freedom is necessary in order to bring about a particular good (for example, the creature's freely offered worship and love of the Creator) that could not be otherwise achieved. Theodicies are to be contrasted with the approach that Plantinga takes in *God, Freedom, and Evil,* where he offers what he terms a "defense," which he distinguishes from a theodicy. The difference is that in a defense one does not attempt to show why God *does* allow evil, but instead one attempts to show only why God *might* allow evil.[4]

A final thing to note about St. Thomas's version of the argument from evil and his response to that argument is that it is entirely philosophical or intellectual. That is, it is addressed to an intellectual issue that poses a problem for belief in God's existence. There is another kind of issue, however, that St. Thomas does not address: the pastoral problem. Plantinga draws attention to this dimension of the problem when he concludes his discussion of the problem of evil with the following passage:

> The existence of God is neither precluded nor rendered improbable by the existence of evil. Of course, suffering and misfortune may nonetheless constitute a *problem* for the theist; but the problem is not that his beliefs are logically or probabilistically incompatible. The theist may find a *religious* problem in evil; in the presence of his own suffering or that of someone near to him he may find it difficult to maintain what he takes to be the proper attitude towards God. Faced with great personal suffering or misfortune, he may be tempted to rebel against God, to shake his fist in God's face, or even to give up belief in God altogether. But this is a problem of a different dimension. Such a problem calls, not for philosophical enlightenment, but for pastoral care.[5]

This problem is not addressed by the various philosophical arguments—at least not in any direct way. It is of little use to the person who has just lost a child or who has suffered a profound injustice to be offered a philosophical argument for the logical compatibility of the existence of God and of evil or an argument for the reasonableness of the belief in God's existence despite the existence of such evil. Such a person might believe in the existence of the God of classical theism and be satisfied that the philosophical arguments pose no problem to such belief, and yet experience a crisis of belief or faith when some particular instance of evil is personally experienced either directly or vicariously. What is called for is something more practical, which we might call the pastoral response.

The pastoral response, then, is addressed to the pastoral problems of evil. These problems arise both for one who believes in God's existence and for one who does not believe. Any suffering can pose a personal challenge that requires a response that is other than purely intellectual in nature. It is a personal and practical response that is required. This personal and practical response is the pastoral response to the pastoral problems of evil. The successful pastoral response must be of a kind that allows the one who is suffering to understand the suffering and to be able to act effectively in the presence of the suffering. This is the kind of response on which Eastwood has focused in his films. Before turning to Eastwood's practical treatment of the pastoral dimension of the problems of evil, however, we must note that he is not unaware of the philosophical dimensions of the problem. This requires a brief look at his film *Mystic River.*

Clint Eastwood and the Philosophical Problems of Evil

Mystic River opens with a shot looking out over the rooftops of what we soon learn is a Boston neighborhood. The camera slowly tracks down to look at particular details in the neighborhood—two men sitting on the second floor back porch of a house, two boys, young Jimmy Markum (Jason Kelly) and young Sean Devine (Connor Polo), running through the backyard below on their way to play street hockey. Eventually, the camera comes to focus on those two boys, now joined by a third, young Dave Boyle (Cameron Bowen), as they play in the street. This prologue to the rest of the film recounts what happens to those three boys on that day and in the four days that follow. They are confronted by two middle-aged men in a dark car, men who represent themselves as policemen and who chastise the boys for having written their names in the wet cement of the sidewalk adjacent to the street. The two men force young Dave into the car for the purported purpose of taking him to his mother so that he can confess to her what he has done to municipal property. Eastwood takes special care to focus on the jewelry worn by one of the men: on his right hand he wears a signet ring that bears the image of a cross and around his neck he wears a small gold cross on a chain. In a series of brief scenes we are shown that Dave has been taken by sexual predators from whom he escapes four days later. As Dave escapes through the woods, Eastwood has his camera point to the little bit of sky that can be seen through the trees and then has the camera spin as the scene goes to black. This prologue ends with young Jimmy and Sean looking up at Dave's silhouette in an upstairs window in his home.[6]

The technique of moving the shot upward and spinning is one that Eastwood uses several times throughout the film. It suggests both an appeal to heaven and the silence that meets that appeal. In visual terms, the shot asks, Where is God? Where is justice for the innocent who have been harmed by the "wolves" who prey upon them?

These questions come to fore in the remainder of the story, which picks up twenty-five years later with an adult Dave Boyle (Tim Robbins), Jimmy Markum (Sean Penn), and Sean Devine (Kevin Bacon). Jimmy has spent time in prison, has a grown daughter, Katie (Emmy Rossum), and has remarried after the death of his first wife. His present wife is Annabeth (Laura Linney), but it becomes clear that Jimmy's world revolves around Katie. Jimmy runs a convenience store in the fictional Buckingham Flats neighborhood of Boston. He is no longer involved in criminal activity, but his second-marriage brothers-in-law, the Savage brothers Val (Kevin Chapman), Nick (Adam Nelson), and Kevin (Robert Wahlberg), seem still to be involved in petty crime. Dave has married Annabeth's cousin Celeste (Marcia Gay Harden) and has a young son. Sean is married to Lauren (Tori Davis), but she has left him and they are separated when we first see the adult Sean. Sean is a Trooper in the homicide unit of the Massachusetts State Police. The event that drives the rest of the film is Katie's murder and the search for her killer(s).

Emergency dispatchers receive a report of an abandoned car, and when police arrive at the scene they discover blood and other evidence of violence. Sean and his partner, Whitey Powers (Laurence Fishburne), are called in to search for the body because the park adjacent to the street where the car was abandoned is under state jurisdiction. Sean learns that the car belongs to Katie Markum and quickly infers that she is likely the victim of murder. The search for Katie's body begins and focuses on the park.

Again, Eastwood draws attention to the presence or absence of God in the midst of this moral evil. Shots of the search for Katie's body are intercut with scenes from the First Communion of one of Jimmy's younger daughters in which we hear the priest repeatedly say "Body of Christ" as he distributes the Host. Jimmy is concerned about Katie's absence from her sister's Communion and, after Mass, eventually makes his way to the crime scene, where he recognizes her car. Katie's body is finally found in the old bear cage at the abandoned zoo in the park. It is significant, again, that the camera gazes skyward from the position of Katie's body as Eastwood shows us Sean's "Oh, Christ" response to the discovery. The next shot is from above as Sean climbs into the pit to examine the body. One of the attending officers notes that Katie's head has been split at the crown and that she has been beaten with a stick. This suggests a religious connection with the "crowning" and beating of Christ prior to His crucifixion, especially since neither crowning nor beating was the actual cause of death in either case. Sean wonders aloud what he will say to Jimmy: "Hey, Jimmy. God said you owed another marker. He came to collect." In the meantime, Jimmy has managed to get through the police barricades and comes rushing toward the body's location. Jimmy is in obvious despair as he is restrained by police and cries out, "Is my daughter in there?! Is she in there?!" As Jimmy understands the answers to his questions, his face turns heavenward and the camera looks down on him from above as he screams out, "Oh, no! Oh, God, no!" The camera pulls back as Jimmy continues to struggle and scream, dissolves into a similarly situated view of Katie's broken and abandoned body, and then pans around and upward to show the leaden heavens through the tops of the trees.[7]

By the way in which he moves his camera, intercuts his shots, and ends with the upward pan to the heavens, Eastwood sets this moral evil in a religious context in which all of the issues of the philosophical problems of evil are affectively present to the viewer. It would seem that Eastwood has set us up for a cinematic consideration of these problems. However, from this point on, the story largely turns into a police procedural and a drama firmly rooted in the everyday world.[8]

The religious and philosophical issues remain in the background, but they are never directly addressed and never resolved. Near the end of the film, Jimmy has come to believe that Dave killed Katie and he takes him out by the Mystic River in order to execute him. Jimmy tells Dave that, years ago, he had executed "Just Ray" Harris, who had betrayed him to the police and prevented him from being with his first wife as she was dying of cancer. Jimmy says, "I could feel God watching me, shaking his head. Not angry . . . but like if a puppy shit on the rug." He goes on to say, "We bury our sins here, Dave. We wash them clean." Then he kills Dave by shooting him, which we see from Dave's perspective as he looks up into the white light of the muzzle blast. The camera then tracks downward and we see that the muzzle blast has become the light of the sky of the following morning. As the camera continues to track, we see Jimmy in the old neighborhood, sitting on the curb and drinking from a bottle. Sean arrives and tells Jimmy that they have caught Katie's killers. Jimmy's face shows us that he slowly realizes that Dave was innocent.[9]

The final shot of the film begins as a repetition of one that has occurred several times throughout the film: the camera moves in across the dark surface of the water and toward the neighborhood on the far shore. This time, however, the camera slowly descends into the water and the darkness beneath its surface. There are no answers coming from the heavens.

The point of this summary of various scenes and shots from the film is twofold. First, the upward movement of the camera at key points seems to me clearly to indicate an awareness of the philosophical problems of evil, the challenge that it poses to religious belief. That there is an awareness of the religious dimension of the problems of evil is reinforced by the intercutting of shots (the Catholic Mass and the search for Katie's body) and the dialogue ("I could feel God watching me.... We bury our sins here...."). But, second, this awareness is not followed up within the context of the film. There is no explicit discussion of God's justice, of God's response to the evil and suffering the film's characters experience. Instead, the focus is on practical matters of how people deal with their experiences of loss and pain. The focus is on different ways of thinking of earthly justice, different ways of handling the problems of evil in the everyday. Jimmy handles these problems by seeking vengeance, especially after he comes to believe that Sean and the authorities are not having success in solving the crime and that he knows the killer's identity. Sean handles these problems by using proper police procedures to try to find those responsible for the crimes. Sean also handles these problems by being humble and admitting his failings. He tells his estranged wife that he is sorry for having pushed her away. The result is that his wife will return home and that she finally tells him the name of his daughter, who has been born while father and mother have been separated. It is probably significant that the daughter's name is Nora, which means "honor"—a name of which Sean approves. In dealing with Katie's murder, Sean has sought to be honorable, upright, in pursuing justice. This stands in stark contrast with Jimmy, who, according to a code of tribal honor much different than the one Sean seeks to uphold, has pursued vengeance and deceived his childhood friend Dave in order to exact that vengeance. Eastwood's visual telling of the story is very much focused on this world and shows little interest in attempting to resolve or pursue grand philosophical problems.

Clint Eastwood and the Pastoral Problems of Evil

Eastwood's evident awareness of the philosophical problems of evil and his decision not to address these problems in their intellectual or cosmic dimension are significant in that it tells us that his orientation is practical and personal. He argues visually that no matter what one has to say about the philosophical and cosmic dimensions of the problems of evil, one must still confront in a practical way the pastoral and personal dimensions of these problems. We see this very clearly in his direction in *Hereafter.*

The film tells the stories of three major characters—stories that eventually intersect and intertwine. The first major character we meet is French journalist Marie Lelay, the beginning of whose story I summarized earlier. The second character is George Lonegan (Matt Damon), a bachelor from the San Francisco Bay area who as a child was ill with encephalomyelitis and, while being operated on, died several times on the operating table, only to be brought back each time. At some point after the operation, George began to experience migraines and to have nightmares and what he calls "connections," or visions. Doctors diagnosed him with passive schizophrenia and gave him medication, but George found the medication not only ended the visions, but also "pretty much stopped everything else." George decided to stop taking the medication and to live with the visions, but found that his psychic visions are not a gift but a curse. As he says, "It ruins any chance I have at a normal life."[10] The third major character is Marcus, the younger identical twin of Jason (Frankie and George McLaren). The boys live in London with their mother, Jackie (Lyndsey Marshal), a drug addict who has decided finally to get clean. When Jason, in Marcus's place, goes to the chemist's to pick up medication for his mother, he is confronted by some bullies, runs into the street in an effort to escape them, and is hit by a truck and killed.

Each of these characters experiences the kind and degree of suffering that would naturally give rise to the philosophical problems of evil. There is the tsunami, critical illness, one's own death, the death of tens of thousands, the death of a beloved twin brother, a terrorist bombing, unjust treatment at the hand of a colleague, the loss of a possible romantic relationship. But with respect to each of these instances of suffering and loss, Eastwood focuses not on the philosophical problems but on the pastoral problems. He seems concerned not so much by the possible future reality and nature of a hereafter as he is concerned with the present reality and nature of the here-and-now sufferings of his characters. Even as he was wrapping up *Invictus* and, thus, before he began filming *Hereafter,* Eastwood said the following in an interview with Scott Foundas for *LA Weekly*: "[There's] a certain charlatan aspect to the hereafter, to those who prey on people's beliefs that there's some afterlife, and mankind doesn't seem to be willing to accept that this is your life and you should do the best you can with it and enjoy it while you're here, and that'll be enough. There has to be immortality or eternal life and embracing some religious thing. I don't have the answer. Maybe there is a hereafter, but I don't know, so I approach it by not knowing. I just tell the story." In an interview with Geoff Boucher of the *Los Angeles Times* in September 2010, at which point *Hereafter* was completed and was shortly to premiere at the 35th Toronto International Film Festival, Eastwood said of the afterlife: "People ask me what I believe. . . . I say, 'I don't know yet.' I'm not closed off to it. There are points in my life when I thought I knew all the answers and other times when I was sure I didn't know any of them. Right now, well, I'm waiting to see. Aren't we all?" Eastwood's focus is on the practical. He doesn't pretend to have the answers. "I just tell the story." The story of these characters—their suffering, their needs, and their pursuit of practical ways of addressing their suffering and needs—he thinks to be well worth the telling, quite apart from the grander philosophical and religious issues about the reality of the afterlife.[11]

Each of the major characters in the story confronts problems that arise largely from the reality of death. Marie has died and been revived, as has George. But George has the additional complicating factor that his encounter with death has left him with an apparent ability to connect with the dead. Marcus, of course, has seen his dead twin brother and is confronted with trying to figure out how to live his life without the older brother (older by five minutes) to whom he has always looked for advice and direction. Insofar as their sufferings are connected by the reality of death, their needs are also connected: each of them needs a way to understand, a way to make sense of how to live in light of the reality of death. Marie needs to understand what happened to her when she died. She needs to make sense of what she experienced. George needs to understand how he can live his life without his psychic curse making it impossible for him. Marcus needs to understand what his life is now that his brother is no longer alive to guide him.

In keeping with his practical approach, we should not expect Eastwood to offer us a one-size-fits-all solution to the pastoral problems of suffering each of the characters confronts. However, there are certain themes or patterns that do emerge when we take a closer look at all three of the stories.

When Marie returns to Paris after the tsunami, she attempts to return to work as a television anchor and investigative journalist but finds herself so distracted by her memories of what she experienced when it appeared that she was dead that she is unable to concentrate. Her producer-boyfriend, Didier, advises her to take some additional time off in order to recover and to write the book about which she had long talked. Marie does this and gets a contract with a publisher to write a hard-hitting look at François Mitterrand. At a celebratory dinner with Didier, Marie asks him what he thinks happens at death. Didier responds, "That's a strange question. . . . When you die, you die. The lights go out, that's it." Despite Didier's dismissal of her concern and even while researching the book, Marie is haunted by memories of her experience and eventually searches the Internet in an effort to see what others might say about such experiences. She discovers the website for the (fictional) Hospice du Couchant–Centre médicalisé Suisse, which is directed by Dr. Claudia Rousseau (Marthe Keller), and arranges a visit. Dr. Rousseau indicates to Marie that she is a former atheist whose decades-long experiences at the hospice have changed her views. When Marie asks Dr. Rousseau what she experienced during the tsunami, Rousseau straightforwardly tells her that it was death. She then provides Marie with a great deal of material for research and Marie returns to Paris to write her book. It is no longer a book on Mitterrand but is now a book entitled *Hereafter: The Conspiracy of Silence.* When she meets with the publisher to discuss her manuscript on the day of the London Underground bombings, the publishing executive Michael (Jean-Yves Berteloot) tells her that he cannot publish the book, that she had promised to deliver a different book, and that she needs to return the advance. Marie has dinner with Didier in order to arrange her return to the television newsroom, but finds that she has been replaced both on the set and in Didier's bed by Jasmine (Mylène Jampanoï). Michael, the publishing executive, calls her later in the evening to tell her that on her behalf he has contacted some American publishers who might be interested in her manuscript. Marie sends off the manuscript. Sometime later she receives a phone call from an American publisher. We next see her at the London Book Fair, where she is to read from and promote her book. It is at the London Book Fair where she first meets George. When their hands touch during Marie's book signing, George has a vision in which Marie is floating, apparently lifeless, in the water. For her part, it is obvious that Marie is attracted to George. When she later receives a rather lengthy handwritten letter from him at her hotel, she reads it with interest. A widening smile shows us her delight. We are never privy to the contents of the letter, but we do see her later entering Leadenhall Market, where George is sitting at a table and waiting for her.

Notice that Marie's suffering was addressed in very specific ways. First, there is Dr. Rousseau, who listens to Marie, takes seriously her experiences and questions, and shares from her own experiences. She was present to Marie in that she attended to what Marie had to say and to her concerns. Second, she acted by providing Marie with research materials and encouraging her to believe that she might have something important to say to help others. Michael, the publishing executive, played a role very similar to the one played by Dr. Rousseau. Although he was unable to publish the book that Marie had written in lieu of the book for which he had contracted, he still listened to her and took her seriously enough to contact other publishers on her behalf and to direct her to those publishers. Again, we see the pattern of listening, being "present," and acting compassionately.

George's story only gradually emerges over the course of the film. As mentioned previously, George has "connections" with or visions of those who are dead. He worked for a time as a professional psychic but quit when it became too much of a burden. It is his brother Billy (Jay Mohr) who pulls George back into doing "readings." George does three readings over the course of the film. The first is with Christos Andreou (Richard Kind), one of Billy's business associates who has lost his wife. The second is with a potential love interest, Melanie (Bryce Dallas Howard). The final reading is with Marcus in London.

During the reading with Christos, we learn that George likes briefly to hold the person's hands to establish a better connection. In his reading with Christos, George asks questions to which Christos is to respond with a simple "Yes" or "No." In general, after letting go of Christos's hands, George does not look him in the face but looks downward and off to the side. Based on George's questions and comments, Christos is quite convinced that George has a "genuine gift," as Billy puts it to George.

Melanie and George meet and pair up as chefs at a night school cooking course. During one of the cooking exercises, their hands touch and George has a vision that seems to disturb him, but he says nothing to Melanie. Later, Melanie returns with George to his apartment so that they can cook dinner together. While there, George retrieves a message from Billy on his answering machine telling him that Christos won't say anything to others about the reading and making the comment about George having a genuine gift. Melanie is intrigued and tries to convince George to give her a reading and in the process again touches George's hand, producing another brief vision. George tries to convince Melanie that a reading would be a bad idea, but he eventually yields to her pleading and does as she asks. Again, in general he looks downward and to the side, not at Melanie's face, as he gives the reading. He tries to cut it off after a few innocuous comments about her deceased mother, but Melanie can tell that there is more. Under pressure, George tells her that her father wants to say that he is sorry and that he asks for her forgiveness for what he did to her many years ago, which appears to have been sexual abuse of some kind. Melanie is understandably upset, leaves the apartment, and collapses in tears at the foot of the steps. George, in turn, appears to be in despair, as his "gift" has ruined yet another opportunity for a normal life.

The third and final reading occurs when Marcus spots George at the London Book Fair. He recognizes him as the psychic from a website that he had visited and pursues him until George finally gives him a reading. Again, George briefly holds Marcus's hands and then, generally looking downward and to the side, asks questions and tells Marcus things that would seem to be coming from Jason. George tells Marcus that Jason wants him no longer to use him as an excuse for not making decisions and that he wants him to stop wearing Jason's cap that Marcus has worn ever since the accident. When George says that Jason is leaving, Marcus replies with tearful pleas that he not go. At this point George looks at Marcus, says that Jason has come back, and then, looking Marcus fully in the face, tells Marcus that he is not to be worried about being on his own because he is not: the two of them, Jason and Marcus, are from one cell and so they are the same. When Jason "leaves" and Marcus asks where he's gone, George confesses that he doesn't know.

Later, as George reads Marie's book in his hotel room, Marcus calls to tell him the hotel where Marie is staying. This leads George to go to the hotel the next day, leave a letter for Marie, and then go to the Leadenhall Market to see if Marie shows up. In this case, when Marie and George touch hands, there is no connection to the dead. There is mutual recognition and we anticipate that George may finally have found the possibility for a normal life.

George's suffering was addressed in ways appropriate to his situation but that bear striking similarities to the ways in which Marie's suffering was addressed. First, there is Marcus, who observed George looking at and speaking with Marie at the book fair. He paid attention and saw that George liked her. When Marcus said something about this to George just prior to the reading, George denied it. But it is Marcus who later that night calls George to tell him where Marie is staying. When George again attempts to deny his attraction to Marie, Marcus simply hangs up. Marcus listened not to what George was saying verbally, but to what George had said earlier at the book fair by his facial expressions and bodily posture. Then Marcus acted to help George by giving him a bit of a push. Second, there is Marie. We can see that, at the book fair, she is attracted to George just as he is to her. But it is the lengthy letter that she receives from George to which she "listens." Again, we do not know the contents of the letter, but we can surmise that George has had to tell her about his "gift" and his appreciation for what she has written. She does not dismiss him and what he has to say. She then acts by responding to what would seem to be his invitation to meet him at Leadenhall Market. Just as in Marie's case, we see the pattern of listening, being "present," and acting.

Finally, there is Marcus to consider. After Jason is killed, the twins' mother, Jackie, enters a treatment program and Marcus is sent to live with foster parents until such time as Jackie might be able to care for him. Marcus is quiet and withdrawn both at home and at school, but eventually he begins a search. Since he has always looked to his brother for leadership, he wants to know where his brother is now so that perhaps Jason will tell him what he is to do. Marcus's search begins online. He Googles, "What happens when you die" and watches first a YouTube video of an Islamic teacher (Surinder Duhra), who says that one cannot hide from the Angel of God. When the teacher begins to chant in Arabic, Marcus clicks to the next video, which appears to be from an English evangelical Christian who says "the good news is, if you believe in Christ, you have nothing to fear" from death. Marcus just shakes his head: he's already seen the "comfort" of the church at Jason's funeral, where the presiding priest offered pious platitudes such as "Death is not final. It is merely the beginning," and that Jason is now in heaven "surrounded by all the angels and saints, looking down at us." Religion provides no answer to Marcus's questions. Marcus next travels to the Centre for Psychic Advancement and attends a session with Ellen Joyce (Selina Cadell), the Centre's "Senior Sensitive." Her interactions with Marcus show him that she is a fraud: she says that it is his father who has died. Next Marcus visits a man who purports to have a spirit guide, another man who lauds the utility of an "omnidirectional supercardioid condenser microphone" for listening to the dead, and a mirror-gazer who tells him about the ancient Greeks and the "psychomanteum." Marcus recognizes that none of these people is taking him seriously and that they are charlatans. The last part of his search is again on the Internet, where he comes across what seems to be George's old website, "Genuinely Talks With the Dead." It is Marcus's familiarity with this website that allows him to recognize George when he sees him at the London Book Fair. Although George denies being the person on the website and denies being a psychic, Marcus continues to pursue him until finally George does give him the reading described earlier.

When we reflect on George's reading with Marcus, we see the same pattern as was present in dealing with the suffering of Marie and George—listening, being present, and acting compassionately. In this case, George listens to what Marcus is saying when Jason is purportedly going to leave forever. George hears the pleading in Marcus's voice and recognizes his loss and despair. Matt Damon does an especially good job of conveying the empathy with which George hears Marcus's cry. He looks straight at Marcus's face even as Marcus's eyes are turned downward and then moves his body slightly toward Marcus as he purports to deliver Jason's message of encouragement and comfort. He looks Marcus in the eyes and tells him what Jason is saying, something that George almost never does in his readings. He is physically putting himself even more into Marcus's presence: he is consciously being both literally and figuratively present with Marcus. That action and the action of speaking words of encouragement and comfort to Marcus are the means of addressing Marcus's suffering.[12]

Thus, in the stories of Marie, George, and Marcus, we see Eastwood the practical philosopher at work and addressing the pastoral problem of evil. There are no grand answers: those answers, especially in the form of religion, are ignored or rejected. The answers that are given are practical ones aimed at addressing the specific sufferings of particular people. Although there seems to be a discernible pattern of listening, being present, and acting compassionately, there is no theoretical claim that this pattern must always be followed. Moreover, what will count as listening, being present, and acting may well vary from case to case. Dr. Rousseau literally listens to Marie's account of her experience, whereas Marie figuratively listens to the contents of George's letter and Marcus listens by ignoring George's words. Michael the publishing executive is present with Marie at the meeting even while seeming to dismiss her and her book, whereas George is literally present with and moving toward Marcus at the reading. Marcus acts by making a phone call to George, whereas Marie acts by showing up at Leadenhall Market. But despite the differences in details, the practical pastoral pattern remains the same. In this, we see Eastwood as practical philosopher.[13]

Notes

1. C. S. Lewis, *The Problem of Pain* (New York: HarperCollins, 2001), 14. The quote from Richard McClelland is from a personal communication in the form of comments on an earlier draft of this paper.

2. St. Thomas Aquinas, *Summa Theologica,* Part I, Question 2, Article 3, Objection 1, available online at www.newadvent.org/summa/1002.htm.

3. Alvin Plantinga, *God, Freedom, and Evil* (New York: Harper and Row, 1974). Michael L. Peterson, "The Problem of Evil," in *A Companion to Philosophy of Religion,* ed. Phillip L. Quinn and Charles Taliaferro (Malden, Mass.: Blackwell, 1999), 393–401. There are dissenting voices, of course. See, for example, Michael Tooley, "The Problem of Evil," *Stanford Encyclopedia of Philosophy* (online).

4. Note that St. Thomas's general theodicy depends on his arguments for the existence of God and for the nature of this God as perfectly good and powerful. These are arguments that he goes on to outline in the famous "Five Ways" in Question 2 and in succeeding Questions in the *Summa.*

5. Plantinga, *Evil,* 63–64.

6. The first use of the camera looking heavenward occurs at the 7:15 mark in the film, in the chapter "A Boy's Ordeal." The mark is approximate and is determined by the counter on the DVD version of the film when viewed using Windows Media Player 12. The exact timing mark might vary from one player to another.

7. The sequence of events and camera shots occurs between 24:40 and 34:04, beginning in the chapter "World of Hurt" and ending in the chapter "My Daughter Is There?!?" The music accompanying the final shots described is especially dramatic as it crescendos and emphasizes the significance of the scene and the shot.

8. There is only one exception to this. At 57:14–57:17 ("Getting My Head Right"), the camera's heavenward spiral recurs in the context of Dave's flashback to his escape from the predators.

9. These shots run from 1:57:25 ("We Bury Our Sins") to 2:00:20 ("The Last Time I Saw Dave").

10. *Hereafter* at 40:35 (chapter 5).

11. Scott Foundas, "Eastwood on the Pitch," *LA Weekly,* December 10, 2009, online at www.laweekly.com/2009-12-10/film-tv/eastwood-on-the-pitch/ (accessed 8/27/2012); Geoff Boucher, "With 'Hereafter,' Clint Eastwood Contemplates What's Next," *Los*

Angeles Times, September 9, 2010, online at http://articles.latimes.com/2010/sep/09/entertainment/la-et-clint-eastwood-20100909 (accessed 8/27/2012).

12. This bodily movement is around 1:54:48 (chapter 12).

13. It is beyond the scope of this paper, but there are at least two further lines of thought that seem worthy of pursuit. The first is to connect Eastwood's embodied practical philosophy with the Aristotelian virtue of *phronesis.* The second is to expand the number of films that are considered to see how well the current analysis of Eastwood's treatment of the pastoral problem of evil applies to other of his films from the twenty-first century. I expect that the emphasis on the practical over the philosophical would hold true elsewhere, although there are likely to be refinements of the particular elements of the pastoral response.

The Smile and the Spit

The Motivational Polarity and Self-Reliance Portrayed in *The Outlaw Josey Wales* and the *Dollars* Trilogy

James R. Couch

The characters of Josey Wales and "The Man with No Name," like magnets, have the power of attraction as well as repulsion. Not only did the cigar chewing, unshaven face of the Man with No Name deliver barbs of divisive wit and foreboding scowls, but smiles indicating solidarity and humor. These traits are similarly found in Wales. Yet, even adding the further similarities of verbal adroitness, cleverness, vigilance, and certainly the mastery of the gun, the central characters of the trilogy, *A Fistful of Dollars* (1964), *For a Few Dollars More* (1965), *The Good, the Bad, and the Ugly* (1966), and of *The Outlaw Josey Wales* (1976), at least at first glance, show a decided difference.[1] Where Josey Wales scowls and offers a wad of well-aimed spit to show his contempt for what he finds morally distasteful, the nameless blond man of the trilogy is more at ease, even smiling in the face of danger. Moreover, where Wales struggles to right the unbalanced scales of justice, the Man with No Name struggles to tip the scales of fortune, with gold, in his favor. Though the films differ in respect to their stories and the mannerisms displayed by the central characters, the fundamental and unifying theme of self-reliance is a part of them all. Eastwood's acting brings to life characters that truly navigate according to the self-assurance taken from their own moral compass and confidence in their skills, and as a result reveals the tenuous relationship between the self-reliant individual and other people, a relationship provoking both smiles and spit.

Exploration of Eastwood's two characters and the specific consideration of these characters' actions of smiling and spitting will traverse the following trajectory. The ultimate goal is to bring to light Eastwood's revelatory acting as it shows the problematic relationship a self-reliant individual has with other people and society at large. By first looking at the role of Josey Wales, then examining the Man with No Name of the trilogy, their respective tendencies of spitting and smiling can be contextualized. Such contextualizing can aid understanding how these particular traits fit with the conception of self-reliance. As will be discussed, the self-reliant individual, by following a course of his or her own design, can easily be seen acting in ways antithetical to others. A tension is consequently created between that individual and others. This tension is one of attraction and repulsion, exposing the motivational polarity in which people are moved to either approach or withdraw from Wales as he spits and the Man with No Name as he smiles. In the first section, Wales's acts of spitting will be discussed in regard to what will be called contemptuous disgust, which is to say, an attitude that has a moral component and is capable of both repelling and attracting others. The smile is often more inviting, showing compassion and genuine enjoyment, but it remains plastic and capable of being deceitful, concealing a person's true thoughts and feelings. Consequently, Eastwood's use of the smile in the trilogy again points to the tension fostered in others by the self-reliant, as it is used both to show solidarity and to create discord. I begin with the character of Josey Wales, farmer turned outlaw.

Outlaw Farmer

The Outlaw Josey Wales is a Western that in some ways allowed Eastwood to depart from his earlier roles in the Sergio Leone films. Rather than being a man with no name, in this film Eastwood's character clearly has one, inspiring greater awe in both the characters of the film and the audience with each new feat. The film itself is based on a novel written by Forrest Carter, *The Rebel Outlaw: Josey Wales,* which was later republished as *Gone to Texas.*[2] The story, as Eastwood admitted, is a story that follows the incredible journey of Wales as he travels from farmer and family man to Confederate rebel and outlaw.[3] The tale begins with Wales, living in Missouri with his wife and son, being attacked by Captain Terrill and his band of Kansas "Redlegs." The Union soldiers mercilessly destroy the farm and murder Wales's wife and son. Rising from the ruins of his former life, Wales joins Confederate raiders, to become hardened by his desire for vengeance and his distrust of those who explicitly and implicitly sanctioned the destruction of his former life.

The end of the Civil War did not mean the end of Wales's tale, as he is seen as "the last of the hold-outs," becoming a wanted man due to his refusal to surrender. Kansas senator James Henry Lane (Frank Schofield) sanctions the execution of Wales's fellow Confederates, declaring, "We've gotta clean up this country."[4] All those failing to be loyal to the Union, like Wales, should be hounded to Hell. The attempt by Wales to escape by going south is slowed by not only opportunistic bushwhackers, bounty hunters, and the Union forces now commanded to hunt him down, but by a gradual collection of followers who find companionship, security, or both in accompanying him on his journey "down Mexico way." The story ends with the question of whether Wales, having gained a new family of friends, will settle with them on the once abandoned farm near Santo Rios, Texas, or continue alone to Mexico. Of course, Wales's freedom to make this choice is paid for with the killing of Terrill and his band of Redlegs, who had tracked him to the little homestead on the Crooked River.

The film can easily be understood as a story of a man drawn into the moral haze of war out of the need to avenge the murder of his family, who then at the end of the war attempts to escape his violent past. Eastwood's portrayal here, however, gives greater detail to the central character of that general story. Through the readily identifiable demonstration of disgust, Eastwood's character expresses contempt for those that felt morally bereft. Interestingly, it is the emotions of contempt and disgust that reveal the problematic tension that is found ever lurking between the highly self-reliant individual and the society that intends for him or her to be a part. Not only does Wales, as Eastwood plays him, display his contempt through tobacco spit only after he has become a rebel, but he does so by joining well-timed quips with well-aimed tobacco discharge, while at other times allowing the spit to speak for itself. In both cases the act of spitting provides an exclamation mark to the disgust Wales evidently feels in given situations. When Wales spits, various antagonists are provoked into trying their guns against him. His act of spitting simultaneously warns others, the viewer included, of Wales's swift and precise action—particularly with the gun. As a result of the reactions to the spitting of Wales, the tense relationship between the character and others becomes evident. The discussion of Wales's actions will show that when he feels disgusted by the moral behavior of others, spit and often gunfire result, but what would seem off-putting and repulsive paradoxically attracts others to join him. Consequently, this trait becomes a significant departure from the cigar biting in other films, as the moral disgust of Wales reveals the repulsion and attraction of the self-reliant.

Spitting not only shows the previously mentioned feeling of disgust felt by the one spitting—a refusal to swallow something—but also touches on society's deeper aversion to bodily fluids. Spitting today can be understood in regard to hygiene, whereby it threatens the general health of others by spreading germs, but this would only be a partial understanding. It also recalls the more general prohibition of allowing others to see bodily excretions. Long before the harms of microscopic organisms were recognized, spitting was often understood in a similar way as urinating. Doing either in the presence of others showed a lack of respect.[5] When spitting is considered as an outward sign of a person's attitude of disregard, then a further connection can be made. This connection comes from Michelle Mason's work on contempt being a moral attitude. She argues that "attitude" is a better term than emotion or feeling because it "best captures," in her opinion, "contempt's quality as a form of regard."[6] Consequently, when Wales's attitude is seen as one of contempt, then the regard he has for others who provoke his spit can be connected to his moral distaste. Moreover, when spit is considered as an indicator of Wales's moral distaste, disgust becomes a pertinent element in his attitude of contempt.

What will here be termed "contemptuous disgust" is the attitude Wales exhibits through his spitting. The feelings of contempt and disgust have been discussed as having a moral component and have also been spoken of in relation to each other.[7] The effort to define disgust made by Paul Rozin, Jonathan Haidt, and Clark R. McCauley provides the initial insight, suggesting that "disgust originated as a rejection response to bad tastes, and then evolved into a much more abstract and ideational emotion."[8] The development suggested is one in which a means for defending the body from harm developed into a means to defend the spirit from harm. The physical repulsion to bodily substances felt to be outside of their respective regions, being contaminated, undigested food as an easily recognizable example, relates to the reaction caused by the more abstract fear of becoming impure from coming into contact with those things or people considered polluted. Disgust thereby can be understood as pertaining to moral matters, because the feeling involves the classification of what one *should not* come into contact with. William Miller states in his book *The Anatomy of Disgust*: "Disgust is more than just the motivator of good taste; it marks out moral matters for which we can have no compromise. Disgust signals our being appalled, signals the fact that we are paying more than lip-service; its presence lets us know we are truly in the grip of the norm whose violation we are witnessing or imagining." From the disgust a person feels being linked to the violation of a norm that that person believes should not be violated, Miller notes the feeling's "powerful communalizing capacities." The emotion sets the limit between groups—the morally acceptable from the nonacceptable, the pure from the impure. This capacity is significant in respect to the community that gradually develops around Wales, for the development of the community involves the sharing of certain values and ultimately the sentiments that arise from them. The shared sentiments (like contempt and disgust) are significant, for as Miller finds, "These sentiments supply the motivation for punishing certain kinds of offenses." In other words, Wales's act of spitting can be understood as demonstrating his feelings toward the devaluation of certain moral values he prizes and his response to it. Though his response of spitting often leads to the severe punishment of the moral offender, repulsing some, it still has the power to attract others in seeming moral approbation. Consequently, this act, by having the ability to simultaneously foster feelings of rejection in certain witnesses while fostering feelings of approval in others, can be understood as creating a motivational polarity—impulses either to draw closer or to preserve if not increase the distance from Wales.[9]

The feeling of contempt, differing from disgust, is recognized by the essential aspect of superiority being claimed by the one feeling the emotion. As mentioned above, contempt can be said to be an attitude relating to how one regards other people. Such an outlook immediately speaks to the notion of self-reliance, due to the individual already holding him or herself in a superior position over others in order to consider them unworthy of reliance. Michelle Mason finds the object of contempt to be cast in a lower rank as a result of being viewed as having not met an "interpersonal ideal" to which the judging person adheres. Mason declares, "One comes to see the other as inferior, that is, when measured against the relevant interpersonal ideal."[10] Importantly, the result of this ranking is aversion—which if strong enough might be considered revulsion, allowing the connection to be made with disgust. Moreover, Mason's insight that the failure of the object of contempt to meet an ideal of what it means to be a person affords the possibility that this failure be met with punishment. She, however, does not see retribution as an essential quality of the attitude but does acknowledge that feelings of retribution often do accompany feelings of contempt, which again lends itself to the actions of Wales.

The ability of disgust to reveal the boundaries of "moral categories that separate pure and impure, good and evil, good taste and bad taste" in conjunction with contempt's relation to perceived superiority make their joining in the attitude of contemptuous disgust fitting for the self-reliant Wales.[11] This attitude regards others as inferior as a result of classifying both them and their actions as vile. Not only does the display of this attitude repulse those to whom it is directed, creating an affective barrier between them and the holder of this attitude, but it allows others who recognize a similar attitude in themselves to discover a sense of community that is owed to the shared disgust arising from the devaluation of certain values they hold in common.

With the previous considerations of disgust and contempt in mind, the first several instances of Wales's act of spitting become more significant. Though the first time Wales is seen spitting can easily be dismissed as a result of him simply chewing on a pull of tobacco, the importance of the act of spitting grows as the film progresses. His first display of spitting is seen as he considers surrendering with the other Confederates, but gains significance after the same group of Confederates are witnessed being murdered by the Union soldiers. Eastwood's use of spit from then on becomes a significant indication of his character's utter contempt for those whose moral outlook and actions run in a contrary direction. We see Wales spitting during the verbal exchange with the carpetbagger who was attempting to get him to buy his snake oil. That this is done in front of the old woman managing the riverside store also demonstrates the creation of an unspoken allegiance between herself and Wales, of which both she and the viewers are quickly aware. Presuming that Wales and the old woman did not know each other, this display of disgust suggests further details of Wales's self-reliance. The outward show of his disgust acts as a barrier that repels those held in contempt, while also granting others who share the underlying values for his sentiments greater access to him as a person. The recognition of a shared feeling, particularly in regard to the needs of not only survival, but moral superiority, creates an alliance among those who share the feeling. The view that there has been an evolutionary development of the human psychological abilities to make and detect alliances, or as John Tooby and Lena Cosmides have more precisely argued, "that the human mind was equipped by evolution with a rich, multicomponent coalitional psychology," allows further appreciation of the scene at the trading post, as well as those in which Wales gains other members to his party, even if this was not his intention.[12] Understanding that evolution has provided human beings with the ability to recognize those with whom they can join, even if this is an unconscious occurrence, suggests that there are recognizable values at the basis of any given human coalition.

One of the most pointed instances of spitting comes after Wales and his young, critically wounded companion successfully fend off two bounty hunters. Having killed the men, the young man asks whether the two should be buried, and in response Wales spits on a dead man's head, saying, "Hell with them fellas; buzzards gotta eat, same as the worms." This example reveals at the least an utter disregard for the dead men, but the more apt interpretation is that Wales's character feels an overwhelming contempt for the callous—particularly those who attempt to make money from the misery and death of others. This is evident in his tendency to spit in response to those devaluing the life of others, and becomes more poignant when Mason's notion of contempt, as it involves the violation of an ideal of what it means to be a person, is recalled. The actions of the bounty hunters show them as not meeting such simple criteria as kindness and the avoidance of treachery. Their services were bought by the same corrupt public officials who had condemned Wales, having recast murderous actions as virtuous and patriotic efforts. By treating the dead men as if they were mere carrion, and therefore unworthy of burial, Wales's contempt underlies his disgust. The unwillingness of Wales to treat the bodies with respect ironically shows the character's tendency to exhibit the same type of behavior he finds fault with. Eastwood's attention to the theme of government hypocrisy is again evident when Wales listens to the story of dispossession told by Lone Watie (Chief Dan George). Here he targets a scorpion as the aged Watie tells him of his meeting with government men. The words from a man of the government, "endeavor to persevere," rang hollow to Watie and his fellow Iroquois, who were being coerced into traveling the Trail of Tears. Wales's contemptuous disgust is recognizable as he empathizes with Watie's description of the duplicity displayed by the government in its dealing with a "civilized" tribe. The last example of Eastwood deepening his character's contempt for those abusing power is delivered in the trading post. The two trappers only stop their assault on the Navajo girl in order to try to capture Wales. Consequently, by treating the woman and Wales as commodities to be bought and sold, the trappers trespass against both. Ultimately, this earns the corpse of one of those "pilgrims" spit to the head.

The bodies of the dead were not the only targets of Wales's spit. The three-legged dog that appears also earns several discharges: the first for joining him and Lone Watie, another in witnessing the aftermath of the Comancheros' capture of the travelers from Kansas, and last, for beginning to whine during the hymn being sung by Wales and the guests at the party held in honor of the settlement at the Texas homestead. Apart from disgust and contempt, the spit also functions as a warning. When Wales spits after being sarcastically offered a "good price" for his horse by the same Comancheros who overtook the group from Kansas, the realization that this signals Hell having come to breakfast is made too late. Unfortunately for the Comancheros, they ignored the boundary Wales set, not realizing that Wales's act of disgust meant their death. Similarly, when he runs into the Union soldiers in the small Texas town, he provocatively spits and calmly asks them if they plan to pull their pistols or whistle Dixie. In both cases Wales has already identified those deemed offensive, and as a result the viewer, even if not the antagonists, is forewarned of the consequences of being so categorized by "Mr. Chained Blue Light'n."

The previous warnings of Wales's propensity to violence that are owed to his act of spitting makes his encounter with the Comanche chief Ten Bears (Will Sampson) significant due to the film having foreshadowed gunplay based on Wales's previous acts of spitting. Ten Bears, however, is not antagonized by Wales's spit, but acknowledges that there is iron in Wales's words of life and death. In this case the warning is understood through Wales's seriousness and lack of fear of death. The acknowledgment of this by Ten Bears leads to the making of a blood pact, an oath made by sharing a bodily fluid. This pact corresponds to the thought that bodily fluids outside their respective domains are feared as sources of contamination. Consequently, by making the pact both sides demonstrate a complete lack of this fear. What Wales and Ten Bears have created is a coalitional act that contrasts with the boundary transgression attempted by the Comancheros. From the recognition of shared values, the two characters have agreed that their respective tribes will form a mutually beneficial alliance.

The last examples illustrate the affiliative aspect of contemptuous disgust through Wales's lack of spitting in situations where it is expected that he will spit. After having been chastised earlier by Granny (Paula Trueman) for spitting, when later reaching the homestead Wales twice does not spit. He swallows upon first entering the house and later, while in the house when he is provoked by Granny, he again swallows when she suggests that he may be a Missouri loafer. This goes to show that Wales's character holds this home or Granny to be indicators of where such actions are not to be done. This may well speak to Wales not only recognizing the values he shares with Granny upon being returned to the setting of home and hearth, but the coalitional alliance to which they belong that is created from those shared values.

Drawing these various examples together we find the first curious mixture and even opposing aspects of a self-reliant man. On the one hand there is the all too apparent disregard for certain social norms and expectations, like avoiding violent confrontation or Native Americans. Wales's initial intention to "set things right" runs counter to the law and the Union forces supposedly upholding it, even as it might be an unwitting testament to Aristotle's view that laws may be immoral by being unjust.[13] This opposition, as the action of the film illustrates, immediately makes the society from which he now stands apart want him all the more to conform to its wishes, which can happen by his being brought in either dead or alive. On the other hand, the values that underlie the fixity of his outlook and moral disposition (as well as the accuracy of his guns) draw not only the attention of the authorities, but attract others to join him. This attraction is owed not simply to the physical protection he provides, but to the recognition of others that the values Wales holds are shared with themselves. The actions that result from these values reveal the firmness of his character regarding the unjust and morally suspect forces surrounding him. Such actions lend themselves to a sense of security for those who are like-minded in regard to sharing the same values, while also serving as a threat to those who are not like-minded.

The Coldness and Compassion of the Smile

The *Dollars* trilogy was directed by Sergio Leone, who with the help of other writers (Duccio Tessari, Fulvio Morsella, Luciano Vincenzoni, Sergio Donati, Agenore Incrocci, Furio Scarpelli) created the individual characters Eastwood plays in the respective films. Though each character does have an actual moniker, the designation of the Man with No Name comes to unify them all due to Eastwood acting in each of the roles in a remarkably similar way, each time being directed by Leone, as well as the stories leaving open the possibility that they are episodes in one character's life.[14] Eastwood's involvement in the trilogy has been well discussed, consequently only a few remarks are necessary to remind the reader of Eastwood's roles in the particular stories, as well as to indicate the continuity of character and his break from the conventional Western hero.[15] However, the importance of these considerations for us derives from how they involve the particular smile only Eastwood is capable of giving. The smile, as it is often caught sneaking past the well-bitten cigar, is at times derisive and cynical, while at others compassionate and mirthful. Eastwood's use of the smile reveals, like his previously discussed act of spitting, the motivational polarity produced by the mannerisms of a self-reliant man.

A Fistful of Dollars introduces Eastwood's portrayal of the Man with No Name. The story as well as its lead role were inspired by the Akira Kurosawa film *Yojimbo* (1961) and its male lead, Toshirō Mifune. In Leone's telling of the story, the Man with No Name comes to San Miguel, a Mexican border town divided between warring gangs, the Baxters and the Rojos. Quickly realizing that in such a situation a man could become rich, Eastwood's character begins to play each side against the other. Like Coyote of Native American lore, the Man with No Name delights in seeking his own benefit, even as it means anger and destruction for both himself and those around him. His willingness to defy the odds by the use of his cleverness and combative skills also recalls the cunning Odysseus. Placing the Man with No Name alongside these figures, one imagines them smiling from life's pleasures, as well as using a more derisive smile or even sneer to betray their attitude of contempt toward those felt to be inferior. The Man with No Name offers smiles in both of these senses (delight and contempt) as he seeks his fortune from the battling gangs.

In *A Fistful of Dollars* Eastwood offers smiles in conjunction with his character's discovery of pleasant or advantageous knowledge, as well as using the smile in attempts to conceal his own treacherous plans. Two examples illustrate this. The first example involves both aspects: the expression of pleasure and concealment of intentions. When the Man with No Name reaches town and learns of the warring gangs, he considers the possibility of making money from the hostility and suspicion the war has created and grins in response. There is no doubt that the prospect of easy money can generate a smile, but in this case the money would likely come at the expense of other people's lives. Consequently, the smile that the Man with No Name gives Silvanito (Jose Calvo) suggests his delight at the prospect of money being made; however, his smile also hides the beginning of a devious plan to get it. The second example of Eastwood's use of the smile more explicitly indicates the common human effort of concealment. The smile can at times provide a friendly façade to hide the terrible knowledge, plans, and feelings of which a person does not want others to be aware. In this instance we find art imitating life, with the smile employed by Eastwood in the now famous scene where his character initiates his mercenary plan by effortlessly dispatching four of the Baxter men. The smile Eastwood gives is not the Duchenne smile that is marked by the contraction of both the small muscles around the mouth and the small muscles around the eye.[16] Rather, his grin does not engage the muscles of the eyes, consequently indicating deception in contrast to actual pleasure. Moreover, the deceptiveness of his smile appears to be an unsettling mask that momentarily disarms his opponents by unexpectedly appearing lighthearted and jocular at the tense moment when guns could be drawn. The disingenuous smile grants the time for the hidden and deadly agenda of the Man with No Name to emerge. The four bait him by scaring the mule he is riding, but before the Man with No Name pulls his gun, he suddenly smiles and manages a laugh at the outlaws' attempt to warn him off. Yet the smile vanishes as he demands an apology on behalf of his mule. When no apology comes, the poncho is flipped aside and a sudden fusillade of lethal shots is delivered. As a result the smile is shown to have been a disguise for the Man with No Name's intention of killing these men. The character's smile produces uncertainty; the men are put off their guard regarding the deadly seriousness of the Man with No Name.

The deceptive character of the Man with No Name's smile involves a facial expression, as Miller notes, of contempt as it exposes the canine tooth on one side of the face. Miller finds that "This same expression can imperceptibly metamorphose into a smile, which as Darwin notes, 'may be real, although one of derision and this implies that the offender is so insignificant that he excites only amusement; but the amusement is generally a pretense.'"[17] Interestingly, amusement used as a pretense can be connected to the previously discussed notions of contempt and disgust. This is due to the object of contempt being perceived to be threatening and disgusting, which allows the smile to be used as a defense against revealing the individual's truer contemptuous feelings. Eastwood's character often displays a smile of this sort, particularly when smoking a cigar in the presence of the various gang members.

For a Few Dollars More pairs Eastwood with Lee Van Cleef. In this film the two highly skilled bounty hunters work together to collect the reward offered for El Indio (Gian Maria Volonté) and his murderous gang of outlaws. Indio is wanted for having escaped from prison. He quickly returns to killing and stealing, setting his eyes this time on a heavily fortified bank containing a mountain of cash. Colonel Mortimer (Van Cleef) persuades the Man with No Name to join him in a scheme to bring down Indio. The Man with No Name joins Indio's gang in order to work toward their capture from the inside. Meanwhile, Mortimer carefully tracks the gang from the outside, waiting for the opportunity to offer his safe-cracking skill when the time is right. As the story unfolds, it is revealed that Indio had earlier killed a man and raped his wife. A pair of pocket watches and their eerie melodies serve as reminders to Indio and Mortimer of the past crime. For both Mortimer and Indio their watch is a reminder of an unpunished crime, and by the end of the film the viewer discovers that the watch possessed by Indio had been taken from the woman Indio had violated—Mortimer's sister. The suicide of Mortimer's sister after Indio's crime prompted the colonel's quest for revenge that will only be satisfied with the death of Indio. The Man with No Name, however, is unaware of this connection until Indio is killed at the end of the film. This consequently suggests that he remained true to the mercenary outlook developed in the first film, having agreed to help Mortimer for a share of the reward money.

Eastwood's portrayal of the character in this film again uses the smile as an expression of the delight taken from thoughts of money and the plans to get it, as well as indicating from the actions that follow his smile that there is usually something more hidden behind the bounty hunter's grin. Additionally, once the Man with No Name becomes a partner with the colonel, his smile likewise shows his allegiance to and reluctant admiration for his new partner. The smile in this context becomes an indication of solidarity and companionship, which in turn shows similarity to the coalitional aspect of the act of spitting. Whether the aim of the alliance is protection, revenge, or gold, all recall the coalition-forming power of the self-reliant Wales, and provide a correlation to Eastwood's smile in the next film.

The third film in the trilogy contains all of the central themes previously discussed. The three main characters of the movie are the *Bad,* Angel Eyes (Lee Van Cleef); the *Ugly,* Tuco Ramirez (Eli Wallach); and the *Good,* Blondie (Eastwood). Each of the characters is vying for a cashbox filled with $200,000 in Confederate gold. The deception and savagery found in both of the earlier films are again seen in Leone's third installment, yet Eastwood's character gains further depth in this film. Eastwood's performance, as it involves the occasional act of compassion, reveals the Man with No Name's capacity to be more than a one-dimensional outlaw. It is Eastwood's use of the smile that shows his character to be a man who, despite living amid the moral upheaval created by the Civil War, manages to demonstrate a moral sensibility through his self-reliance.[18]

A shipment of gold disappears after Union forces attack a Confederate wagon containing the payroll for the 3rd Cavalry Regiment. The news of the missing money passes first to Angel Eyes by way of a man whom he had been hired to kill. Angel Eyes quickly decides to pursue the cash box by means of the trail left by a man who had taken the name of Bill Carson (Antonio Casale). Meanwhile, Blondie and Tuco, who had been profitably swindling the hangman, dissolve their partnership. In this partnership Tuco would be turned in by the Man with No Name for a reward, but once the wanted man was dangling at the end of the rope his "blond haired angel" would then provide a well-aimed shot to free him. While repaying the Man with No Name for earlier having forced him to walk through the desert, Tuco and his captive stumble across a Confederate coach carrying the dying Carson. Carson whispers the location of the gold to Eastwood's character, forcing Tuco to nurse Blondie back to life for a share of the gold. The story ends after the Good, the Bad, and the Ugly have all three made their way to the cemetery at Sad Hill. Angel Eyes is killed by a deceptive Blondie, who had unloaded Tuco's gun before the three-way showdown. With the death of Angel Eyes, Tuco again learns that there are those with a gun and those who dig.

Eastwood's use of the smile in this film demonstrates the human ability to show both compassion and treachery. Two iconic scenes reveal Eastwood's portrayal to again be one appreciative of the polarity of the self-reliant. The first time the viewer sees the Man with No Name is when he stops three other bounty hunters from collecting on Tuco. The smile emerges just as it has in the previous films of the trilogy: at the knowledge that money can be made from treachery. Yet, Blondie's double-dealing is later offset by his compassionate offering of both a smile and a cigar, having listened to Tuco's lies concerning his reunion with his brother the priest (Luigi Pistilli). The second example of Eastwood's smile comes at the end of the film. Tuco, tottering at the end of a rope with his share of the gold lying at his feet, is forced again to realize that those with a rope around their neck must rely on others to do the cutting. It is only fitting that this final scene reveals both the sadistic and compassionate elements contained in the smile of the Man with No Name. As he takes aim and shoots the hanging rope, the Man with No Name's willingness to torture a person like Tuco is counterpoised against his willingness to let even the ugly have a share of happiness.

The films Clint Eastwood has chosen to act in have generally cast him in roles that leave the viewer no doubt that his character resembles a modern Odysseus, remaining steadfast until the successful completion of his trials and the overcoming of his tribulations. This can easily be attributed to his "look," particularly his roughhewn appearance in such films as the ones previously discussed. Like Eastwood's later role as Harry Callahan (a man fighting against both the establishment and the criminals from whom he swore to protect it), we find an essential polarity issuing from a character heeding his own moral dictates. The motivational polarity of aversion and approach resulting from the actions of the self-reliant individual raises the question whether one can manage to be true to one's own values without inevitably being divisive, as one's commitment to certain values inevitably generates this polarizing effect. The philosophical significance of this polarity comes to light in the consideration of Eastwood's use of smiling and spitting. The characteristics portrayed in both *The Outlaw Josey Wales* and the *Dollars* trilogy offer a glimpse of men who only rarely are troubled by a conflict between self and society. Though still adhering to various social values and norms, conflicts between their own goals and those of society are resolved for them by already valuing their own autonomy over the authority of society. Unfortunately, this decision is usually detrimental to those on the side of society. For Wales, his willingness to follow the dictates of his conscience quickly places him on an opposing side, when viewed from the perspective of society. Unperturbed by this, Wales spits at those and that which would have him compromise or surrender his values. This results in both the repulsion and attraction of other individuals. More specifically, individuals witnessing the actions of Wales feel themselves compelled to make a choice to either align themselves with him or against him, and the feeling of the polarizing effect of his actions ultimately classifies those who are friends of Wales and those who are his foes. It might easily be imagined that the combination of Wales's skills of violence and the uncompromising nature of his moral outlook places him among those beyond good and evil. The employment of the smile is common enough, often happening unconsciously in everyday life. Yet, as Eastwood's smiling Man with No Name shows, the smile is capable of hiding as much as it reveals. This character similarly acts in ways that place him in a morally nebulous region. The responses to the Man with No Name's smile at the prospect of killing others for money, and his later offering of a compassionate smile to a person who is suffering, are again evidence of the self-reliant individual's ability to create states of motivational polarity in others. This polarity consists of the impulse to approach, whether aggressively or not, and the opposing impulse to withdraw or avoid contact with this character. Consequently, the smiling and spitting in Eastwood's performances are the actions that force a choice by the witnesses: to either join him in a coalition or oppose him. Though it is important to note that those who oppose Eastwood's characters often meet with violence, it is even more significant to note that those individuals possessing confidence in both their values and their ability to apply them, as discovered in their encounters with the self-reliant characters Eastwood portrays, are the very cause of the motivational polarity. The recognition of this power of self-reliant individuals gives better understanding to our own reactions to our encounters with them, which is to say, our own tendency either to smile or to spit.

Notes

1. The dates for the *Dollars* trilogy are for the films' original releases in Italy. The release dates for U.S. theaters are: *A Fistful of Dollars* (January 1967); *For a Few Dollars More* (May 1967); *The Good, the Bad, and the Ugly* (December 1967).

2. Originally the book was published as *The Rebel Outlaw: Josey Wales* (Gantt, Ala.: Whippoorwill, 1973), and was later republished as *Gone to Texas* (New York: Delacorte Press, 1975). *The Vengeance Trail of Josey Wales* (New York: Delacorte Press, 1976), also written by Forrest Carter, continues the story of Wales's exploits.

3. See Patrick McGillian, "Clint Eastwood," in *Clint Eastwood: Interviews*, ed. Robert E. Kapsis and Kathie Coblentz (Jackson: Univ. of Mississippi Press, 1999), 22.

4. *The Outlaw Josey Wales*, 1976.

5. Though the situation or context may provide for exceptions, the lack of respect an individual may have is owed to the belief that all bodily secretions and emissions are contaminated, and the individual disregards others' becoming contaminated by his or her excreta. See in particular William Ian Miller's *The Anatomy of Disgust* (Cambridge, Mass.: Harvard Univ. Press, 1997), 96–108.

6. Michelle Mason, "Contempt as a Moral Attitude," *Ethics* 113 (2003): 239.

7. See Miller's *The Anatomy of Disgust*, 213–234.

8. Paul Rozin, Jonathan Haidt, and Clark R. McCauley, "Disgust," in *The Handbook of Emotions*, 3rd ed., ed. Michael Lewis, Jeanette M. Haviland-Jones, and Lisa Feldman Barret (New York: Guilford Press, 2008), 771.

9. The three quotes in this paragraph come from Miller's *The Anatomy of Disgust*, 194 and 195.

10. Mason, "Contempt as a Moral Attitude," 241.

11. Ibid., 220.

12. John Tooby and Lena Cosmides, "Groups in Mind: The Coalitional Roots of War and Morality," in *Human Morality and Sociality: Evolutionary and Comparative Perspectives*, ed. H. Høgh-Olesen (New York: Palgrave MacMillan, 2010), 191–234.

13. See Aristotle, *Nicomachean Ethics*, book 5, chapter 10, 1137b 13–34, in *The Basic*

Works of Aristotle, ed. Richard McKeon (New York: Random House, 2001). Law should generate equity, for without equity a law becomes unjust.

14. He is referred to in the original script of *A Fistful of Dollars* as "Texas Joe," later in the 1979 script as "Joe, lo Straniero," as "Manco" in *For a Few Dollars More,* and as "Blondie" in *The Good, the Bad, and the Ugly.*

15. Two sources for discussions of the characters in Eastwood's Western films are *Clint Eastwood, Actor and Director: New Perspectives,* ed. Leonard Engel (Salt Lake City: Univ. of Utah Press, 2007), particularly chapters 1, 2, 6, and 9; William Beard, *Persistence of Double Vision: Essays on Clint Eastwood* (Edmonton: Univ. of Alberta Press, 2000), particularly chapter 2 for a discussion of the (anti)hero.

16. For a discussion see P. Ekman, W. Friesen, and R. Davidson, "The Duchenne Smile: Emotional Expression and Brain Physiology II," *Journal of Personality and Social Psychology* 58 (1990): 342–353.

17. Miller, *The Anatomy of Disgust,* 218. The passage from Darwin is found in *The Expressions of the Emotions in Man and Animals* (Chicago: Chicago Univ. Press, 1965), 254.

18. I am arguing, then, that smiles can both signal sociability and conceal hostility. For empirical support for this view (applied both to Duchenne smiles and non-Duchenne smiles) see M. Mehu, A. Little, and R. Dunbar, "Duchenne Smiles and the Perception of Generosity and Sociability in Faces," *Journal of Evolutionary Psychology* 5 (2007): 133–146.

The Representation of Justice in Eastwood's *High Plains Drifter*

Erin E. Flynn

A defining feature of the Western is that the civil order it depicts lacks developed institutions, particularly political institutions. Sometimes this absence has to do with questions about the legitimacy or desirability of the direction in which the civil order is headed in so many Westerns: toward the institutions of lawmaking, of political action, representation, and organization. At the very least, in the matter at hand in certain Westerns, the political is depicted as at best irrelevant, at worst corrupting. Or so I shall argue in what follows.

There is another feature of such Westerns, which I believe functions as a correlate to the absence or distrust of political authority. That feature is a representation of a kind of moral law, and in particular of justice. These two features suggest that certain Westerns can be read as representing a moral law in a particular relation to the civil order and its burgeoning political dimension. In the potential normative vacuum created by the absence of political authority, the moral law steps forward in such Westerns as the first law that must be kept. It is natural or transcendent, in the sense that its authority does not depend on any civil or political order. It not only provides a normative center of gravity for such Westerns, but it also implies a condition of the legitimacy of the coming political order. In such Westerns, the value and legitimacy of the civil order is therefore depicted as rooted in a certain kind of moral law.

After outlining a classic instance of this vision of the moral law in relation to the civil order, I will present Eastwood's *High Plains Drifter* (1973) as offering a variation on the vision, one that amounts to an evolution of it. Despite the appeal of the vision, I will argue that the variant of it in *High*

Plains Drifter should alert us to certain of its shortcomings. In particular, I will argue that conceiving of the moral law as transcending civil institutions in a particular way can in fact undermine our ability to determine and live up to that law.

The Representation of Justice in *High Noon*

In order to see this Western representation of justice, and of the legitimacy of the civil order as rooted in a certain relation to the moral law, let us first consider another Western standing clearly in the background of *High Plains Drifter,* namely *High Noon* (Zinnemann, 1952). In *High Noon,* the town of Hadleyville proves itself unworthy of the law when it fails to back Will Kane (Gary Cooper) against the return of outlaw Frank Miller (Ian MacDonald), sworn to vengeance against the lawmen who put him away. Miller has been pardoned, which (as the act of a political official) indicates that the civil order is here under siege due to a political failure. Indeed, as I shall argue, Hadleyville's failure is depicted in *High Noon* as a failure of the political, even of the political as itself a kind of failure.

Hadleyville's failure is foretold in a scene in which Judge Mettrick (Otto Kruger), who sentenced Miller, delivers a hasty "lesson in civics" to Kane, the marshal who arrested Miller. During that lesson, the judge takes down the U.S. flag, packs up his scales of justice and law books, and explains to Kane that the civil order is by nature weak, and that people will accept tyranny and fall in line behind the powerful, no matter how unjust the powerful might be. That is why the judge is hurrying to get out of town, and he recommends that Kane do the same. The civil failure is crucially depicted sometime later in a sort of impromptu town hall meeting in the church. There the townsfolk, while acknowledging their debt to Kane for having brought law and order to Hadleyville, blame "politicians up north" for pardoning Miller. Furthermore, they claim that the conflict between Kane and Miller is now a private matter, since Kane has recently resigned as marshal. In order not to discourage the investment of those same northerners, the townsfolk ultimately encourage Kane to run, so that the inevitable fight with the Miller gang might not occur on the streets of Hadleyville. It would give the town a bad name, after all, recalling the days before Kane came to make the town safe for "women and children." In sum, this political discussion is shown not merely to be ineffective, but to reinforce and even extend the town's hypocrisy and cowardice. The town, in other words, proves the judge's point.

Interestingly, it may well be the words themselves, the very political dialogue, which the picture regards as corrupting. More than once Kane is asked why he is compelled to stay and fight Miller. He is generally unable to explain why, and often he, or others speaking on his behalf, refer to his reasons as something that cannot be explained if not already understood. Kane's predecessor and patron, the old marshal Martin Howe (Lon Chaney Jr.), tells Kane that he is not surprised the town won't stand behind him, since people "got to talk themselves into law and order," and that they don't really care about or value the law and the lawman. Since Kane's reasons are something that cannot be explained, we already know that no amount of talking is going to improve their situation. The upshot of all of this is that when Kane eventually vanquishes the Miller gang, he throws his tin star in the dirt and leaves town as the residents of Hadleyville flow slowly back into the street. Despite being saved from the Miller gang, the town has shown itself to be unworthy of the law. Bad times are coming for Hadleyville, in the form of either more Frank Millers or the northern politicians who pardoned him, or both.

What is it that Hadleyville lacks, making it unworthy, illegitimate, and ultimately incapable of defending itself against Frank Miller? Howe suggests that it is lack of care or respect for the law. But that answer is ambiguous. The town, after all, is courting the developed political order to the north, an order already revealed to be complicit in the problem the town now faces. It is not concern for the positive law, much less political order, that is at the heart of what Hadleyville lacks—not merely laws on the books, or a judge, or even a marshal.

To get at what Hadleyville lacks, *High Noon* invites us to ask another question. What compels Kane to stay and fight? It is no longer his professional duty. It is also not the need to protect Hadleyville. It is made clear throughout the movie that some citizens of Hadleyville, notably the saloon owner, Gillis (Larry J. Blake), and the hotel clerk (Howland Chamberlain), actually think that their interests were better served when Frank Miller rode roughshod over the town. Things were livelier then, and business in the saloon and the hotel was likely better. Regulation, it seems, has always been bad for business. Certainly we sense that something is at stake for Hadleyville, but not the town's destruction. Whatever Miller threatens in the civil order cannot easily be accounted for in terms of safety, welfare, or private interests.

What compels Kane, I contend, is the fact that Miller has committed serious and violent wrongs, wrongs that strike at the dignity and status of persons as such, wrongs which must be opposed and negated. The reason Kane has trouble explaining this is that it cannot be easily or properly accounted for in terms of consequences to the interests of people, including even his own interests. The reasons of prudence do not necessarily lead to the conclusion that such wrongs must be opposed and negated. Rather, justice itself demands it.

This then is what Hadleyville lacks: clear insight into a demand of justice, a moral or natural law defining right and wrong, and especially the will or courage to execute that law. We may summarize this trait as *rectitude.*[1] In such a Western, the right kind of gunfighter represents this moral law, which prefigures, transcends, and grounds the legitimacy of the civil order. It transcends that order in the same sense in which it is a natural law. That is, its authority and perhaps even its actualization do not depend on the civil order, or on any legal or political system of institutions. On the contrary, the authority of these depends on it.[2] I will therefore sometimes refer to it as the law that stands behind the law.[3] Crucially, it is represented as a law that cannot be properly known or determined by political discourse or legislative action or perhaps any collective communicative or discursive actions of persons. This also suggests an epistemic sense in which the law is natural. Our knowledge of it, as in Kane's case, is a matter of clear moral sense or intuition, perhaps incommunicable to others. Deliberation regarding what the moral law is or ought to be, what amounts to a violation of that law, and what is required in its defense has little place in this vision and is sometimes actively derided. At the very least, such deliberative practices are as likely to obscure as to clarify the moral law.

With this representation of justice and the civil order in view, I turn now to Eastwood's *High Plains Drifter.* My main contention will be that that the representation of justice in *High Plains Drifter* is an evolution of the representation described above, one that follows from this depiction of the law that stands behind the law.

A Synopsis of *High Plains Drifter*

High Plains Drifter is set in the fictional mining town of Lago. In the opening shots, the Stranger (played, of course, by Eastwood) rides down into the distant and isolated town, out of a cinematic haze of heat and hills.[4] Jane

Tompkins argues that the landscape shot, common to the opening of the Western, establishes the preeminence of nature and the absence of culture and society.[5] But the haze in *High Plains Drifter* is initially indistinct and disorienting, a misty blank that only gradually gives way to a landscape in focus, as if to suggest that the earth, along with the Stranger, is materializing before our eyes.

A marshal has been murdered in Lago, killed by assassins hired by the owners of the mine. He was bullwhipped to death in the street. Eventually we learn that the marshal, Duncan (Buddy Van Horn), had discovered that the mine was on government land, a fact that would invalidate its claim, drive the Lago Mining Company out of business, and presumably ruin the town. The marshal was murdered before he had a chance to reveal what he knew.

Lago is waiting for revenge to rain down on it. The marshal's killers are soon to be released from jail. After the murder they were railroaded, framed for stealing a gold ingot from the company. Having recognized their power in a town in which power had expelled the law, the assassins had begun to take liberties. The town, compounding its sins, got rid of them. But the people of Lago are sure Stacy Bridges (Geoffrey Lewis) and his partners, the Carlin brothers (Anthony James and Dan Vadis), will return for revenge, and so they have hired three gunfighters for protection. It is worth noting that Sheriff Shaw (Walter Barnes) seems not even to be a candidate for protecting the town. He is an ineffective placeholder occupying a meaningless office. Because it has deprived itself of the real law, the town must resort to hiring out the work of protection to second-rate killers. Unfortunately for Lago, within minutes of his arrival the Stranger kills the three gunfighters. The ease with which he kills them is remarkable. When the gunfighters interrupt his drink, attempting to intimidate him by asking whether he thinks he's fast enough for life in Lago, he grabs a bottle of whiskey before they can reach their guns and replies, "a lot faster than you'll ever live to be." When they pursue him to the barbershop and threaten him again, interrupting his shave in the process, he shoots them all dead, after which he rapes Callie Travers (Mariana Hill), who has knocked the cigarillo out of his mouth and insulted him on the street.

In a sign of both its desperation and its turpitude, the town turns to the Stranger for help. Though initially disinclined, he agrees to help after he has been assured a free hand in the town. Under the pretense of preparing Lago to defend itself against the Bridges gang, what unfolds is, I shall argue, a perfect exposure and negation of Lago's corrupt civil order.

In the course of these preparations, the Stranger dreams more than once of Duncan's murder, appears to dream of himself as Duncan murdered, in fact. After an attempt on his life, which he effortlessly escapes, he rides out to torment the Bridges gang, already close to town. Invisible in the hills, he fires down on them with uncanny accuracy, only to frighten them and stoke Stacy Bridges's vengeful fury. When the time comes, the Stranger, having had the town painted red in preparation for a "welcome home" celebration, abandons Lago to its destruction by the Bridges gang. That evening, as the gang's revenge is near to climax, the Stranger returns unseen and kills the assassins one by one, in the very place they had bullwhipped the marshal to death.

The Representation of Justice in *High Plains Drifter*

The justice in *High Plains Drifter* is distinctively retributive. It is a matter of answering for a crime, of getting precisely what is deserved. Consider, for example, the reversals and exposures that unfold once the Stranger is placed in charge. The greed that led to the town's corruption is turned on its head. Economic exchange is reversed, as the Stranger appropriates and redistributes goods according to his whim. He drives guests from the hotel, and when the preacher (Robert Donner) calls the dispossessed his brothers, the Stranger suggests that he take his "brothers" in, which the preacher does, at the same rates the hotel was charging. He exposes the loveless marriage between the hotel owner, Lewis Belding (Ted Hartley), and his wife, Sarah (Verna Bloom). We learn in flashback that Belding had restrained his wife when she tried to intervene on Duncan's behalf.

These reversals occur while the Stranger ironically attempts to teach the town the courage it needs to defend itself. Hence, in the process of teaching Lago the importance of courage, the Stranger exposes the corruption that flowed from the town's lack of moral courage when it acquiesced to Duncan's murder. That lesson is fully learned when Mordecai (Billy Curtis), the town "runt" who had cowered beneath a porch during Duncan's murder, kills Belding as Belding aims to shoot the Stranger in the back. It is the final killing in the movie, marking Mordecai's moral elevation and ensuring Sarah's liberation.

At the heart of these reversals is punishment for Duncan's murder, and the punishment is startlingly precise. The wicked are killed; the weak are terrified. Those who bullwhipped the marshal are whipped in turn. The mayor (Stefan Gierasch) and the sheriff, who abdicated their duty to the law, are stripped of even the trappings of their false authority, replaced in their offices by Mordecai. Callie Travers, who used her sexuality to curry favor with powerful men, is raped. It would be no overstatement to say that in the universe of *High Plains Drifter* desert is the only engine that drives the narrative.

The Stranger avenges Duncan's murder, but he also forces Lago to acknowledge its guilt, which is essential to the retribution. This is clearest at the movie's climax, when the townsfolk fearfully realize that the assassins are being killed by bullwhip at the site of the marshal's murder. It is telling that nearly everything the people of Lago have said about themselves and their town has been false. Indeed, the movie's first piece of dialogue seems designed to tell the viewer just this. The lead thug informs the Stranger that most people find life in Lago a little too fast for them. But we have just seen the Stranger ride through a motionless town, its inhabitants pinned behind their doors and windows, fearfully watching him. What follows is a series of lies in which Lago attempts to hide its true identity. Of course, all of the lies flow from the town's attempt to cover up its crime, a crime motivated by the need to keep the marshal from revealing the truth about the mining company's claim, and so also about the founding and the legitimacy of the town itself.[6] Sarah and Mordecai are the only townspeople who speak sincerely to the Stranger. Reflecting on the threat the Stranger poses, Sarah says: "You are a man that makes people afraid, and that makes you dangerous." The Stranger replies: "It's what people know about themselves inside that makes them afraid." He is out to expose what they know inside, but everywhere he would turn to discover the truth he finds only lies. Instead, the truth about the murder is revealed in his dreams. The dream sequences recall the disorienting effect of the haze at the beginning of the movie. At first the viewer cannot discern what is going on, who is being whipped, and why. But gradually the disorientation fades and the truth about Lago is revealed, even as the denizens of the town try to obscure it, thereby revealing all the more about themselves.[7] The Stranger need not bother with ordinary methods of discovery, and the viewer has access to what he knows via his dreams, which are perhaps revelations to him, but seem more likely to be tormenting reminders of something he already knows. And given the precision with which he metes out punishment, he seems to know it perfectly. The use of dreams makes the Stranger a kind of seer of hidden truths, and we are privy to his vision. They tell us, among other things, that knowing the relevant truth here, namely the guilt of the town, will not require investigation or argument. In short, no trial or deliberation will be necessary for justice to be done to Lago. Instead, what is required is clear moral vision, vision here associated with revelatory dreams, and the courage to act in accord with it.

The Stranger materializes out of the heat and descends from the mountains, killing and raping with ease. He paints Lago red, renames it "Hell," and burns it clean in a ritualized acknowledgment of and atonement for its crime. He punishes all transgressors. He liberates Sarah and elevates Mordecai, the only two citizens who seem to have acknowledged and felt genuine remorse for Lago's crime. Above all he avenges the murder of the marshal. When he leaves the town, though it has been decimated, the remaining inhabitants can breathe and even smile at last, their bloodguilt having been lifted, their civil order cleansed.[8] He leaves Lago in the direction from which he came, through the cemetery. He was not passing through; Lago was his destination, his goal.[9] Having done what he came to do, the Stranger returns into the haze of the hills, into whatever stands behind nature, on the other side of the cemetery.

As the Stranger leaves town he passes Mordecai carving Duncan's name into a grave marker. Duncan has been acknowledged, and this is a sign that the civil order has returned to legitimacy, each individual having received his due and recognition. Mordecai looks up at the Stranger and remarks that he still doesn't know his name. "Yes, you do," the Stranger replies. The scene invites speculation about the identity of the Stranger.[10] One possibility is that the Stranger's name is Duncan, the dead marshal's brother.[11] Or perhaps the Stranger is the ghost of Duncan himself, who like the ghost of Banquo has returned to avenge his own murder.[12] But the Stranger's enigmatic claim that Mordecai knows his name also suggests that the name of the Stranger has been announced sometime before, or is eternally known. Death is his name. He rides a pale horse. Hell follows him. The first man he shoots, he shoots in the forehead, the crimson hole gaping as if to indicate that he did not have the seal of God on him.[13] And though he kills the Bridges gang for their murder of Duncan, he also uses them as instruments of Lago's destruction. Those three, Bridges and the Carlin brothers, are the other riders of this apocalypse.[14] Hence the Stranger is an agent of God's punishment. It is important that he remain nameless, though we are told that we know his name. This fact keeps him as close as possible to God the unnamable, to a strange and remote God. It keeps him from being one among the named inhabitants of the civil order.

His strangeness and his precision are further keys to understanding the relation between the civil and the moral orders depicted in the movie. I spoke above of the moral law of some Westerns as transcendent in the sense of having authority independent of civil institutions. But here that transcendence appears to involve an authority beyond even nature itself. It is supernatural in contrast to the worldliness of the civil, and outstrips even the power of nature. It enjoys absolute authority over the civil order. It is supreme. When the civil order strays, its transgressions trigger retribution from beyond. This civil order of Lago cannot keep its own justice. To be righted and provided with at least the possibility of legitimacy, Lago needs an emissary, an executioner of the law beyond. *High Plains Drifter* represents that law as not only absolutely authoritative, but also as perfectly, metaphysically precise. The Stranger's retribution is without error and in perfect keeping with the nature of Lago's various crimes. He turns Lago inside out, cleanses it, while he and his law are utterly independent of it. The purity of his authority requires such transcendence. Far more radically than the gunfighter riding into the sunset, the Stranger rides out of materiality, out of corporeality, and into another world, into the domain of a perfectly just and, for all we know, merciless God.

The Evolution of the Western's Representation of Justice in *High Plains Drifter*

High Plains Drifter therefore depicts the law that stands behind the law, as divine law. This is the law that gives Marshal Kane's tin star meaning. It is the law that *Warlock* (Dmytryk, 1959) distinguishes from two deficient kinds of law: the law identified with the peace and order the powerful man brings, the law the town of Warlock *buys* when it hires Marshal Clay Blaisedell (Henry Fonda), and the positive law associated with the distant political order, the law advocated for in *Warlock* by the disabled and often drunk Judge Holloway (Wallace Ford). In addition to providing a fabulously satisfying mythical template for the telling of a classic revenge story, the representation of such law as divine in *High Plains Drifter* can also be understood as an evolution, an unfolding of what we might call the logic of the representation of justice in certain Westerns.

I argued above, via *High Noon,* that some Westerns not only depict the civil order as vulnerable, they also tend to regard with suspicion, if not outright cynicism, the political and legislative aspirations of that order.

Law books and political association are regarded as at best irrelevant to the matter at hand, and at worst corrupting, especially emasculating ventures.[15] The people of Hadleyville or Warlock may long for law and order, but the Westerns themselves are wary of the moral value as well as the efficacy of securing law and order through political association and legislative action. To avoid disintegration, the civil order seems poised between two normatively undesirable options: order imposed by the powerful or order secured through political association. I have maintained that a Western resolution of this dilemma is to appeal to a law that stands behind the law, a moral or natural law, which grounds the legitimacy of the civil order. But in the context of the Western, to call this law a *natural* law is problematic. For the nature commonly presented in the Western is a nature shorn of moral sentiment,[16] a nature reflected in the attitude of Abe McQuown (Tom Drake), leader of a gang of cowboys, who explains that he terrorizes Warlock and runs off its lawmen to remind the town that he was there first, and that he will call the shots as long as he wants to. In the face of that kind of nature, the natural law is the law of a stronger man, exactly the law Warlock buys when it hires Marshal Blaisedell. What the natural law provides is therefore something more like a Hobbesian sovereign than the law that stands behind the law in *High Noon.* In the Western, the moral law cannot be rooted in nature.

The Western's doubts about our capacity to make our own law, as well as about rooting the moral law in nature, come to explicit aesthetic representation in *High Plains Drifter*'s depiction of the moral law as divine, as beyond our civil institutions and beyond nature. This logic is reflected in Eastwood's own Western persona, notably the one that made him famous: the Man with No Name of the Leone pictures. The Man with No Name is surely a drifter, but hardly a representative of the moral law, even in *The Good, the Bad, and the Ugly,* where he ironically stands for the Good. He is the gunfighter as antihero; his independence is not associated with moral authority. On the contrary, his independence is a function of moral disorder, the disorder that flows from the deficiencies of the forms of law discussed above. The biblical proportions of *High Plains Drifter* indicate that Eastwood could not reclaim No Name from moral disorder simply by returning to the lost innocence of moral intuition and the courage of the good man.[17] If the attitude toward nature and society grows too cynical, the moral authority that might establish the latter's legitimacy (or redeem the former) requires that the moral law be increasingly remote, absolutely authoritative, and perfectly precise. It also requires that its agent be something more than the good man. This turns the gunfighter into the Stranger, executioner of a divine law whose authority is strange and terrible.

High Plains Drifter's self-consciousness is already implicit in the peculiar nature of Lago's misdeed. The marshal discovered that the mine was on government land. The very order about which the Western is typically so cautious, sometimes to the point of cynicism, here is the linchpin of the wrongdoing. In killing the marshal, Lago deprived itself of law in many ways. Not only does the town eliminate the law's enforcer, but also its connection to the state as a whole; political authority is evaded. It is not clear that the nullification of the company's claim would have been fair, so I don't mean to suggest that the movie encourages us to adopt the federal perspective. But the fact remains that the core of Lago's corruption, its violation of the moral law, involves its repudiation of the legitimacy of the government's claim to the land. This fact, in turn, erodes any legitimacy the civil order of Lago might have generated out of its own political and legal institutions. Lago's own act of cynicism toward political and legal authority (the fact that the mine is on government land is at one point referred to as a "mere technicality, really") serves to isolate it in its corruption. Lago exposes itself to transcendent retribution by severing its ties to worldly accountability.

High Plains Drifter therefore reclaims the idea of a law standing behind the law, but does so as if aware that the civil order, or a common attitude in Westerns toward that order, has created out of itself the need for transcendent retribution. When the normative authority of the civil order breaks down, when we doubt our own normative resources, justice itself must be depicted as transcending our civil order, as an ideal toward which we strive or from which we have fallen. To think the relation between the civil order and justice would then require thinking a world beyond the civil (and, in the Western, beyond nature), from which the moral law may descend and into which it may return.

The Good and the Bad in the Political Morality of *High Plains Drifter*

How are we to think of this conception of the law behind the law, which seems in part generated by the Western's own doubts about lawmaking and political association? Though the reclamation of this idea in *High Plains Drifter* is self-consciously mythic, it is not for that reason ironic. In fact, the moral attitude of the movie is fairly clear: have the "guts" to defend what's right, lest a remorseless, unforgiving angel be sent to turn your world upside down. More than once the movie makes clear that our humanity depends on this courage, and that moralizing rationalizations of wicked deeds (for the good of everyone, the price of progress, according to Belting) are self-serving hypocrisies. The Stranger even tells the sheriff that the only thing wrong with Lago is a serious lack of guts. In fact, the Stranger's various conversations with the sheriff may be taken as a civics lesson meant to contradict the lesson given by Judge Mettrick in *High Noon.* Sheriff Shaw begins *High Plains Drifter* as an ineffective, ironic representative of the law, but one of the movie's last shots is of his cautiously smiling, sunlit face as he looks up at the departing Stranger. It is as if a burden has been lifted from him in particular, so that now he may be free to function as a genuine representative of the law. This in turn suggests that what I have deemed the Western's distrust of the civil order might best be characterized as expressing the idea that without this moral underpinning the civil order will be defective and easily corrupted.

There is something deeply satisfying (and perhaps quite right) about the movie's depiction of the law that stands behind the law as emanating from or expressive of a divine authority, for such a depiction expresses the sort of claim this law has on us, a claim not subordinate to our individual preferences or inclinations. It indicates that the law has a necessity and authority that outstrips our private pursuits, including the vain and selfish ends to which political association and positive law can be put. This is perhaps part of what Marshal Kane finds impossible to explain. When we fail to stand and oppose serious wrongs done to ourselves and others, the kinds of wrongs that strike at the very dignity of the person, then we forfeit our own status as persons and allow that we may be treated as mere things. Such a law is not one among many options for *us.* It is rather constitutive of us as persons. If we fail to keep it, no matter how much security and satisfaction might be guaranteed by a civil order, we fail to be persons.[18] The general lack of dignity exuded by the people of Lago attests to this fact.

The depiction of this law as divine may also capture something constitutive of us in a slightly different sense, something deeply rooted in our psychological nature, for despite the fact that we often speak of punishment as being for the purpose of deterring crime and maintaining order, our punishment decisions are in fact often rooted in retributive motives.[19] We have, it would seem, a very deep sense that an unpunished wrong is an intolerable affront to justice. This is so, irrespective of the actual future threat the unpunished wrong poses, and perhaps even of the "progress" or common "good" the wrong may have advanced. And so, with perhaps a little exaggeration, we might say that the Stranger is an emissary of a god of our own nature, our own deep attunement to the law he represents. Lago is discordant, its craven selfishness having muted the call for justice.

Nevertheless, there is to my mind something unsettling and even deficient in this representation of the law that stands behind the law, and I will spend the rest of this essay exploring some of what I take to be its shortcomings. Perhaps I can begin this exploration by pointing out a possible tension in this representation of the law. I claimed above that the punishments meted out by the Stranger are startlingly precise and, I venture, quite satisfying to most viewers. We recognize that justice has been done. But inasmuch as the Stranger is also clearly marked as an agent of divine justice, to what extent may we call this *our* justice, and is it appropriate to imply that the legitimacy of the civil order is answerable to or grounded in such a conception of justice? Though the narrative allows for Duncan's *personal* desires as victim ("damn you to hell," he says to his killers) to mingle with the absoluteness of this moral law, the mingling is in fact what Duncan says it is: a call to a higher authority. We may be reassured by this call as well as unsettled by it, but it is unavoidably a call beyond ourselves, certifying the desire for revenge by means of the transcendent moral authority. The call may well be prophetic,[20] which I take in part to imply that it is meant to restore us to our true, better, higher selves. But that does not imply that we should necessarily endorse it.

The danger of such a call and such a conception of the law that stands behind the law might begin to come clear if we consider the strangeness of the Stranger. His isolation belongs to him: he enters town with it and he insists upon it. The town attempts to embrace him, but he rejects the embrace. This is another mythic reversal of *High Noon,* in which the town is to blame for the isolation of Kane, who turns to them again and again for help. The Stranger eschews many norms of the civil order, and in many respects taunts our moral assumptions and expectations, even if we see in his deeds a perfect justice. Such taunting is perhaps most acute in the Stranger's rape of Callie, which occurs very early in the movie.

What is the meaning of this fusion of pristine justice and its uncanny, taunting agent? It is part of the prophetic or apocalyptic fabric of the story, a warning that there is a law to which we are answerable, but a law that is distant and strange. We will recognize it as perfectly just, but also as alien and awesome. But something else is in play here as well, something perhaps brought out by Sarah's initial reaction to the Stranger. Sarah exhibits moral courage otherwise unknown in Lago. One might therefore have expected her to gravitate immediately to the Stranger. Instead, she initially regards him with disdain, itself a sign of her courage. Presumably she sees in him just another man wielding violence selfishly, raping women and killing men according to his whim. This marks his law as strange, even to those who would respect and keep it. Seen from Sarah's initial perspective, it brings the Stranger eerily close to the very injustice he has come to overturn.

In keeping with the typical Westerner, the Stranger is taciturn.[21] His silence is attractive, especially since it is commonly contrasted with a use of words that is either ineffective or corrupt or plainly false. As we have seen, the law the Westerner keeps is sometimes presented as ineffable. If you have to talk about it, if it is subject to discursive determinations, hope is lost. This is why it is important for Westerns such as *High Noon* or *Warlock* or even *The Man Who Shot Liberty Valance* to portray outlaws whose deeds clearly express contempt for their victims, a brazen denial that the victim has any right not to be treated as such. These are situations, as the minister in *High Noon* shamefully confesses, in which right and wrong are clear and the demands of justice plain. Seeing them requires no expertise and few words. Such situations help focus our attention on the importance of courage, which is part of their moral value. But if talk won't help us determine the moral law, a death struggle or violent conflict is what settles matters. This kind of avenging justice can make for difficult mutual recognition, and so for an unstable ethical order. In *High Plains Drifter*, there is thus a telling point of contact between the absence of deliberation or adjudication and the fact that the Stranger's presence is the result of a call for revenge. How do we know that he is not an agent of private vendetta, rather than of the law that stands behind the law? How do we know that Duncan's claim is *right*? We see it. It is revealed to us. Here is the danger. The need for communicative action is suppressed, sidestepped, even derided. But without it, how can we make that law that stands behind the law *our* law? How can we make it more than just a private call for revenge, at best avenging justice? And here perhaps is the warning also implicit in the "prophecy." The law that stands behind the law might well be private vengeance. That is, this law may not ground or justify the civil order at all; it may rather be the law that emerges when that order fails to keep its own justice, the law that emerges when it severs its ties to civil accountability. It would then be a law that will undermine community. So there is after all in *High Plains Drifter* a trace of the idea that what has come to Lago is not retributive or even avenging justice, but merely the violence that follows from the dissolution or corruption of positive law and civil order.

That is not, of course, what is ultimately depicted in *High Plains Drifter,* in which the revenge appears to be just.[22] There may be such avenging justice. Perhaps it is even God's law. But it is unlikely that we can determine the content of this law except through our ordinary processes of deliberation, and it is even less likely that these processes of deliberation can be shorn from their normative social context. Furthermore, if *we* are to keep this law, it would seem that there is no way to keep it except through some sort of civil institution, something that constitutes us as a *we.* The suggestion that we might know the law, perhaps by intuition or revelation, independently of our ordinary processes of deliberation (much less our institutionalized processes of adjudication), and that the law might be actualized independently of civil institutions therefore stands at least in considerable tension, if not outright contradiction, with what would seem to be requirements of our actually keeping this law. Truly to keep this law we would need to bring it down to earth, so to speak. To the extent that we remain doubtful about our own capacities to deliberate and adjudicate the claims of justice (or about the consistency of such adjudication with the courage necessary to execute justice, and so about our ability to exhibit a just character), to that extent we also remain doubtful about our ability to live up to the moral law, and so to answer its call adequately. Hence it would seem that the Western cannot afford too much cynicism about the civil order, just as it would seem that the concept of a moral law independent of social practice might lack the content needed for us to look after our own justice and keep our own law.

Our position, then, is this: to talk about justice can indeed be a sign of moral cowardice and selfishness, inventing complications where none really exist. We know the sophistry that puts words in the service of injustice. But to insulate justice from sophistry by depicting it as divine can be its own kind of sophistry. It can encourage the view that justice need not be discussed to be determined, since we have intuitive or revelatory insight into its demands, treating complications as though these are the products of weak-minded or weak-willed attempts to serve our own interests. Our moral judgments may require intuition, but we should be wary of depicting those intuitions as of something absolute or divine. For in that case we may obviate the need to justify them by ordinary discursive means. And if we do not justify them that way, we should be wary that these intuitions are rationalizations of our own selfish ends, undermining our attempts to recognize each other's claims within the normative structure constituting our community, and so too the requirement that those who suffer at the hands of our justice ought to be able to recognize their own justice in it. In that case, the idea of the law that stands behind the law may just be an expression of our dissatisfaction with the necessary conditions of actualizing justice in the civil order, treating that order with unwarranted contempt. The appeal to justice beyond the civil, especially the kind of retributive or avenging justice so wonderfully mythologized in *High Plains Drifter,* should therefore be regarded with suspicion. It may enable violence and injustice in the very people who use violence in the name of justice, and especially order. In the words of that later Eastwood Westerner, William Munny, it may deliver us to a condition in which "deserve's got nothin' to do with it."

Notes

1. The perpetually upright Gary Cooper was, after all, exceptionally well cast.

2. This is one symbolic reason why the gunfighter is cast as an outsider even in Westerns that depict the civil order as somehow dependent on him, as in *Shane* (Stevens, 1953), for instance. But even where the gunfighter is depicted as a more troubling, antisocial figure, I suggest that one will often find that he keeps this law, if only or primarily privately, as with Tom Doniphon (John Wayne) in *The Man Who Shot Liberty Valance* (Ford, 1962). The law is integral to him as an independent person.

3. Hence, I am ambivalent about Bazin's claim that the Western emphasizes the need for law in the context of fragile human morality. For the positive law in many Westerns is also depicted as weak, and the civil order it establishes as not always justified or desirable. See André Bazin, "The Western," in *What Is Cinema? Vol. II* (Berkeley: Univ. of California Press, 1971), 145–146. The question of how my observations relate to the Western genre is a complicated one. It may be that the traits I identify are common only to those Westerns Bazin calls "superwesterns" and Warshow calls "aestheticized Westerns," *Shane* and *High Noon* being the favorite examples. See Robert Warshow, "Movie Chronicle: The Westerner," *Partisan Review* (March–April 1954): 190–203, and Bazin "The Evolution of the Western," in *What Is Cinema? Vol. II.* For a broader account of the genre willing to embrace more of the elements I have suggested, see Raymond Durgnat and Scott Simmon, "Six Creeds That Won the Western," *Film Comment* (September–October 1980): 69–84.

4. For a compelling synopsis and brief analysis, see Lawrence F. Knapp, *Directed by Clint Eastwood* (Jefferson, N.C.: McFarland, 1996), 55–64.

5. See Jane Tompkins, *West of Everything: The Inner Life of Westerns* (Oxford: Oxford Univ. Press, 1992), 69–87.

6. For an extended discussion of Westerns as meditations on our myths of "founding" the American West, rather than as themselves mythologizing that West, see Robert B. Pippin, *Hollywood Westerns and American Myth* (New Haven, Conn.: Yale Univ. Press, 2010). While he does not discuss *High Plains Drifter*, this aspect of the movie and the way in which Lago has denied itself legal standing with a series of false "claims" fits reasonably well with Pippin's account. However, *High Plains Drifter* seems much less interested in the necessity and the fate of mythologizing the founding. It is rather a narrative about exposing (and rectifying) a particular falsification.

7. The Stranger's dreams in fact fuse with one other flashback of the event: Mordecai's traumatized recollection of it from his own perspective, on the ground like the dying marshal, hiding beneath a porch. That recollection ties Mordecai to Duncan and the Stranger all the more decisively.

8. In this I disagree with Drucilla Cornell, for whom the movie implies no serious moral repair, but instead depicts the trauma survivor's reproduction of evil. See Drucilla Cornell, *Clint Eastwood and Issues of American Masculinity* (New York: Fordham Univ. Press, 2009), 10–18.

9. Thanks to Rayna Patton for alerting me to the anagram of "Lago" and "goal."

10. This is a speculation that I take to be in marked contrast to the anonymity of the Man with No Name, the Eastwood persona of the Leone pictures.

11. Eastwood himself apparently, fantastically in my view, has favored this interpretation. See Knapp, *Directed by Clint Eastwood*, 61.

12. Buddy Van Horn, who plays Duncan, was Eastwood's stunt double.

13. See Revelation 7:3 and 9:4. I thank Richard McClelland for encouraging me to acknowledge in greater detail the movie's explicit references to prophetic and apocalyptic literature.

14. See Knapp, *Directed by Clint Eastwood*, 61.

15. John Ford's *The Man Who Shot Liberty Valance* is a brilliant meditation on the attractions and deficiencies of positive law and political association. See also Pippin, *Hollywood Westerns and American Myth*, 61–101.

16. See Tompkins, *West of Everything*, 72–73.

17. A number of critics have seen in the Stranger such a project of reclamation. See François Guérif, *Clint Eastwood*, trans. L. Nesselson (New York: St. Martin's Press, 1984), 95–96. See also Paul Smith, *Clint Eastwood: A Cultural Production* (Minneapolis: Univ. of Minnesota Press, 1993), 37–42. Smith follows Guérif, and reads Eastwood-directed Westerns generally as attempting to restore the form after the subversion he helped Leone execute against it. And see Knapp, *Directed by Clint Eastwood*, 58, who especially emphasizes the supernatural dimensions of the reclamation.

18. This basically Kantian idea has a long philosophical lineage, and defending it is far beyond the scope of this paper. But for a classic articulation of it, see Peter Strawson,

"Freedom and Resentment," *Proceedings of the British Academy* 48 (1962): 187–211. For an articulation of it in terms of punishment, see Herbert Morris, "Persons and Punishment," in *On Guilt and Innocence* (Berkeley: Univ. of California Press, 1976), 31–88. For a discussion of it in terms of vindictiveness, see Jeffrie Murphy, "Two Cheers for Vindictiveness," *Punishment and Society* 2 (2000): 131–143.

19. See, for instance, Livia B. Keller et al., "A Closer Look at an Eye for an Eye: Laypersons' Punishment Decisions Are Primarily Driven by Retributive Motives," *Social Justice Research* 23, no. 2/3 (September 2010): 99–116; Kevin M. Carlsmith, "On Justifying Punishment: The Discrepancy Between Words and Actions," *Social Justice Research* 21, no. 2 (June 2008): 119–137; and K. Carlsmith and J. Darley, "Psychological Aspects of Retributive Justice," *Advances in Experimental Social Psychology* 40 (2008): 193–236. Thanks to Richard McClelland for alerting me to this literature.

20. The editors of this volume have suggested this to me.

21. On the Western's distrust of language, see Tompkins, *West of Everything*, 49–55.

22. I am therefore not claiming that revenge cannot be just, though our tradition of moral thought does tend to take a dim view of revenge. Retributivist theories of punishment, for instance, are often criticized for rationalizing vengeance. Hence retributivists often distinguish sharply between retribution and revenge. Yet revenge is not without its moral defenders. See, for instance, William Ian Miller, *Eye for an Eye* (Cambridge: Cambridge Univ. Press, 2005), and Peter French, *The Virtues of Vengeance* (Lawrence: Univ. Press of Kansas, 2001). For a defense of the emotions underpinning vengeance, see Jeffrie Murphy, "Two Cheers for Vindictiveness," and Thane Rosenbaum, *Payback: The Case for Revenge* (Chicago: Univ. of Chicago Press, 2013).

Bad Men at Play

On the Banality of Goodness in *Unforgiven*

Richard Gilmore

> Bad Men from Bodie weren't ordinary scoundrels, they came with the land, and you could no more cope with them than you could with dust or hailstones.
>
> —E. L. Doctorow, *Welcome to Hard Times*

Clint Eastwood is not obviously a philosopher. There are, however, two parallel traditions of Western philosophy, both of which can be said to originate with Plato. One tradition, associated with the middle and later works of Plato, is the idea of philosophy as the pursuit of knowledge, which becomes for Plato knowledge of the Forms. There is another tradition, another idea of what philosophy is about, in the earlier, so-called Socratic works of Plato. The idea of philosophy in those earlier works is of philosophy as a kind of wisdom, specifically, the wisdom to understand that we do not always really know what we think we know. It is this wisdom that I see Eastwood developing in *Unforgiven* (1992). Most profoundly, what we do not know that we think we know is: what we want. We think we want a certain kind of power, the power of the gun, for example; or the power to do whatever we want, to instill fear in others, to dominate. We want this power in order to flee the banality of our obsequious and conforming lives. These desires, I see Eastwood arguing in *Unforgiven*, are more complicated than they may seem, and our real desires may not be as we think they are.

Metaphysical Levels of Mise-en-Scène and Metaphysical Levels of Reality

Unforgiven begins with a complicated series of cuts that suggest multiple narrative levels and even multiple metaphysical levels. The opening shot is of a house, a man, and a tree just after sunset. The house, man, and tree are seen in silhouette as they are backlit by the orange of fading day. The man has finished the work of filling in a grave, the grave of his dead wife. We know it is his dead wife because accompanying this image is a text that explains who this man is, who his wife was, and what happened to her. The text provides particulars to the silhouetted forms that the image alone does not provide. As silhouetted forms, without particular characteristics identifiable, the image suggests that these are primordial, universal forms, the frontier house, Iggsydryl, the original tree, Man, in his primordial, universal activity, burying a loved one.

Just this opening shot implies multiple levels of reality. "Mise-en-scène" refers to anything that is "put" in the scene. In this case, the mise-en-scène includes both the text and the silhouetted figures of man, tree, and house, which implies at least two levels of reality. There is the reality of the man at work burying his dead wife. There is the reality of the text on the screen. And there is also the reality suggested by the point of view of the camera, a point of view bearing witness to this painful scene, which then points to still another reality beyond the reality of the framed shot because we, as the audience, share this point of view, and this act of bearing witness.

The ambiguity of the opening shot compels the audience to interpret it, which is to compel the audience to reflect and think, which is part of what it means to do philosophy. I take it that part of what *Unforgiven* is about is a reflection on the nature of what it means to be a human being, and perhaps more specifically, even though there are some very strong women characters in the film, what it means to be a man. Some of the issues the movie addresses have to do with what love means, what friendship means, what loyalty and duty mean, what family means, and what life means. These are deep philosophical issues and each of the characters in the movie will encounter these issues in different ways and arrive at different solutions to the problems these issues pose. It is not clear to me that the movie itself proposes a preferred solution for the life issues it addresses so much as it suggests the tragic inadequacy of all attempts to resolve these issues in a fully satisfactory way.

The second shot of the movie is another long shot, also beautiful, but beautiful in a very different way from the first shot. Whereas the first shot is beautiful as elegiac composition, the second shot is beautiful as Sublime Nature: a powerful thunderstorm in some distant mountains descending on a small, vulnerable-looking town. Again, the scene contains text that gives particulars to this universal (universal in the sense of archetypal) image of raw nature: "Big Whiskey Wyoming, 1880." The music has been replaced with the sound of the distant thunder. The next shot is an almost claustrophobic shot, at night, of the main street of a very small pioneer town in pounding rain. The empty street is lit by light from the building windows, but that light ends in an opaque blackness where the streets head out of town into the night. This shot will be repeated near the end of the movie when William Munny (Clint Eastwood) returns for his vengeance. This shot is followed by a weird dreamlike panning shot across the rain-drenched outside of a building, picking up strange shadows acting out uninterpretable scenes behind shaded windows. This dreamlike ambiguity is resolved in the next shot of a man vigorously sexually riding a woman in a bed. She is urging him on. From the next room comes a cry, the man's buddy calling for him. The man runs to his buddy's aid in the next room, and there we see the other man attacking a young woman, another prostitute, with a knife, slashing her face, screaming violent things at her. The knife is very large, compensation, no doubt, for what we will learn is his surprisingly small penis. Knives and guns are generally compensations for our inadequacies, which is not to say that they are not also extremely useful tools. The philosophical point is to remember that both are often true.

Freud's Primal Scene and Philosophy

These scenes near the beginning of *Unforgiven* of shadows moving behind screened windows, shadows of people performing some kind of weird, eerie movements that we, the audience, do not know quite how to interpret, but which seem vaguely disturbing, invoke Freud's idea of the Primal Scene. The Primal Scene, according to Freud, occurs when a young child happens to witness his or her parents making love.[1] The child, according to Freud, cannot tell if this is a scene of violence or affection. What makes it primal is that the child is compelled, due to the intense nature of the scene, to form an interpretation of what is going on before he or she has any conceptual tools for really understanding what is going on. In this way, Freud's primal scene stands as well for the primal scene of philosophy. Philosophy is all about trying to understand what we do not understand, trying to invent new conceptual tools to understand something for which we have only weak or inadequate conceptual tools for understanding. A version of the Primal Scene (perhaps not quite as Freud meant it) is, therefore, recapitulated every time one finds oneself in a situation in which one can recognize that there is more going on than one can understand, especially if what is going on has overtones of violence or sex or both. Many good movies put us into this position at their outset, in the position of sensing that there is something important going on, something to do with violence or sex, but we cannot tell quite what it is.

Slavoj Žižek has argued that this is a repeated trope in the films of Hitchcock, for example. In Hitchcock, the representation of the Primal Scene repeatedly takes a very similar form: we, the audience, as well as some of the characters in the movie, will see a couple in the distance, usually on some kind of hillock, engaged in some kind of intense communication, and we cannot be sure whether it is a violent argument or an intense declaration of love.[2] We are forced, given the intensity of the scene, to try to interpret what it means without sufficient information to make a reliable interpretation. This is what Eastwood is doing at the beginning of *Unforgiven*. Intentionally or not, the dreamlike quality of the images that do not seem to make any sense recapitulates for us the sense of the Primal Scene, of bearing witness to something of evident importance that we do not have the resources to parse and understand. That it is intentional is certainly suggested when the shadows we see through the window get translated into a man having vigorous, if not violent, sex with a woman (which is the Primal Scene just as Freud described it, although not including the detail of *a tergo*), and then the connection with actual violence is made explicit via a montage from that scene of sex to the next scene of the cowboy yelling at the young prostitute and then cutting her face.

What Eastwood is doing here is a form of philosophy done with images instead of words. Hitchcock called this "pure cinema," when concepts are generated by means of linked images, or montage.[3] The concepts generated by Eastwood in this opening sequence have to do with the human condition, which is what makes them philosophical. We all live with the specter of death in the background. We all live with raw nature towering above us, and working inside us to challenge our civilized veneer. We all repeatedly recapitulate the basic pattern of the Primal Scene, the experience of finding ourselves in situations beyond our understanding, especially situations that involve sex and violence, where we have to try to interpret what is going on without sufficient conceptual tools. Philosophy is about trying to come up with some better conceptual tools, beginning with some better questions, for dealing with our lives.

Eastwood and the Western

Eastwood is a master of the Western, both as an actor and as a director. The genre of the Western invokes mythic themes: good versus evil, civilization versus barbarity, man versus nature. The hero, therefore, must be a superior person, at least in the sense of being better equipped to deal with the particular situations presented in the narrative of the movie. As an actor Eastwood conveyed this sense of a mythic figure in the spaghetti Westerns with Sergio Leone through a combination of minimal talk and a maximum of gunfighting skill, these combined with an ironic detachment that made him seem to be concerned with otherworldly things even as he obsessively pursued this world's riches. As a director, he does it in movie after movie through various narrative techniques, such as giving his protagonists a mysterious past or just an inner commitment that is different from and unknown to the rest of the people that surround him. His characters are both subject to fate and superior to fate. They both endure horrible beatings, hardships, and cruelties, and emerge from all hardships somehow essentially unscathed, as if they had some secret connection with the realm of the immortals.[4] His protagonists have a dignity that manifests itself not continually but in moments. It shines through the worst degradations of dirt and violence. We see in these moments a glimpse of something redemptive. In *Unforgiven,* these moments are especially striking because the character of William Munny is so generally unpleasant, unattractive, and distinctly unheroic.

Consider a couple of such moments from one of Eastwood's early movies directed by Sergio Leone. In *The Good, the Bad, and the Ugly* (1966) there are two moments of this kind of redemptive dignity that are especially striking. One is when Tuco (Eli Wallach) and Blondie (Clint Eastwood), in an uneasy truce, are trying to find the graveyard where the money for which they are searching is buried. They come across a drunken Union general (Aldo Giuffrè) who has orders to take a particular bridge. The opposing Confederate general clearly has the same orders. Each day both sides attack, meeting at the bridge. Many men are killed and wounded, in what seems to be a futile campaign for both sides. In a very uncharacteristically selfless gesture, Tuco and Blondie decide to blow up the bridge. It is the last thing that the now wounded and dying general sees, an end to this waste of men's lives in the exploding bridge. These two Bad Men, Bad Men in the sense that they live outside the law, perform a supremely moral act, an act that the system of law itself cannot accomplish—the end of the senseless killing of hundreds of men.

Another moment of surprising redemptive poignancy is when Tuco and Blondie are at the monastery where Tuco's brother, Father Pablo Ramirez (Luigi Pistilli), is a monk. There is a tense scene between Tuco and his brother. It is a scene that is meant to be in private, but Blondie bears witness to the scene through a doorway. In the scene, Tuco's brother tells Tuco of the death of their mother, and then viciously denounces Tuco. Tuco is clearly hurt by these accusations, but when he comes out he tells Blondie how much his brother loves him. Blondie just says, "Yeah," but as they are riding away on a buckboard Blondie hands Tuco his cigar for a puff, a gesture of solidarity between unloved outcasts and a silent affirmation that in this world the good are not always so good and the bad may have some good in them yet.

In *Unforgiven* three such moments can be identified. One moment is the complicated scene in which the two cowboys, Quick Mike (David Mucci) and Davey Bunting (Rob Campbell), return to town with the horses for the owner of the whorehouse, Skinny Dubois (Anthony James). One of the cowboys, Davey, the one who did not do the cutting, brings a special horse for the cut prostitute, Delilah (Anna Levine). There is a moment of temporal suspension when the various moral issues are weighed. On the one hand, the cowboys are honoring their promise and even going beyond what they promised in an attempt at restitution. They are doing something "good." On the other hand, the very act of restitution seems to affirm the commodity status of the women, that justice for them can be achieved via a commodity exchange. But the cowboys also bring a gift, an additional horse, for the woman who was cut, which would seem to transcend the mere exchange of commodities. Delilah, the cut prostitute, her face healing, seems to respond positively to this offer of a gift, as do we, the audience, but the woman who is leading the demands for justice for the prostitutes, Strawberry Alice (Frances Fisher), refuses the horse. It is a complicated moment because all of the various claims—moral, practical, political—are brought into salience. We feel and see the rightness of Strawberry Alice's insistence on the insufficiency of this gesture by the cowboys for rectifying the terrible injustice that has been done, and we feel the strong desire for this gift to be accepted and the hope that all can move forward and escape the terrible logic of strict justice via vengeance. We feel the need and desire of the cowboys to try to do something to ameliorate the pain and injustice that they caused. We see the desire in Delilah to be able just to accept the horse, to be just a regular person again instead of the center of a cause, to begin to put the whole thing behind her. We see Skinny, in some sense the real source of the deepest forms of the injustice by his demand for financial restitution for the damaging of his "property," watching, more or less indifferent to the issues raised by this gesture refused. It is a scene of great and ambiguous moral complexity that emerges from what would seem to be a straightforward exchange. The multiplicity of perspectives that the scene engages reflects a multiplicity of narratives present simultaneously.

Another scene of subtly rendered moral complexity would be Munny's surprising reflection on what it means to kill a man: "It's a hell of a thing, killing a man. You take away all he's got, and all he's ever gonna have." The Schofield Kid (Jaimz Woolvett) says, "Yeah, well, I guess they had it coming." Munny replies, "We all got it coming, Kid." This is surprising because up to this point Munny has been as verbally unreflective as he has been inept with a gun or a horse. This display of depth, his sympathy for the killed and his sense of justice, suggest redemptive aspects of his character that we had not expected.

A final example is the scene between Munny and Delilah, in which Munny speaks movingly of his wife and refuses Delilah's offer of "a free one" (in other words, sex with no charge). Delilah is clearly hurt by his refusal. She seems to understand the rejection as being because of her disfigurement, that Munny thinks she is too ugly to have sex with. Munny sees her pain and says, "You ain't ugly like me. It's just that we both got scars. But you're a beautiful woman and if I was to want a free one, I'd want it with you. I guess, more than with them other two. It's that I can't on account of my wife." It is a touching scene because Delilah is trying to do something nice for Munny and Munny is trying to do something nice for Delilah. It is a scene of remarkable tenderness within a movie of remarkable violence. The scene humanizes them both, revealing still more layers of moral and human complexity. Again, our expectations are upended, our ability to read a person's character is called into question, we are confronted with the fact that we may not really know what we think we know. We realize that things are more complicated than they initially appeared. This is perhaps the most fundamental philosophical realization, and it changes our view of the film.

Wilderness and Civilization

A recurrent theme in the genre of the Western film, and especially in the Westerns of John Ford (for example, *The Man Who Shot Liberty Valance*, 1962), but also as the theme of Sergio Leone's *Once Upon a Time in the West* (1968), is the theme of historical transition from a time when wilderness and wildness dominate to a time when civilization and order dominate (usually marked in Westerns by the construction of tracks for, or the arrival of, a train). There is a macrocosm/microcosm corollary that is also a part of this historical transition in that just as a society must become more ordered and law-bound, so too must the individuals within that society. As the society becomes more civilized, the society's heroes will be more civilized. They will be bringers of civilization rather than wildness. An individual with self-control and a society under the rule of law make possible a stable, well-ordered, bourgeois life. This is a great gain. What is lost is the intensity, the spontaneity, the deep satisfaction of doing what one wants, of being the source of the law as opposed to being subject to law. Stability and order are gained, but at the price of meekness, docility, and cooperativeness.

At the beginning of the movie Munny has given up drinking and violence for a life as a pig farmer, a life that is more stable, well-ordered, and with the potential for a lasting happiness. He has married, had children, acquired a farm—all of these require more and more self-control in turn. All of these require a suppression of one's inner wildness, and Munny had been, by all accounts, exceptionally wild, but, as he says to Ned (Morgan Freeman), "I'm not like that anymore. I'm just like anybody else."

For Munny, however, this life of being the same as everyone else is not going so well. His wife dies, the pig farming is a struggle, and the future for his children is very uncertain. Then an opportunity appears in the form of the Schofield Kid, an opportunity to make a substantial amount of money for something that he used to do for free. At first he resists the offer, but finding himself face down in pig shit he reconsiders. That is where civil society leaves most of us, deep in our own shit. That is, for the great benefits of living in a civilized society we must repress, as Freud says, our wildness. We cannot discharge our anger freely when we feel anger. We cannot act on our lusts freely when we feel lust. We cannot act on our impulses to violence when we feel the impulse to commit violence. On the one hand, thank God that we do not, and that others do not as well. On the other hand, the suppression of all of those impulses does not make those impulses go away. They accrue and become a kind of sty in which we wallow.

Westerns represent a kind of dream of freedom from all of those repressions civil society demands of us. In Westerns, men are wild, one with nature, out in nature; they fight when they are angry, they whoop when they are happy, they pursue the woman they desire without equivocation or art. The Bad Men are frightening, but also fascinating. You don't have to be (or even want to be) a Bad Man to be fascinated by that kind of immediate connection between desire and action. Even the Good Men in Westerns tend to be liminal figures, halfway between the wildness of the bad and the tameness of the good. They have some self-control, some sense of deference to law, but are also prone to and able at violence if the situation calls for it. John Ford's Westerns contain many examples of such figures: Tom Doniphon (John Wayne) in *The Man Who Shot Liberty Valance* (1962), Ethan Edwards (John Wayne) in *The Searchers* (1956), Wyatt Earp (Henry Fonda) in *My Darling Clementine* (1946). These films explicitly mark the transition in societies from pre-civilized, pre-law-ruled to societies civilized and under the rule of law. The times are thrilling in the pre-law, pre-civilization portion of the films, and wistful in the sequences when the transition has been made. Ford does not seem to be saying in these films that lawlessness is better than law, but only that something is lost when law and civilization are fully instantiated. The question, then, is what do we really want? Do we really want the order and banality of civilized society, or do we really want the wildness that is displayed in the figure of the Westerner, the power of the gun, the closeness to wild nature? The wildness of the Westerner is a kind of play, but it is play for mortal stakes.

Bad Men at Play

> You don't know how to play.
>
> —Cheyenne (Jason Robards) in Leone's *Once Upon a Time in the West*

There are several references to Bad Men as a specific type in *Unforgiven.* Little Bill explicitly denies that the cowboys who were involved in the cutting of the prostitute Delilah are Bad Men. When he is considering what the appropriate justice is for the cutting of a whore, he considers whipping, but settles finally on a fine: five ponies from one of the cowboys and two from the other. Alice is aghast and says, “It ain’t fair Little Bill. It ain’t fair.” Little Bill takes her aside and says, “Haven’t you seen enough blood for one night, huh? Hell, Alice, it ain’t like they was tramps or loafers or bad men.” When Will Munny goes to his friend Ned Logan to have him ride with him and the Schofield Kid to kill the cowboys and get the reward, Ned says to him, “Hell, Will. We ain’t bad men no more. Shit, we’re farmers.” Little Bill is a Bad Man still (even though he is also still the Law), and so is English Bob, though not quite so Bad as Little Bill. And Little Bill has got nothing on Will Munny when he returns to his Bad Man ways. The Schofield Kid thinks he wants to be a Bad Man, and pretends to be one based on the stories he has heard, but he will change his mind once he has a taste of what it really means to be a Bad Man.

The theme of many classic Westerns is that of Bad Men at play. Johan Huizinga, in his book *Homo Ludens,* suggests that along with *Homo faber,* Man the Maker, and *Homo sapiens,* Man the Knower, we should be known as *Homo ludens,* Man the Player. Huizinga’s book is a sustained argument for the idea that there is an element of play in all manifestations of culture, that “culture itself bears the character of play.”[5] Much of culture, especially under capitalism, will seem to be anti-play, to be about profit, not play. This is the version of capitalism as an expression of the Protestant work ethic, and the early influences of Puritanism in the founding of America, which is also a Christianizing of America.[6] Huizinga equates play with freedom: “Here, then, we find the first main characteristic of play: that it is free, is in fact freedom.”[7] Where society oppresses and forces us to repress, play is the release from oppression and repression. We are fascinated with Bad Men, in part, because they live for a particular kind of play that most of us cannot afford to engage in, and, in that pursuit, are free in a way most of us are not.

Sergio Leone, to whom (along with Don Siegal) *Unforgiven* is dedicated, was the master of the Bad Men at play theme. In *The Good, the Bad, and the Ugly,* the gold the three men are looking for is a MacGuffin. None of them cares about the gold. What would they do with it if they got it? Open a nice little dry goods store? The gold is just an opportunity for the Bad Men to play together. It is just the flag in a game of “capture the flag.” The fun is getting it, and winning the game. It is in competing with the other Bad Men for it. There are some minimal rules to the game, but the game itself is at least partially outside societal laws and concerns. The only thing the three Bad Men really care about is each other and playing the game together.

The philosophy of the Bad Man is best articulated in Leone's *Once Upon a Time in the West.*[8] The philosophy of the Bad Man has to do with a serious kind of play, specifically, to engage in play at mortal stakes. This is explained and illustrated by Cheyenne in the scene in the roadhouse. The scene in the roadhouse is itself set up by a marvelous illustration of this principle of play for mortal stakes that we hear, but do not see. That scene is set up from the point of view of the barkeep. As we stare, with him, at the door of the roadhouse, we hear a buggy drive up to the roadhouse, a fight, yells, gunshots, then quiet. Through the door walks Cheyenne. His first word is "Whiskey." His hands are still handcuffed. He pulls the cork from the whiskey bottle with his teeth and drinks. He seems unperturbed. He is a Bad Man.

After his drink of whiskey he looks around at the other people in the bar, sizing them up. At one point one of the men in the saloon, who is seated and in the somewhat dandified dress of a gambler, slowly starts to reach for his pistol. Cheyenne spots it and only wags his finger at him. "Tch, tch, tch," he says, "You don't know how to play." The man, acknowledging this truth, returns his gun to his holster. Cheyenne, as if to prove his point, instructs the man to pull his gun, holding out his manacled hands. As the man draws his gun, Cheyenne aims his own gun at the man's head. He says to the man, "Shoot." The man shoots the manacles, freeing Cheyenne's hands. Just at that moment we hear the haunting sound of a harmonica from some unseen source. Cheyenne goes over to a dark corner, from where the harmonica sound seems to be coming. A man sits in the shadows, playing. Cheyenne slides over a light hooked on a line to reveal Harmonica (Charles Bronson). Harmonica's playing is an announcement that he knows how to play. Cheyenne tries to intimidate him, but Harmonica cannot be intimidated. Cheyenne can see right away that this is also a real Bad Man. The ground rules for Bad Men at play are shown, not said: You must be completely confident in your skill with a gun; you must be willing to kill; and, finally, you must be willing to die.

It is a matter of integrity. Real Bad Men, as opposed to the pretend Bad Men like the Schofield Kid or the gambler man in the saloon, are what they seem to be, and they will do what they say they will do or die trying. This, too, is part of their fascination. Most of us who live in today's complex world are forced to make many compromises. We must make many adjustments to deal with constantly changing circumstances. Our many commitments to various competing projects make us very sensitive to ambiguity and the need for flexibility. What gets lost may be our sense of integrity, our sense of a commitment to a single idea that we follow to its end. This is what the Bad Men possess. It is something that they recognize in each other.[9]

The culmination of the Bad Men at play philosophy is most fully articulated by Frank (Henry Fonda) near the very end of *Once Upon a Time in the West.* Frank is a very Bad Man, but he knows himself and he knows Bad Men and he will give the best account of how a Bad Man thinks. Leading up to the final confrontation of the film, Harmonica is sitting on a fence, whittling, waiting for something, or someone. When Jill (Claudia Cardinale) asks Cheyenne, "Cheyenne, what's he waiting for out there? What's he doing?" Cheyenne answers, "He's whittlin' on a piece of wood. I got a feelin' when he stops whittlin', something's gonna happen." Frank rides up through a horde of men working on laying railroad tracks (civilization is coming, but it is not there yet) and dust flying. It is a classic shot, contrasting the past, Frank, with the future, the multicultural mix of men working on the railroad, the machine line that will literally bring the future to the West. Frank is steering straight for Harmonica. Harmonica has his gun propped on the fence post in front of him, not threateningly, but as an obvious precaution for dealing with a man like Frank. When Frank rides up to him they have the following conversation:

FRANK: Surprised to see me?
HARMONICA: I knew you'd come.
[*Frank dismounts from his horse, slowly, carefully, keeping his eyes on Harmonica.*]
FRANK: Morton once told me I could never be like him. Now I understand why. It wouldn'ta bothered him knowing you were around somewhere alive.
HARMONICA: So, you found out you're not a businessman after all.
FRANK: Just a man.
HARMONICA: An ancient race. . . . [*Harmonica looks up, wistful, looks off at the railroad workers.*] . . . Other mortals'll be along, and they'll kill it off.
FRANK: The future doesn't matter to us. Nothing matters now, not the land, not the money, not the woman. I came to see you, because now I know you'll tell me what you're after.
[*Harmonica gets off the fence in the same way that Frank got off his horse, carefully, slowly, eyes on Frank.*]
HARMONICA: Only at the point of dying.
FRANK: I know.[10]

Huizinga argues that play is an essential feature of human nature. Capitalism is in its essence anti-play in the way that it makes capital—the idea that everything has a price—the basis of our relationship to the world. Capitalism wants everyone to be an economic person, after all, whether as producer, consumer, or entrepreneur. Bad Men preserve the spirit of play. Pure play is inherently pointless. Or rather, it is its own point. For the Bad Man, as Frank says, it's not about the land, not the money, it's not even about the woman, it is about the play. This is play beyond good and evil. When Frank maneuvers to have the sun in Harmonica's eyes for the final showdown, that is not evil, and Harmonica shows no emotion about the development. It is precisely what he expects from Frank. When Cheyenne is trying to explain to Jill about men like them, he says, "You don't understand, Jill. People like that have something inside, something to do with death." It is an obvious statement, on the one hand, since Frank is certainly a killer, and Harmonica kills some men himself, but that obscures the real meaning of the claim. The important way in which men like Frank and Harmonica have something to do with death is that they are not afraid of it. They are not trying to buy or earn their way out of the deal. The games they like to play summon death as a player. Death is explicitly a part of the game they play. There would be no game if death were not present.[11]

The Banality of Goodness, the Goodness of Banality

Slavoj Žižek has written about a secret terror at the heart of the bourgeois, well-socialized, good capitalist life, especially for men. It is the terror of banality. Talking about David Lynch's *Lost Highway* (1997), Žižek contrasts the opposition of two horrors confronting the modern bourgeois man: "the fantasmatic horror of the nightmarish *noir* universe of perverse sex, betrayal and murder, and the (perhaps much more unsettling) despair of our drab, 'alienated' daily life of impotence and distrust."[12] The one terror is of falling out of the bourgeois world into a lawless noir world of pure id. The other terror, the more unsettling, is to maintain one's place in the bourgeois world. The bourgeois capitalist life, for those who can achieve it, is very well protected against the assaults of the world. The price paid for that security is a sense of the absolute banality lurking at the core of that existence. This is what Thoreau described as "lives of quiet desperation."[13] Bad, desperate men avoid that particular existential night of the soul. There may be other nights of the soul for Bad Men, but not that one.

William Munny has given up his Bad Man ways and taken on the values of the Christianized morality of his wife for his wife's sake, for his children's sake, but also, no doubt, for his own sake. The material counterpart of this soul renunciation is the renunciation of alcohol, which always accompanied his Bad Man play. Throughout *Unforgiven* Munny is offered many opportunities to take a drink, something he and everyone else knows will make what they have to do a lot easier, and in every case he refuses the drink. One plotline this refusal introduces into the narrative of the movie is the question, When will Munny take a drink? What will it take to make him take a drink? Bad Men may not have any sort of morals according to societal standards, but they do have principles that resemble a moral code, each his own, I suppose, but clearly for Munny there is something in his code about honoring men he has ridden with who have proved themselves worthy. Munny takes a terrible beating from Little Bill, a beating that almost kills him, but does not turn to drink on that account. Instead, he turns the other cheek and continues to live up to his version of Christian values. When Munny learns that Little Bill has beaten and killed his friend Ned, however, that is another thing altogether. It is time to drink.

Drink releases the Bad Man in Munny, the man secreted inside the man that Munny has tried to make himself into. The ending of the movie begins with a return to the opening shots of the streets of the town of Big Whiskey at night and in the rain. William Munny is riding into town, swigging whiskey all the way. Now it's not about the land or the money, or even the women. He's come to see Little Bill. Now we see what all of those rumors and stories about him are really about. He is a cold-blooded killer. He doesn't mind talking about killing things, as he says, "I've killed women and children. Killed just about everything that walks or crawls at one time or another." But what he is here for is actually to do some killing, which he does with much aplomb. It is the aplomb, and the integrity, of Bad Men at play.

Our reaction to this killing spree by Munny is complex. In a sense, of course, we, the audience, have been wanting him to take a drink, to return to his old ways, to give up this pathetic, incompetent persona of Christianized "goodness." We have come to see a Western, for heaven's sake. On the other hand, just as the earlier, poorly executed killings were painful to watch because they were so inept, these killings are terrifying to watch because they are so ruthlessly efficient. When his gun misfires, Munny does not miss a beat. He proceeds with the next step in killing everyone in the place as though it were obvious and easy. The innocent (if there are any) and the guilty alike are shot. When Little Bill says, "I don't deserve to die like this." Munny replies, "Deserve's got nothin' to do with it." And that is a terrifying possibility. If our death has nothing to do with deserts, then that raises the question of our lives as well. God ensures deserts. It is a godless world in which "deserve's got nothin' to do with it." That is not what we want, to be confronted with the possibility of the meaninglessness of our death, the possibility of the meaninglessness of our life. Eastwood begins by giving us what we think we want: mete and proper vengeance for wrongs done. He ends by confronting us with our worst fears about the possibility of meaning in our lives, which it is the role of philosophy to consider.

It is a hard life being a Bad Man. It may have its joys and intensities, but the price is extremely high—no real friends, no wife, no children, no love, no community. The most you might get, if you are lucky, is someone you ride with about whom you have no complaints. Munny and Ned both gave it up. When we see Munny revert to his Bad Man ways, which is what we want to see, we are horrified by what we see, and by our own desires to see them. What nags at us throughout the movie is the banality of Munny's barely sustained goodness. What we long for is the Bad Man to emerge. When the Bad Man does emerge, we are reminded of what it really means to be a Bad Man, what it really looks like and what the costs are. The message of the film, I think, is that there is no living without a remainder of dissatisfaction. Goodness, being law-abiding, will cost us a certain intensity and freedom in our lives, but get us love, a family, some partial security against the travails of the world, which includes friends and community. Being a Bad Man may sound like fun, but the costs are extremely high, and there is always a badder man out there, as Little Bill discovered. Good may be banal, but badness is downright terrifying.[14]

Notes

1. A general discussion of the Primal Scene occurs in chapter 4 of "From the History of Infantile Neurosis" in volume 17 of *The Standard Edition of the Complete Psychological Works of Sigmund Freud,* translated by James Strachey in collaboration with Anna Freud, assisted by Alix Strachey and Alan Tyson (1917–1919; reprint, London: Hogarth Press, 1973), 17:29–47.

2. Slavoj Žižek, *Everything You Always Wanted to Know about Lacan (But Were Afraid to Ask Hitchcock)* (New York: Verso, 2002), 235.

3. Hitchcock says to Peter Bogdonovich, "I believe in pure cinema." He goes on to

say, "I think montage is the essential thing in a motion picture." Hitchcock describes the experiment by the Russian director Vsevolod Pudovkin, who showed audiences the face of an actor, then a coffin, then the identical image of the same actor and a young woman. What the audience sees in the expression of the actor is very different in the two cases. The generating of a specific response from the audience by means of a series of images on the screen is what Hitchcock means by "pure cinema." Peter Bogdonovich, *Who the Devil Made It: Conversations with Legendary Film Directors* (New York: Ballantine Books, 1997), 476.

4. The idea of Eastwood's characters having some secret connection with the realm of the immortals connects with the very nature of the medium of film itself, since on film actors are, as it were, immortalized, taken out of time, at least in the contexts of the films in which they star. I owe this insight to Richard McClelland, commenting on an early draft of this paper.

5. Johan Huizinga, *Homo Ludens* (Boston: Beacon Press, 1950), i.

6. Peter French, in his *Cowboy Metaphysics: Ethics and Death in Westerns* (New York: Rowman and Littlefield, 1997), focuses his analysis of the Westerner on the division between the Christianized Easterners and the un-Christianized Westerners. He associates Easterners not just with being Christianized, but also with being feminized: "A rising tide of civilizing and Christianizing not only was led by women, but threatened to wash away the very activities and beliefs that men held to be their special domain, what they cared most about" (*Metaphysics,* 15). I read Eastwood's treatment of the Westerners in *Unforgiven* as trying to make problematic any simple dichotomy of Eastern = bad or feminine and Western = good or masculine (or vice versa).

7. Huizinga, *Homo Ludens,* 8.

8. *Once Upon a Time in the West* was a film that Sergio Leone originally offered to Clint Eastwood (as the Harmonica character), but which Eastwood decided not to do. Christopher Frayling, *Sergio Leone: Something to Do with Death* (New York: Faber and Faber, 2000), 273.

9. My thanks to Richard McClelland for raising the issue of the integrity of the Bad Men for me.

10. I am quoting directly from the film.

11. Peter French calls this "deep play." As he says, "I define 'deep play' as any activity in which the stakes are so high that it is irrational for anyone to engage in it" (*Cowboy Metaphysics,* 111). Mention of death and games recalls also the famous chess scene in Bergman's *The Seventh Seal* (1957).

12. Slavoj Žižek, *The Art of the Ridiculous Sublime: On David Lynch's Lost Highway* (Seattle: Univ. of Washington Press, 2000), 13.

13. Henry David Thoreau, *Walden, or, Life in the Woods* (New York: Vintage Books/Library of America Edition, 1991), 9.

14. I owe considerable thanks to Richard McClelland and Brian Clayton for their many comments on earlier drafts of this paper.

Aristotle, Eastwood, Friendship, and Death

Jason Grinnell

Much of Clint Eastwood's work displays the complexities of friendship. Friends are vital to a good, flourishing life, but being a good friend can pose difficult challenges. In particular, friendship can make us confront our own deepest commitments and values. The manner in which we confront those challenges is what makes true friendship possible, and perhaps all too rare. Two films in particular, *Million Dollar Baby* (2004) and *Gran Torino* (2008), illustrate a broadly Aristotelian perspective on friendship, but also explore some of the tensions within Aristotle's view.

For Aristotle, the most complete friendship is that of "character-friends" who value each other for each other's sake. This is clearly at work in both films, but Frankie Dunn (Clint Eastwood) and Walt Kowalski (Clint Eastwood) each struggle with how to be this sort of friend, and what this sort of friendship requires of us when we don't endorse a friend's goals. In many ways, *Million Dollar Baby* and *Gran Torino* are similar films. Both movies feature lonely, cranky, perhaps miserable old men who struggle with loss and have little connection to family or friends, and both movies explore how difficult it is for those men to befriend a lonely and lost younger person. These men, while perhaps not meeting Aristotle's standards for excellence of character in all respects, are good in the ways that matter. The end of each film, while differing in the details, addresses the fundamental question of how much one must do for a friend. At the end of one, a man helps his beloved friend die, despite his desire to preserve her life. At the end of the other, a man brings about his own death despite the desire of his beloved friend not to lose him. In each case, the demands of character and excellence present the apparent paradox that friendship may require one friend to bring about a death and end a friendship.

While Eastwood aptly illustrates the complexity of friendship, a broadly Aristotelian understanding of friendship can help us resolve this paradox. For example, Aristotle tells us that character-friends value each other for each other's sake. While precisely what this means is something of an open question, it can help us better appreciate the struggles of Frankie and Walt to honor their friends and retain their goodness of character. Thinking about the films in loosely Aristotelian terms can, at the very least, enrich our movie-watching experience.

Classifying Friends

Many of us are rather casual in how we think of "friendship." Coworkers, neighbors, those who link to our social media pages, fellow regulars at the coffee shop, people with whom we went to high school, close confidants, "significant others," and persons with whom we have a long history of shared affection and admiration may all fall under the category "friend." The term the ancient Greeks used for "friendship," *philia,* was similarly broad, encompassing things of which one is fond, family relationships, business relationships, political relationships, and the deepest sort of bond between persons. In the fourth century BCE, the philosopher Aristotle offered an insightful classification of friendship (*philia*) that can help us to think more carefully about how we use the word, how we understand what it means to be a friend, and what friendship in its various forms provides for and requires of us.

Common to all the varied uses of "friendship" for Aristotle is an attitude of mutual goodwill. Both parties wish good for one another, and each recognizes that the other feels the same. Aristotle writes, "Let 'being friendly' be wanting for someone what one thinks are good things for him, not what one thinks benefits oneself, and wanting what is potentially productive of these good things. A friend is one who loves and is loved in return, and people think they are friends when they think this relationship exists mutually."[1] Aristotle tells us that we love (befriend) for one of three reasons. What is loved is loved either because it is good, it is pleasant, or it is useful.[2] These reasons form the basis of three forms of friendship. One can befriend another because he is useful, because he is pleasant to be around, or because he is good. The first two sorts of friendship are incomplete in important ways, while the third is the complete form of friendship.

Those we befriend because they are useful are not loved for themselves, but only for what they can do for us. This sort of friendship is unstable, as what is useful to us will depend on the situation. This is also the case for friendships based on pleasure: our ideas of what is pleasurable can change quickly and often, so these friendships too tend to be fleeting. As a result, friendships based on utility or pleasure tend to be both superficial and unstable. Because of this, it seems reasonable to think of them as incomplete friendships. As Aristotle describes them: "And in fact these friendships are friendships incidentally, for the one loved is not loved by reference to the person he is but to the fact that in the one case he provides some good [in other words, usefulness] and in the other some pleasure."[3]

What is often called "character-friendship," however, is different. It is this sort of "friendship between good people, those resembling each other in excellence, that is complete; for each alike of these wishes good things for the other in so far as he is good, and he is good himself."[4] In this sort of friendship, friends value each other as persons, not merely for useful or pleasant traits. This sort of friendship lasts as long as the character of each remains good, and "excellence is something lasting."[5] Character-friends, then, are friends who love the excellence they see in the other: one's character, in Aristotle's view, is the stable core of one's real self, and so character-friends love each other for who they are, not merely for what they can do. This is the best kind of friendship, friendship between persons of good character who value this good character in one another. Aristotle warns us that we should expect such friendships to be rare, since such people are rare. He also reminds us that they take time to develop. Both parties must learn to accept one another, learn to trust one another. As *Million Dollar Baby* and *Gran Torino* show, character-friends are Aristotelian "other-selves," dedicated to helping one another flourish. The kinds of sacrifices that this may entail are not made lightly.

Because of the importance of equality in character-friendship, Aristotle had reservations about the possibility of friendship between older and younger people, between men and women, between people of different social status and power,[6] and between people of different ethnicities.[7] Shared interests, shared experience, and shared background are important components of friendship, and to the extent that each of these similarities is less likely to be present between those who differ in age, sex, power, and culture, friendships will be less likely and more difficult as well. The friendships of Frankie Dunn and Maggie Fitzgerald (Hilary Swank) and of Walt Kowalski and Thao Lor (Bee Vang) may have surprised Aristotle, but their love and character are such that their friendships will become character-friendships nonetheless.

Aristotle warns us that character-friendships take time to develop. Eastwood develops the central friendships of his films in recognizable stages, and those stages are recognizable as the sorts of friendships Aristotle describes.

Incomplete Friendships

Many of the relationships depicted in *Million Dollar Baby* and *Gran Torino* are incomplete friendships. These sorts of friendships are based on what one can offer to the other that is of value, such as a service or pleasure. In such friendships, there is goodwill toward one another, and the friends benefit from or enjoy each other's company. What they lack is any foundation in the character of the friends themselves. The friends do not share the same values and the same commitment to excellence; the friendship is thus not based on mutual admiration of the friends' good character. When the circumstances of the service or pleasure change, the friendship has nothing to hold it together.

A good example of this sort of friendship in *Million Dollar Baby* is that between Frankie and the fighter he is training, "Big" Willie Little (Mike Colter). Willie treats Frankie merely as someone he can use to improve his skills. For his part, Frankie seems to care about Willie as something more than a mere business partner, and perhaps finds pleasure in his company or in watching him fight, but the men don't seem to respect and admire each other's character or share their deepest value commitments. While Frankie is committed to protecting his fighters, and values thorough preparation and safety more than the prestige of a title fight, Willie cares most about winning the title. They disagree about which is more important—about what is the highest good—so Willie hires a new manager.[8] As Aristotle would remind us, incomplete friendships are often fleeting.

In *Gran Torino* Walt's friendship with Tim Kennedy (William Hill), the construction superintendent, also seems to fall into the incomplete category. It appears that they have known each other for some time, and Tim trusts Walt well enough that he hires Thao when Walt "vouches" for him, but there is little that would suggest a deep character-friendship between the men. There is nothing wrong with incomplete friendships, of course, but they are very different from complete friendships based on mutual admiration of character.

In both films, the central friendships (Frankie and Maggie, Walt and Thao) begin as incomplete friendships and then develop into much more.

Indeed, as the characters (particularly the characters played by Eastwood himself) originally see each other, they appear so different that any sort of friendship seems unlikely. They certainly don't appear at first glance to have any shared history, experience, or values that could serve as the foundation for a complete friendship.

Frankie is suspicious of Maggie when he first meets her, asking if he owes her money, or if he "knew her mother." When he learns she has come to him for training as a boxer, Frankie is surprised and contemptuous. Frankie doesn't train women, as in his view women's boxing is the "latest freak show." Women's boxing is too far from what he knows to be interesting or respectable to him, and doesn't fit the image he has of his sport, nor would training a woman fit the image he has of himself or his character. Maggie, however, refuses to accept Frankie's dismissal of her potential as a fighter, her goals, and her dedication to reaching them and comes to Frankie's gym to train anyway. Frankie's first instinct is to throw her out, but he lets her stay because she has paid six months worth of gym dues. His gym needs the revenue, so he tolerates her presence. At this point, she has no value to him beyond his need for dues, and he has no value to her beyond what he can teach her about fighting. Their relationship certainly could not be considered pleasant. Frankie is offended by Maggie's presence and he is less than kind in the way he treats her.

Maggie has nothing else in her life but her love of boxing. *This* is something she has in common with Frankie. They both value boxing more than (almost?) anything else. She is single-mindedly committed to it; it is the goal toward which all of her other activities are directed. Frankie is finally worn down by her persistence and agrees to train (but *not* to manage) her until she's ready and can get a manager. Sal, the first manager with whom Maggie works, treats her as a utility friend, a tool. He is willing to pit her against fighters for whom she is not yet ready—and who could severely injure or even kill her—if it will advance another of his fighters' career. When Frankie realizes this he has to intervene. As little respect as he may have for her, he is too conscientious and dedicated to the safety of the fighters he trains to let her risk herself this way. He doesn't want to manage her, but he does care about what happens to her. As cranky and insulting as he can be, when it really matters his good character asserts itself, and he sacrifices his own desires to protect his new "friend."

Gran Torino follows a similar plotline. Walt is old and set in his ways, and has a thorough disdain for others. When he first meets Thao, the young man that lives next door, he is contemptuous and abusive. Thao has come to ask for jumper cables, and Walt denies having any and rudely sends Thao away. Despite his contempt for his neighbors, however, we soon see Walt helping to jumpstart the balky car. Much like *Million Dollar Baby*'s Frankie, his basic decency is strong enough to break through his crankiness when necessary.

Soon, a Hmong gang tries to recruit Thao. His cousin Spider (Doua Moua) is already a member, and the gang has aided Thao in the past, so Thao reluctantly agrees to steal Walt's prized Gran Torino as his initiation into the gang. Thao is caught but flees before Walt recognizes him. Thao seems to have had enough of gang life, but the gang won't take "no" for an answer and comes to his home to try to take him by force. In the struggle, Walt appears with his rifle and saves Thao by ordering the gang to "get off my lawn."

At the behest of Thao's family, Walt reluctantly agrees to let Thao work off the dishonor resulting from his attempted theft of Walt's car. Walt initially doesn't want him around, but he eventually relents. He is still contemptuous of Thao, but it soon occurs to him that he can use the situation with Thao to his advantage. Thao becomes a utility friend to Walt, fixing neighborhood eyesores. As Walt watches Thao work hard on these tasks without complaint, it appears that he is beginning to respect Thao's work ethic and recognize their shared values, despite his earlier "unlike you, I'm not useless and I maintain my own property" comment. The foundation of a character-friendship is becoming apparent.

As *Million Dollar Baby* unfolds, Frankie and Maggie begin to find satisfaction and pleasure in each other's company. After intervening in Maggie's relationship with her first manager, Frankie takes over managing duties as well, and pledges to her that he won't ever leave her. Maggie's close call and Frankie's role in it triggers a change in him. He's spent much of his life feeling guilty for what happened to his friend Eddie "Scrap-Iron" Dupree (Morgan Freeman), and for whatever caused him to become estranged from his daughter. He seems resolved not to let down anyone again. His loyalty and commitment to excellence have finally found a worthy counterpart in Maggie. He comes to admire her dedication to her training and begins to see (and respect) her as a fighter, rather than as a *female* fighter. Maggie listens to his advice and is a good student, but her stubbornness remains. Frankie begins to see the spirit and potential excellence in her that will allow her (and their friendship) to flourish. Maggie also helps Frankie to address one of his own character issues, excessive caution, and pushes him to allow her to move up a class and fight tougher competition. She's too talented and committed to hold herself back, and Frankie can't help but respect that. Maggie embarrasses so many other fighters with quick knockouts that Frankie has to begin bribing other managers to allow fights. It appears as though Maggie has convinced him that her own excellence won't be held back by his caution. He comes to love her as a person and not merely as someone paying gym dues. With the emerging complete friendship comes the recognition that he must allow her to excel even when he is reluctant to do so. He sacrifices for the good of the friendship and finally goes against his cautious nature, takes a chance, and moves Maggie up a competitive level.

In *Gran Torino,* too, Walt and Thao begin to see each other as more than merely useful. As Walt spends time with Thao and his sister, Sue (Ahney Her), it dawns on Walt that he has "more in common" with the Hmong "than with my own spoiled rotten family." His attitude changes, and now he seems able to enjoy time spent with his neighbors as pleasure-friends. When Thao's honor-debt has been paid, Walt seems to want to praise or thank him, but can't quite bring himself to do so. Watching the gang members shadow Thao, Walt ruefully mutters, "This kid doesn't have a chance." He has begun to care about and respect Thao as a person, and respects him even more when Thao finally stands up to him while moving Walt's old refrigerator: "*You* listen, old man. I'm here because you needed help."

Thao's sister, Sue, tells Walt that he is a good man, and accuses Walt of liking Thao. Walt gruffly denies any affection for Thao at all, of course, but it is obvious that Sue is right. As their friendship progresses, Walt decides to help Thao get a job, date Youa (Choua Kue), and learn to talk and act "like a man." In other words, Walt wants to help Thao refine the character traits that Walt believes reflect excellence and realize his full potential to have what Aristotle would call a "manly nature."

Each film's central pair has spent enough time together to discover a similarity of character, and the age, sex, and culture differences Aristotle notes as obstacles to friendship are starting to lose their importance. The friends are beginning to love one another for their similar excellences of character, and this sort of love has an equalizing effect on other differences. As Aristotle writes: "This [loving] is the way, most of all, that even unequal parties will be friends; for in this way they will be brought into equality with each other."[9] The central friendships in both films have grown to the point where the friends are on their way to complete friendships of character, and in these, "friendship is said to be equality."[10]

Complete Friendship

Aristotle tells us that complete friendship, the friendship of character-friends, is much rarer than the incomplete forms described above. It has several important features. First, character-friends have similarly excellent character, and because of this they respect and admire one another. Second, they also function as a sort of mirror, with "the friend being another self" who is able to see his own good characteristics in the other.[11] "The actions of the good, if they are friends, are pleasant for those who are good themselves. . . . Living in the company of good people may also provide a training in excellence."[12] Third, because they are attending to the other's good, they are able to act for the other's sake, and pursue each other's goals as if they were their own. Fourth, this commitment to each other's goals may require significant sacrifices. Unlike the incomplete forms of friendship, character-friends value each other for each other's sake, not merely for the pleasure or utility they offer. Frankie and Maggie, and Walt and Thao, eventually develop a friendship recognizable as character-friendship.

In her first fight after moving up a level, Maggie is badly beaten up and given a broken nose. Frankie tells her he has to stop the fight, but Maggie pleads with him to use his skill as a cutman to allow her to keep fighting. Her commitment to excellence is too strong to bear the thought of conceding. Frankie agrees, reluctantly, but tells her she only has twenty seconds before his temporary fix will fail and she'll have to concede. Faced with the time limit, Maggie rises to the challenge and quickly dispatches the opponent that had been giving her so much trouble. Frankie softly mutters "mo cuishle" in admiration as he watches her win the fight. She has earned his respect as another self—he is now calling her by a Gaelic name meaning "my darling, my blood."

Frankie is still Frankie, however, and remains overly cautious, turning down fights on Maggie's behalf. Maggie gets an opportunity to work with a more aggressive manager, the manager for whom Frankie's first fighter left him. Maggie tells the manager that she is *never* leaving Frankie. Even though she chafes under his conservative managing, she is too loyal and respects and admires Frankie too much ever to leave.[13]

Throughout the movie we see that Frankie is very reluctant to take a risk, even when it seems appropriate, but Maggie eventually makes Frankie set a fight for her with the British champion. True character-friends help us to refine our own character, and by earning Frankie's trust and pushing him to change, Maggie helps Frankie address his own character flaw of excessive caution. By this point, Maggie is such a beloved friend that Frankie buys her a robe with "mo cuishle" on the back, but remains too gruff to tell her what the phrase means. The contrast in relationships is stark when Maggie has an unpleasant encounter with her family. She tells Frankie afterward "I got nobody," to which Frankie responds, "Well, you've got me."

The friendship of Walt and Thao reaches a similar level of respect, admiration, and mutual affection. In order to get him a job in construction, Walt "vouches" for Thao, but also reminds him not to "lie down" in his interview. In other words, Walt has such faith in Thao's excellence of character that he is willing to guarantee it by putting his own reputation on the line. After Thao gets the job, Walt loans him the money he needs to buy a tool belt and offers him the use of his tools. Thao is moved and appreciative, offering sincere thanks, to which Walt offers a self-consciously deliberate handshake. Walt sees working hard as central to being a man, and in Thao he has found someone who shares his commitment to the value of work. Despite the difference in age and ethnicity, it is clear from this scene that the men have come to value and admire one another's character.

When the gang members catch up with Thao, they break some of Walt's tools and burn Thao's face. Thao's overriding concern is that he has let his friend down, so he dismisses his injury and tells Walt he'll replace the broken tools. Walt doesn't care about the tools and is more concerned for Thao's well-being, but Thao insists that this is not Walt's problem. He wants to protect Walt from getting involved.

Walt is more concerned about his friend than his own safety, and so attacks and beats the gang leader, warning him to leave Thao alone. By this point Walt and Thao are complete friends. Walt even offers Thao the use of his Gran Torino, his most prized possession, so that Thao can take Youa on a date in style. Thao has become another self, and Walt trusts him even to drive his irreplaceable car, if it will help Thao better achieve his goals and take his place in the world.

The excellence of each of the friends has been established, and genuine character-friendships have been formed. Each of the friends values the other for the friend's sake, and they have become to each other what Aristotle would consider other selves. Characteristic of this idea of the friend as other-self, though, is the notion of acting in the friend's interest, even if it means sacrificing your own. As Aristotle argues: "The decent person is thought to act because of what is fine, and the better he is, the more so, and for the sake of a friend, while setting his own interests to one side."[14] Acting for the sake of the friend, and the friendship, is fine and noble. Aristotle goes on to tell us that: "Good people will also freely forgo money when this means that their friend will get more; for while the friend gains money, the good person gains what is fine. . . . It may be that he will even forgo opportunities for action in favor of his friend, and that to have been the cause of his friend's acting is finer than his acting himself."[15] Each of the friends has already made sacrifices, but character-friends may require more than delaying a title fight or risking a car. Precisely how to handle such a situation must be explored, and each film does so in a fascinating and troubling way.

Tests of Friendship

Aristotle argues that the social nature of humans and the dangers of chance make true friendship necessary. He tells us: "No one would choose to live without friends, even if he had all the other good things." Friendship is a crucial component of a successful, flourishing life: "And in poverty and all other kinds of misfortune people think of their friends as their only refuge."[16] In both *Million Dollar Baby* and *Gran Torino,* the role of friends as refuge from misfortune will be severely tested. As noted earlier, complete friendship is friendship grounded in the excellent character of the friends, but Frankie and Walt will each be confronted with the realization that the excellence they came to love in their friends is in jeopardy. When that character is in jeopardy, so is the friendship.

In her fight for the title, Maggie underestimates the ruthlessness and maliciousness of her opponent, and—breaking Frankie's absolute rule, "always protect yourself"—lowers her guard after a round-ending bell. She gets punched from behind and hits her head on the corner stool as she falls, resulting in a complete break of her spinal cord and full paralysis. The paralysis threatens her continued autonomy of action, and also means the end of her hitherto all-consuming goal, excellence in boxing. Despite her own situation, her commitment to her friend is such that she fears she has let Frankie down and believes she needs to apologize for failing to protect herself. Frankie, for his part, is distraught at what has befallen his friend and distraught that he has allowed this to happen to her. He calls every doctor he can in an attempt to find one that will offer a prognosis of hope, but nothing can be done. Maggie's loathsome family again appears, having gone to Disneyland before bothering to visit her. They have a lawyer with them, and have come to get Maggie to sign over her assets to them. It is clear that all of her family relationships lack the mutual goodwill Aristotle recognizes as necessary for friendship, and that her family sees her as little more than something they can use. As she discussed with Frankie earlier, she has no one she can rely on but him. When she needs help, Frankie is the one she trusts.

Maggie's condition is bleak, and it is getting worse. She requires a ventilator to breathe, and it takes several hours even to get her into a wheelchair. Because she can't move, she develops ulcers that eventually lead to the amputation of her leg. The spirited, irrepressible fighter completely dedicated to excellence in the boxing ring will never walk, much less fight, again.

Frankie tries to make the best of the situation. He offers to buy her a wheelchair and suggests she think about getting an education. Maggie has other ideas, and asks a favor of him. She wants Frankie to euthanize her, just as her father had done for their dog when she was a girl. Frankie is horrified to think about losing her, and even more so to think of participating in her death:

FRANKIE: Don't even think about that.
MAGGIE: I can't be like this, not after what I done. . . . My daddy said I fought my way into this world, and I would fight my way out of it.

Maggie doesn't want to live like this. She believes she has lived a full and excellent life and wants to end it on her own terms. Her injury has deprived her of much of the autonomy that was central to her self-image, and made continued excellence as she understands it impossible.

MAGGIE: I got what I needed—don't let 'em take it.
FRANKIE: I can't. Please. Please don't ask me.

Maggie, when faced with Frankie's refusal to help her do what she believes she must, tries to do it herself, biting her tongue in the hope of bleeding to death. Frankie rushes to her side, horrified, but when the doctors get it fixed she rips out her stitches and tries again. The very same spirit and stubbornness that Frankie has long admired in her will not allow her to accept what others believe her fate should be. Frankie is horribly conflicted, and caught between what he wants for his friend and what his friend wants for herself. He does not know what is really good for Maggie, nor how to honor his friend while keeping his own character intact.

Frankie goes to church and talks to his priest, Father Horvak (Brían F. O'Byrne), with whom he has had, so far, a most irreverent and sarcastic relationship. Frankie tells his priest about Maggie's marvelous character, her excellence, and her spirit.

> Frankie: But now she wants to die. . . . and I just want to keep her with me . . . and I swear to God, Father . . . it's, it's committing a sin by doing it. By keeping her alive I'm killing her. Do you know what I mean? How do I get around that?
>
> Father Horvak: You don't. You step aside, Frankie. You leave her with God.
>
> Frankie: She's not asking for God's help, she's asking for mine.
>
> Father Horvak: Whatever sins you're carrying, they're nothing compared to this. . . . If you do this thing, you'll be lost . . . you'll never find yourself again.

Frankie visits Maggie again. She is being kept sedated to prevent further suicide attempts. Frankie, seeing her in this state, is obviously torn apart and suffering immensely, but still can't bring himself to do as she has asked. That night, as Frankie begins to assemble his ringside medical equipment and syringes, "Scrap-Iron" Dupris comes to visit.

> Dupris: People die every day Frankie. Mopping floors, washing dishes. You know what their last thought is? "I never got my shot." . . . If she dies today you know what her last thought will be? "I think I did all right." I know I could rest with that.
>
> Frankie: Yeah . . . Yeah.

Frankie makes his decision and tells Maggie he will do as she asks. He finally confides in her what the inscription on her robe means: "my darling, my blood." Maggie is overjoyed at the prospect of finally being released from her current state of existence. Frankie both removes her ventilator and injects a lethal adrenalin overdose, to be certain that this will be the last attempt to bring about her death. He doesn't want her to suffer through any more horrors.[17] Scrap's voiceover tells us that afterward "Frankie had nothing left," and that he disappeared.

In *Gran Torino,* Walt's friendship with Thao will demand a great deal from him, too. By way of retaliation, the gang shoots up Thao's house and abducts Sue. While she is missing Walt fears the worst and alludes to losing "friends" in the war. Sue finally arrives badly beaten and raped. Walt, enraged and distraught, tears up his kitchen. Walt's priest, Father Janovich (Christopher Carley), later arrives at Walt's home to talk about the situation.

> WALT: Thao and Sue are never going to find peace in this world . . . as long as that gang's around. Until they go away, you know, forever.
> FATHER JANOVICH: What are you saying?
> WALT: You know what I'm saying.
> FATHER JANOVICH: [Thao is] sitting out there right now staring at your front door. You know what he expects, Mr. Kowalski.
> WALT: What would you do? What should Thao do?
> FATHER JANOVICH: If I was Thao I guess I'd want vengeance. I'd want to stand shoulder to shoulder with you and kill those men. . . . I know you're close with these people, Mr. Kowalski, but this pisses me off too.
> WALT: I'll think of something. Whatever it is, they won't have a chance.[18]

Thao comes over the next day. He is understandably very agitated, and wants to go to war. He tells Walt that "thinking time is over," but Walt counsels caution. Thao demands of Walt: "Don't let me down!" Walt tells him to remain calm and come back at four o'clock. He assures Thao that "What needs to be done will be done."

Walt prepares himself. He mows the lawn, gets a haircut, a shave, a new suit, and a bath. He also goes to confession. He tells the very worried priest, "Oh, I am at peace." When Thao returns, Walt has his weapons out, and Thao is convinced they are preparing for battle. Walt gives Thao the Silver Star he earned in Korea as a symbol of their bond and his regard for Thao's character, but then he locks Thao in the basement. Thao is furious and demands that Walt let him participate in what he believes is a plan for vengeance. Walt tells him that he, Walt, has blood on his hands, and that he is going it alone. He won't allow Thao to risk his own life and—perhaps even more importantly—his character as part of Walt's plan. An act of vengeance by Thao would send him down both the criminal path Walt has fought to keep him from and the lifetime of guilt that has scarred Walt himself. He tells Thao, "I'm proud to say that you're my friend. You have your whole life ahead of you." Walt and Thao are true friends. Unlike *Million Dollar Baby*'s Frankie Dunn, however, Walt Kowalski does not acquiesce in his friend's desire.

When Walt confronts the gang we discover his true plan. He bluffs and taunts the gang members into murdering him in front of enough witnesses to ensure a successful prosecution. With one act he achieves an autonomous death instead of waiting for his cancer to kill him, protects Thao from destroying his own excellence in an act of vengeance, and brings the gang to justice. He both accomplishes fine and noble things for himself and allows his friend (and neighbors) opportunities for fine action in the future. As the movie ends we see the postscript to Walt's complete love and friendship for his friend: To the horror of the family members that had loved him for his utility as a possible benefactor, Walt's will leaves his Gran Torino to "my friend, Thao Lor."

Sacrifice and One's Other-Self

Eastwood presents us with two deep and rich friendships. Despite their difficult beginnings, both would be recognizable to Aristotle as friendships of character. In each case, however, the outside world intervenes and the friends must rely on their friendship to guide them through misfortune and hard decisions about what really is good for the friends and the friendship.

In the case of *Million Dollar Baby,* Frankie shares and understands Maggie's deep commitment to autonomy, and his friend directly asks him for his help. She has no one else that she trusts enough and loves enough to ask. Frankie understands her request, but he doesn't agree with it, and he certainly doesn't share the goal of ending her life. In the end, however, Frankie does as his friend wishes, despite his horror at doing so and the toll it will take on him. True friendship, as Frankie understands it, requires him to put aside his own interests and help his friend.

In the case of *Gran Torino,* Walt completely understands his friend's desire to seek vengeance and agrees wholeheartedly that something must be done to stop the gang. He and Thao share the goal of an end to the gang's activity, but he will not acquiesce to Thao's desire to participate in a violent end to the conflict. Walt deceives his friend in order to protect him from himself, and to keep Thao from a lifetime of guilt and regret of the sort Walt has suffered. Thao's desired ends are straightforward. He wants to participate in the response to the gang and he wants his friend Walt to live. Walt allows him neither, substituting his judgment for Thao's.

What are we, as viewers with friends of our own, to make of this disparity in the presentation of similar issues in two of Eastwood's films? Are we to conclude that a true friend does as his trusted friend wishes, or that he substitutes his own judgment and does what he thinks best for the friend? A bit more investigation and analysis reveal a possible answer.

Aristotle tells us that in complete friendships, character-friends promote one another's good and view their friends as other selves. "Friendship in its superior form resembles one's love for oneself."[19] In Aristotelian terms, "the good" refers to that which helps one to flourish and be successful at the difficult task of being an excellent human being. When this idea is applied to the particular situations presented in the films, the picture becomes clearer.

As presented to the audience, in both films one of the character-friends must die, and in both cases the character played by Eastwood himself must bring about that death. He does this in order to respect and value his friend and the friendship. In the case of *Million Dollar Baby,* one friend (Maggie) desires as an end the death of one friend (Maggie) over the express wishes of the other friend (Frankie), and it falls to one friend (Frankie) to bring about that end. In *Gran Torino,* the plot presents the same scheme. One friend (Walt) desires as an end the death of one friend (Walt) over the wishes of the other friend (Thao), and it falls to one friend (Walt) to bring about that end.

While complete friends share interests and history, the true test of a friend's role as another self is the willingness to sacrifice for the friend. Aristotle argues that "it will be true for the person of excellence that he does many things for the sake of friends . . . even dying . . . if need be." Such a person will also choose "a year's life lived in a fine way rather than many years lived indifferently."[20] Understood thus, death on one's own terms can be a fine and noble thing. Aristotle goes on to tell us that sacrificing one's life for others is also a fine action done on a grand scale, and as such it is perfectly consistent with a life of excellence. Character-friends share similar excellences and reflect the excellences of each other, pursue one another's good, and will make sacrifices when necessary for that pursuit.

Frankie and Maggie have forged this sort of friendship. Befriending Maggie has allowed Frankie to pass on his practical wisdom about what matters and how to pursue it, establish a connection with a person he can respect and admire, overcome his overly cautious nature, and act on his own excellences of character. Through her friendship with Frankie, Maggie has refined her talent and combined it with her indomitable spirit to reach her dream and heights of success she had only imagined before. Together, their friendship has achieved a fine and noble thing. The good for Maggie is an end to a state of existence she regards as intolerably empty, so that she need not linger in a state neither she nor Frankie can respect or value as flourishing.

As Aristotle argues, it is precisely when we are dealing with bad fortune that we most need our friends.[21] Frankie has made Maggie's flourishing possible with his friendship, and the sacrifice of his own well-being in deference to her desire will allow that fine and noble accomplishment to endure. As Maggie sees it, the longer she lingers in her state, the more diminished their accomplishments and the goodness of her life as a whole become. By sacrificing his emotional well-being—his priest tells him he'll be "lost"—for his friend, Frankie is doing something noble. Their shared commitment to autonomy and excellence is the foundation of their friendship and respect for one another. Maggie's character is central to the character-friendship, and helping Maggie die both protects and preserves her excellence. It is a good and noble act on Frankie's part, and the one most faithful to the friendship.

In *Gran Torino,* Walt and Thao have also forged a character-friendship. Befriending Thao has allowed Walt to pass on his practical wisdom about what matters and how to pursue it, establish a connection with a person he can respect and admire, overcome some of his ill-temper, and act on his own excellences of character. Through his friendship with Walt, Thao has developed what Aristotle would call a "manly nature": he is mature and responsible, and has moved far down the path to a successful life.[22] The relevant good is the continued flourishing of Thao and his continuation as a sort of other-self of Walt. Walt has made Thao's flourishing possible with his friendship, and he allows it to continue with his sacrifice. Had he permitted Thao to participate in a bloody act of revenge, he would have been destroying any chance for Thao's continued excellence, and thus the foundation for their character-friendship. He himself is old, sick, and likely dying, and his sacrifice allows him to die on his own terms, as a man of action, and represents one last noble thing he can do for his friend and their friendship. Walt's sacrifice is likely to be the most noble thing he can do for his friend, and insofar as it both allows Thao the continued pursuit of his own excellent character and allows Walt a meaningful end to his life, it is excellent for both friends.[23]

Frankie and Walt are initially contemptuous of Maggie and Thao, respectively. They see them as too different to matter at all, much less to befriend. Over time each comes to recognize and nurture the excellences of the younger person as they themselves become better men through the opportunities provided by their new friends. The genuine character-friendship that develops, however, forces difficult choices on both men. The excellence Frankie admires in Maggie compels her to seek an end to her life, and Thao's commitment to his character puts his life in danger. Maggie makes the excellent person's choice of a short life lived well, rather than a long but undistinguished life.[24] Frankie agonizes over her choice and what it requires of him, but however much it may pain him, as her friend he will value her goals and help her die, thus preserving what they can of Maggie's whole-life excellence. Walt, by contrast, does not support Thao's self-destructive goal of revenge, and even deceives his friend to stop him. He does recognize that dying for a friend is a fine and noble end, however, and sacrifices himself to allow Thao to flourish, secure his own autonomous death, and bring the gang to justice.

As Aristotle tells us, "Friends, too, can help young people in avoiding mistakes, older ones by caring for them and making up what they cannot do because of weakness, and those in their prime towards fine action."[25] The friendships between the central characters demonstrate precisely this sort of friendship, which becomes possible only with respect and admiration for one another's character. In the face of the obstacles the world poses to a life of excellence, true friends provide a crucial respite, and allow us to flourish in a way we could not otherwise. Frankie and Maggie are friends, and that friendship is celebrated in a death Frankie brings about. Walt and Thao are also friends, and that friendship is celebrated in a death Walt brings about. True friends value each other as other selves, and while that can seem paradoxical or incoherent, Eastwood has offered us an illustration of how it is possible.

Notes

I, too, need my friends to help me flourish: I would like to thank John Draeger, John Burnight, Kimberly Blessing, Sarah Ellen Caputi, and Danielle Morris for a great deal of helpful criticism and commentary on several drafts of this essay. I would also like to thank Brian Clayton and Richard McClelland for their many helpful suggestions and for making this volume possible.

1. Aristotle, *Rhetoric* II.4.2 1381a 4, trans. George Kennedy (New York: Oxford Univ. Press, 2007), 124.

2. Aristotle, *Nicomachean Ethics* VIII.2, 1155b 17–20, trans. Sarah Broadie and Christopher Rowe (New York: Oxford Univ. Press, 2002), 210.

3. Aristotle, *NE* VIII.3, 1156a 17–19 (Broadie and Rowe), 211.

4. Aristotle, *NE* VIII.3, 1156b 7–10 (Broadie and Rowe), 211.

5. Aristotle, *NE* VIII.3, 1156b 12–13 (Broadie and Rowe), 211.

6. For difficulties of elders with youth, parents with children, gods with mortals, kings with commoners, see *NE* VIII.7, 1158b 12–1159a 5 (Broadie and Rowe), 215–216. For justice in such unequal relationships, see *NE* VIII.11, 1161a 10–1161b 10, 220–221, and *NE* IX.2, 1165a 14–36, 226.

7. The term Aristotle uses, *homoethnesi,* is sometimes translated as "same clan," other times as "same race," other times as "same species." In any event, it is clear that Aristotle believes it is easier to be friends with those to whom we are similar. Aristotle, *NE* VIII.1, 1155a (Broadie and Rowe), 209. Cf. *NE* VIII.12, 1161b 11–16, 28–35, 221, and 1162a 4–14, 222.

8. When Frankie reminds him that he can't learn anything from the new manager, as he is only a "businessman," Willie tells Frankie that Frankie has already taught him everything he needs to know. Frankie's gym assistant, Eddie "Scrap-Iron" Dupris, tells Frankie that Willie left because of Frankie's character flaws: he didn't believe in Willie, he was too cautious, and he didn't trust that Willie was ready for the championship fight.

9. Aristotle, *NE* VIII.8, 1159a 33–b2 (Broadie and Rowe), 217.

10. Aristotle, *NE* VIII.5, 1157b 33–36 (Broadie and Rowe), 214.

11. Aristotle, *NE* IX.9, 1169b 6–7 (Broadie and Rowe), 236, and *NE* IX.9, 1170b 5–7 (Broadie and Rowe), 238. Aristotle also discusses the value friends place on sharing their lives: "And whatever it is that for each sort of person constitutes excellence, or whatever it is that it is for the sake of which they choose to live, it's this they wish to spend time doing in company with their friends." Aristotle, *NE* IX.12, 1172a 1–5 (Broadie and Rowe), 240.

12. Aristotle, *NE* IX.9, 1169b 30–1170a 15 (Broadie and Rowe), 237.

13. In Aristotelian terms, both are missing the mark a bit. Ethics concerns the difficult task of precisely fitting one's behavior and attitude to the situation in the way one should: "To be affected when one should, at the things one should, in relation to the people one should, for the reasons one should, is both intermediate and best, which is what belongs to excellence" (Aristotle, *NE* II.6, 1106b 21–25 [Broadie and Rowe], 117). Frankie is too cautious in his approach to life; Maggie is perhaps too loyal.

14. Aristotle, *NE* IX.8, 1168a 34–35 (Broadie and Rowe), 234.

15. Aristotle, *NE* IX.8, 1169a 27–35 (Broadie and Rowe), 236.

16. Aristotle, *NE* VIII.1, 1115a 5–12 (Broadie and Rowe), 208–209.

17. Interestingly, in performing both acts Eastwood is eliminating any possibility of finding ethical wiggle room in a distinction between what we allow (her death when removed from the ventilator) and what we do (causing her death through the injection of the adrenalin overdose). By any interpretation, Frankie is morally responsible for Maggie's death.

18. Walt's priest apparently had a far closer relationship to Walt's late wife, and has spent the movie attempting to get a contemptuous Walt to accept and trust him. It is only in this scene that Walt begins to treat the priest with any sort of respect. In another

similarity between films, the Eastwood character in both movies clashes with a priest, but also sincerely listens to the priest when he must make his most difficult decision.

19. Aristotle, *NE* IX.4, 1166b 1 (Broadie and Rowe), 231.

20. Aristotle, *NE* IX.8, 1169a 20–24 (Broadie and Rowe), 235–236.

21. Aristotle, *NE* IX.11, 1171a 25–26 (Broadie and Rowe), 239.

22. Aristotle, *NE* IX.11, 1171b 6–7 (Broadie and Rowe), 239.

23. Just as Maggie's death allows her to preserve her excellence and her image of herself, Walt's death allows him to end his life preserving his own self-image. As Walt once told Youa, he is a man who "fixes things."

24. Aristotle, *NE* IX.8, 1169a 20–24 (Broadie and Rowe), 236–237.

25. Aristotle, *NE* VIII.1, 1155a 12–15 (Broadie and Rowe), 209.

Giving up the Gun

Violence in the Films of Clint Eastwood

Karen D. Hoffman

The early films of Clint Eastwood's career feature him portraying heavily armed cowboys and officers of the law who do not hesitate to use weapons to defend themselves and others. Such characters meet violence with violence and are defined by their proficiency with their guns. As Eastwood's career unfolds, his films begin to evince more concerns about the use of violence and its impact not just on those who are on the receiving end but also on the agents wielding the weapons. In films like *Unforgiven* (1992), which Eastwood also directed, he depicts a character who initially appears to have rejected his violent past in favor of a life of quiet domesticity but who soon reveals that his violent past has merely been dormant. Over a decade and a half later, Eastwood directed *Gran Torino* (2008), a film in which he portrays Walt Kowalski, a character who is initially quick to reach for his guns but who ultimately relinquishes his weapons. Eastwood's films, which begin with enthusiastic portrayals of gunslingers whose masculinity is understood largely in terms of self-defense, display an increasing concern about the consequences of violence and eventually culminate in a depiction of a character who asserts his masculinity even as he gives up his gun and sacrifices himself in order to save others from gang violence.[1]

In what follows, I discuss the shifting understanding of the proper uses and problematic abuses of violence in Eastwood's films, particularly focusing on the gun as an instrument of violence and on the consequences of violence for the shooter. I begin by discussing the *Dirty Harry* films responsible for Eastwood's association with the .44 Magnum, placing particular emphasis on the identification of the character with his gun and on Harry's belief that the proper way to respond to violence is to wield a bigger gun. I then turn my attention to two of Eastwood's 1970s Westerns: *High Plains*

Drifter (1973) and *The Outlaw Josey Wales* (1976), which depict the use of the gun to avenge moral wrongs. Both films present audiences with characters who have a score to settle. But, while Eastwood's character in the former film does not put down his gun until the fighting is over and the criminals are dead, the actions of his character in the latter film suggest that it is possible to give up the gun—at least when facing honorable men, who similarly agree to holster their weapons. Having discussed two of Eastwood's Westerns from the 1970s, I turn my attention to a 1980s Eastwood Western: *Pale Rider* (1985). Here Eastwood's character's refusal to put down his weapon expresses a commitment to the use of the gun to defend that which is rightfully owned. Suggesting that "real" men refuse to be bullied, the film ultimately depicts the act of wielding a gun as a courageous display of masculinity.

Moving to a discussion of Eastwood's films from the 1990s, I argue that *Unforgiven* takes a very different attitude toward the individual who fires the gun. Despite the fact that Eastwood's character of William Munny raises his gun to avenge the wrongs done first to a woman and then to his friend, the film depicts the human costs of firing the gun, both in terms of those killed and in terms of those who must live with having caused their deaths.

I then explore how, having problematized the gun and the use of violence to answer violence, Eastwood's *Gran Torino* suggests that one can give up the gun while exemplifying rather than renouncing masculinity. The gun that is initially representative of power and strength and drawn in defense of self and others may be cast aside in favor of a courageous act of self-sacrifice.

Thus Eastwood's films can be interpreted as moving from a celebration of the masculine power of the .44 Magnum to a concern about the dangers of the escalating violence of using such a weapon. Moreover, his films depict a shift from an early emphasis on the gun as a tool to enact physical violence—either the death threatened by a serial killer or the protection offered by an officer of the law—to a later accent on the gun as a tool of psychological violence that may damage the one who wields the weapon.

Walt Kowalski's physical demise is not the most importance consequence of the violence depicted in *Gran Torino.* Nor is Walt's sacrifice made so that his neighbors will be merely physically alive at the film's conclusion. Walt gives up his gun and his life with the hope that doing so will help the family next door to minimize the psychological (as well as physical) violence of the gang and will save Thao (Bee Vang) from picking up a gun and violently responding to his sister's rape. Unlike the *Dirty Harry* films, where

Eastwood's character aims to survive his encounter with the killer and to prevent the killer from ending the lives of any more victims, *Gran Torino*'s Walt aims to sacrifice himself so that others may escape the psychological scars of violence.[2]

Dirty Harry and the .44 Magnum

Although most of my discussion will focus on films that Eastwood directed, it seems appropriate to begin with one of the films which crystallized his association with the gun: *Dirty Harry* (1971). Although Eastwood was already recognized as the Man with No Name, the gunslinger from the Sergio Leone Westerns *A Fistful of Dollars* (1964), *For a Few Dollars More* (1965), and *The Good, the Bad, and the Ugly* (1966), it was his role as maverick inspector Harry Callahan that arguably made Eastwood a true American film star and made his gun, the .44 Magnum, iconic. From the opening scene of *Dirty Harry,* in which the camera peers through the scope of the rifle of Charles "Scorpio Killer" Davis (Andy Robinson) as he kills a woman swimming in a rooftop pool, guns play a central role in the film. Harry Callahan is defined by his .44 Magnum; absent his gun, he isn't Dirty Harry. Don Siegal's direction reinforces this identification. The camera often shoots Callahan from a low angle, so that his gun occupies the foreground; the man stands in the background, of secondary importance to his weapon. It is possible that the camera angle here is intended to turn Callahan's handgun into something that resembles a much larger crew-served weapon, such as a heavy machine gun, cannon, or rocket launcher.[3]

Harry's gun represents power. More than once Callahan notes that his weapon is "the most powerful handgun in the world, and would blow your head clean off."[4]

By 1973, when *Magnum Force,* the second of the Dirty Harry films is released, Harry's gun has become so iconic that it is the focus of the opening sequence of the film. Displayed against a red background for the entire duration of the opening credits, the long-barreled .44 Magnum waits to be fired. After several minutes, the hand holding it cocks the hammer and turns the pistol toward the camera. The voice-over recites the inspector's most memorable lines from the first film about how his gun is the most powerful. Back in action, ready to start the next film, the gun fires. Commenting on the opening scene, Paul Smith notes that it aims "to fetishize the gun and its violent shot in an almost pornographic way."[5] Drucilla Cornell agrees: "The projection of the image of magnum force is explicitly phallic in its identification of man with gun."[6]

Although the politics of the series shifts as Callahan goes from playing a near vigilante in *Dirty Harry* to being the one to take down a group of vigilante traffic cops in *Magnum Force,* Harry's gun and his willingness to use physical violence to defend the interests of justice remain constant. As he explains in the first film, shooting is fine "as long as the right people get shot." Notice that the focus here is on the gun as an instrument of justice and as a tool to protect the innocent and to physically disable the villain. No mention is made of the psychological consequences of violence or of the potential damage it inflicts upon the person wielding the gun. The concern is that one shoots the right people.

By the second film of the series, Callahan makes it clear that the right people can include police officers who act on their own initiative as executioners. The vigilante cops who expect Harry to join them in "ridding society of killers that would be caught and sentenced anyway if our courts worked properly" are mistaken in thinking that, because of his reputation for violence, he will support their cause. As Harry explains to Lieutenant Briggs (Hal Holbrook), "I hate the goddamn system. But until someone comes along with some changes that make sense, I'll stick with it."

Of course, what Harry means by sticking with the system does not seem to require abiding by the letter of the law. In the final minutes of the film Harry reactivates a bomb in the car that Briggs drives, thereby bringing about the death of his corrupt supervisor. Harry hasn't used his gun, but he has still resorted to violence, ostensibly in the name of justice.[7]

Because of the violence of the *Dirty Harry* films and Callahan's seeming emotional indifference to it, Pauline Kael considers the films to be "deeply immoral."[8] Viewing them as an extension of the Westerns that shaped Eastwood's early career and "turned the Western into pure violent reverie,"[9] she argues that "Eastwood's gun power makes him the hero of a totally nihilistic dream world."[10]

Eastwood's gun power is still in full swing ten years later, when, in 1983, he releases *Sudden Impact,* the fourth of the *Dirty Harry* films and the only one of the series that Eastwood directs.[11] In a memorable early scene, Callahan interrupts a robbery in a diner, explaining to the criminals that they need to put down their guns because "We're not just gonna let you walk outta here." When asked "Who's 'we,' Sucker?" Harry replies, "Smith and Wesson and me" and draws his gun. He fires two shots and hits both men.

When threatened by the one who still has a gun, Harry responds with his now-famous retort: "Go ahead. Make my day." Although he lacks a human partner to help him foil the robbery, Callahan has his gun, which provides him with all the physical power that he needs.

Ultimately, the *Dirty Harry* films implicitly defend the use of the gun as a proper response to violence—arguably, even as a proper response to the threat of violence. Rather than escalating physical violence, Callahan's gun ends it. The gun's possible negative impact on the man pulling the trigger is not considered. The gun here is an instrument of power that enables rather than diminishes its user. Therefore, the films suggest that, as long as one is shooting the right people, it is better to be the one wielding the gun and, in cases of the justified use of force, to be faster than one's opponent in pulling the trigger.[12]

Vengeance and the Gun: 1970s Westerns *High Plains Drifter* and *The Outlaw Josey Wales*

Making its appearance between the first two *Dirty Harry* films, *High Plains Drifter* combines the spaghetti Western's nameless gunslinger with Callahan's questionable conception of justice and willingness to transcend the boundaries of the law. Early in the film, the Stranger (Clint Eastwood) who mysteriously appears in the tiny frontier town of Lago quickly shows his aptitude with a gun as he dispatches three men who attempt to get the better of him.[13] Thus begins a violent tale in which the people of Lago hand over the town to him, promising that he can have and do whatever he likes so long as he protects them from the three gunslingers (Geoffrey Lewis, John Quade, and Dan Vardis) who have been released from jail and are en route. As the town's protector, the Stranger initially appears to be a possible savior for the frightened people of Lago—one who will shield them from the physical violence of the approaching villains.

However, through a series of flashbacks it soon becomes apparent that the people of the town are not innocents in need of a protector: they are guilty of having hired the very murderers they now fear. Paid by the townspeople to kill the town's Marshal Duncan (Wayne Van Horn), the criminals violently whipped Duncan to death in the main street of the town. The townspeople witnessed the murder but merely stood aside and watched the hired hands kill the lawman.[14] They then deposited the body in an unmarked grave and arranged for the death squad to be sent to prison.

As the Stranger prepares the town for the final showdown, it becomes increasingly clear just how spineless the townspeople really are. Following his instructions, they paint the town red, making literal the town's figurative existence as a kind of hell. While they may believe they fear the Stranger, he claims that it's really "what people know about themselves inside that makes them afraid." The people of Lago have not given up the gun; they have paid others to serve as their hired guns. The Stranger uses his gun to exact retribution.

The Outlaw Josey Wales, which Eastwood directed in 1976, also raises questions about the use of the gun to right moral wrongs. The film opens with a scene of domestic tranquility that is quickly marred by the appearance of Union soldiers who kill Wales's wife and son. Wales seeks revenge by joining a group of Confederate soldiers. Finding themselves outnumbered, the small band of soldiers is given an opportunity to surrender to the Union. Fletcher (John Vernon), a man the Confederates trust, arranges the surrender to Captain Terrill (Bill McKinney) and assures his men of what he has been told: they will not be harmed. All but Wales mistakenly agree to give up their guns. But, as soon as they turn them over, the unarmed men are ruthlessly gunned down. Wales enters the scene in a desperate attempt to help his comrades but manages to save only young Jamie (Sam Bottoms), who is wounded in the shootout and dies soon afterward.

Rather than attempting to avenge the deaths of the Confederate soldiers, Wales heads south with Terrill in pursuit. Wales eventually settles at a ranch in Texas that had belonged to the son of Grandma Smith (Paula Trueman), a woman he befriends on his journey. He makes other friends along the way and arrives in Texas with a group of people fiercely loyal to him, several of whom he has defended from immediate physical harm. When Terrill and the Union soldiers finally catch up to him, they are surprised to find that he is not alone: many guns appear alongside Wales's in the shootout that follows. When the gunfire dies down and Wales finally finds himself alone with Terrill and able to exact revenge on the captain, both men find themselves out of bullets. After firing a long series of shots that results in the mere click of an empty chamber, Wales is compelled to toss his guns aside. The captain draws his sword, intending to use it to kill Wales. But Wales manages to redirect the blow, so that Terrill dies by his own blade.

With Terrill dead, Fletcher is the remaining man among the Union soldiers who can identify Wales. But when the two men come face to face, Fletcher pretends not to recognize the man he has been forced to pursue through several states. Calling Wales "Mr. Wilson," Fletcher explains that, if he found Wales, "I'd try to tell him the war is over." He thereby communicates that he has no interest in seeking the reward for Wales's capture or in exacting any kind of revenge. Wales seems to accept that any quarrel the two men might have had with one another is now over; he responds to Fletcher by noting, "I guess we all died a little in that damn war." In the end, the guilty Terrill, who arguably deserved to die, has been killed. But Fletcher, whose guilt was never clear, is spared.[15]

So *The Outlaw Josey Wales,* which begins when Wales picks up his gun seeking vengeance, ends with emptied guns and a mutual agreement not to reload. The man who loses his family in the opening scene finds a new family of friends by the film's end. For these reasons, Knapp calls the film a "Western epic of rage and redemption."[16] Brett Westbrook notes that, while "[i]n the classic Western, the hero protects the family *from* violence *with* violence," Wales tries to eschew violence in at least four places in the film: (1) instead of firing on the soldiers as they attempt to ferry across the river, Wales shoots the rope they are using to cross, diverting them downstream without killing them; (2) instead of immediately killing several bounty hunters he encounters when he stops for supplies, Wales tries (and fails) to talk them into walking away; (3) instead of picking up his gun against the Comanches, Wales goes to talk to their leader, Ten Bears (Will Sampson), and comes to an agreement that avoids bloodshed; and (4) instead of killing Fletcher, Wales agrees that the war between them is over.[17]

The character of Wales thus provides an early exploration of the value of imposing limits on violence and revenge. As Wales notes in his conversation with the Comanche leader Ten Bears, "dying isn't hard for men like you and me. It's living that's hard when all you really care about has been brutalized and raped." As the two men come to the resolution that they do not need to face death by fighting one another, Wales continues: "I ain't promising you nothing extra. I'm just giving you life and you're giving me life. And I'm saying that men can live together without butchering one another." The two men cut their palms and become blood brothers in an act that both solidifies their commitment to nonviolence toward one another and signals their mutual respect.

In contrast to *High Plains Drifter,* a film in which the people are not honorable and in which justice seems to justify violence, *The Outlaw Josey Wales* is a film in which there are at least some honorable men for whom justice can be accomplished through nonviolent means. The film thereby suggests one possible way of giving up the gun: a mutual surrendering of weapons among honest men. Wales relinquishes his guns not in self-sacrifice but as part of a mutual disarmament.

It's important to note, though, that the mutual surrender of weapons in *The Outlaw Josey Wales* occurs in a context in which it is not clear that there has been insult or injury or in which possible insult and injury have to a certain extent been answered. In the case of Wales's encounter with Ten Bears, the two men display mutual respect for one another's honor—honor which seems to be revealed in the willingness each has to risk injury and possible death as part of their confrontation. Arguably, it is because Ten Bears recognizes Wales's bravery in riding alone in Comanche territory that he allows the man to live. The fact that "dying isn't hard" for men like Wales and Ten Bears and that both men recognize this fact gives them a shared bond. Both seem to abide by a similar code of honor, according to which individuals display a willingness to use violence to defend themselves against insult or injury, even at the risk of death or serious bodily injury.

Writing about such codes of honor, particularly as exemplified in the American South, Richard Nisbett and Dov Cohen note that honor requires an individual to "project a stance of willingness to commit mayhem and to risk wounds or death for himself. Thus, he must constantly be on guard against affronts that could be construed by others as disrespect. When someone allows himself to be insulted, he risks giving the impression that he lacks the strength to protect what is his. Thus the individual must respond with violence or the threat of violence to any affront."[18] Honor is here understood in terms of a "reputation for strength and toughness."

Ten Bears and Josey Wales both possess such strength and toughness. And they mutually recognize and respect this quality in one another. Respect, rather than insult and injury, forms the substance of their exchange. Thus, their ability to resolve possible conflict without resorting to violence seems to be something that supports the code of honor rather than something that challenges such a code.

The mutual disarmament of Wales and Fletcher, however, might seem to question whether honor requires a violent response to insult and injury. Fletcher's actions have led to the death of many of Wales's friends—and would have led to Wales's own death if he had participated in the surrender. Fletcher's pursuit of Wales compounds that injury. Even if Fletcher did not know what would happen to the Confederates who surrendered to Terrill, and even if he was coerced into helping Terrill pursue Wales, it seems fairly clear that Fletcher has injured Wales. A code of honor like the one Nisbett and Cohen describe would seem to require a violent response to such injury.

Arguably, though, that violent response occurs in the form of the final shootout between the Union soldiers and Wales's newfound friends. The final scene of the film, in which Fletcher and Wales seem to acknowledge an end to their conflict—"the war is over"—strikes me as similar to an exchange that men following a code of honor might have *after* a duel as well as in lieu of one. The fact that Fletcher and Wales agree to put down their weapons after participating on opposite sides of a gunfight suggests that traditional codes of honor that require violence as a response to injury might still be being followed by these characters. The fact that they have already engaged in a violent exchange of bullets might help to facilitate their mutual disarmament.

The Gun and Defense of Self and Others: *Pale Rider*

Pale Rider, a film Eastwood directed in 1985, indirectly raises questions of revenge but places more emphasis on the use of violence to preserve life and property and to defend individuals against the loss of either. A group of miners pick up their guns in the hopes of defending themselves against Coy LaHood's attempt to remove them from land that he wants to mine for gold himself. When LaHood (Richard Dysart) hires Marshal Stockburn (John Russell) and his deputies to force the miners to leave, the Preacher (Clint Eastwood) picks up his gun to save them. An undercurrent of the importance of settling old scores remains: Stockburn and the Preacher have already had at least one violent confrontation. It appears from the scars on the Preacher's back that Stockburn shot him six times. Near the film's end, the Preacher picks up his gun and kills the deputies and Stockburn, giving the marshal six similar marks on his torso and one additional bullet in his head. Even so, the overarching focus of the film does not seem to be about avenging past injury so much as it is about preventing future injury by defending the possession of what is rightfully owned.

Much like the Stranger in *High Plains Drifter*, the Preacher in *Pale Rider* has an ethereal quality about him. Both men emerge out of the elements as lone riders on horseback. Surrounded in mystery, both appear to originate from a supernatural realm. Although the Preacher has physical scars that testify to previous injury and connect him to a corporeal past, he is not like other men. The pale rider appears to be summoned by Megan Wheeler

(Sydney Penny), who requests the appearance of a savior as she recites an annotated version of Psalm 23 over the grave of her little dog, one of the early victims of the violence of LaHood's men.[19] Because the Preacher appears for the first time in the mining camp as Megan recites a passage from Revelation, the implication seems to be that the pale rider is both savior and avenging angel.

His initial action in the film is to interrupt the beating of Hull Barret (Michael Moriarty), a man who has gone to town for supplies in defiance of LaHood's orders. LaHood's thugs are using large pieces of hickory to pummel Barret and are preparing to set his cart afire when the Preacher douses the would-be arson with a bucket of water. Rather than pulling his gun, the Preacher selects his own piece of hickory and proceeds to beat back all of Barret's attackers. Part of what makes this scene interesting is the fact that the guns one might expect to see used in such a situation are not employed. When one of the men attempts to fire his pistol, the Preacher knocks it out of his hands, sending it flying through the air. As the camera briefly follows the weapon, one wonders if any gun would be effective against the otherworldly hero that the Preacher represents.

The scene is also worth noting because of the way in which the thugs taunt Barret before assaulting him: they question the sexual nature of his relationship with Sarah Wheeler (Carrie Snodgrass) and her daughter, Megan, and ask what it takes to get Barret to "fight like a man." Barret tries to avoid the conflict by noting that he didn't come to fight, but to no avail. Failure to defend himself does not save him from being beaten. Moreover, the challenge to fight is explicitly tied to a challenge to Barret's masculinity and honor. Barret is emasculated and grouped with women and children as an individual in need of protection. He shows courage in coming to town for supplies, but he seems to be incapable of defending himself. He thus violates the aforementioned code of honor, according to which individuals who are insulted are required to defend themselves. The Preacher appears, becomes Barret's masculine protector, and saves the day.

It is interesting to note that, later in the film, it is Barret who, with the Preacher by his side, convinces the other miners not to accept LaHood's offer to buy them out, even though he knows that LaHood will resort to violence should they refuse. Emboldened by the Preacher, Barret notes that the miners still outnumber LaHood's hired hands and that "we know how to pull a damned trigger, don't we?" With the pale rider by his side, Barret wants to stand and fight. Throughout the film, he changes from being a man who does not abide by the code of honor to becoming one who does. Ultimately, it is also Barret who accompanies his hero out of the camp en route to town for the final showdown. And it would have been Barret who probably would have been killed at that showdown had the Preacher not stopped to dynamite LaHood's hydraulic mining operation and succeeded in spooking Barret's horse, thereby stranding the man without a ride into town.

In the end, though, it is Barret who finally saves the pale rider. In a close parallel to the penultimate scene of *High Plains Drifter,* in which Mordecai (Billy Curtis) saves the Stranger by shooting the marksman who is about to shoot him, Barret manages to walk to town and shoot LaHood just in time to stop the man from shooting the Preacher.[20] The pale rider's attempt to protect Barret from the violence of the gunfight ultimately—and fortunately—fails. Barret arrives in town in time to assert his masculinity and save his newfound friend.

Barret's use of the gun strengthens rather than diminishes his character and his masculine identity. The man who began the film by backing away from a violent encounter finds his voice through his willingness to draw his gun and ends the film by picking up his weapon and entering the fight. The film suggests that his act of wielding his gun is a courageous one; he is to be congratulated for the heroism he displays in firing the final shot. He finally becomes a "real man" and begins to live according to the code of honor that such men follow. Even though the Preacher tried to stop Barret from entering the gunfight, it seems likely that he did so more out of a concern that Barret lacked the skill and experience—and perhaps even masculinity—needed to fight well than out of a desire to protect Barret from having to live with the consequences of having killed a man and become a perpetrator of violence. The film suggests that Barret is a better man for having fired his gun.

Despite their otherworldliness, both the Stranger and the Preacher appear to need the assistance of an unlikely hero—a man who appears to be in need of another's protection and who apparently uses violence only very reluctantly and as a last resort. The myth of the lone gunman is undone; the man who truly stands alone appears unlikely to survive the encounter. Yet, if one's cause is just and one acts to defend one's self or others, the message seems to be that one may be morally justified in refusing to give up the gun. Moreover, use of the gun can strengthen honor and construct masculine identity.

A Failed Attempt at Giving Up the Gun: *Unforgiven*

Unforgiven (1992) represents a shift away from the Westerns Eastwood directed in the 1970s and 1980s, which, as we have seen, often depict the role of gunslinger as one that may be justified in order to right moral wrong or to defend one's self and others. By the time Eastwood directs *Unforgiven* in the early 1990s, he has become increasingly concerned about the consequences of violence for those who wield the gun as well as for those who are its victims. William Munny, the character Eastwood plays in the film, is not a noble hero who rides into town to save the day. He is instead a broken man who carries the heavy burden of his violent past. As the film unfolds it becomes increasingly clear that, although Munny has temporarily lain down his weapons, he hasn't really given up the gun.

The opening scene of the film depicts a ramshackle Midwestern farm in the latter half of the nineteenth century with a lone figure, probably Munny, digging a grave to bury his wife. After a cut to a shot that establishes the landscape of Big Whiskey, Wyoming, where most of the action of the film occurs, Eastwood's camera takes viewers to the town whorehouse on a stormy evening. Prostitute Delilah Fitzgerald (Anna Levine) is attacked by customer Quick Mike (David Mucci), who repeatedly slashes her face as a furious response to the fact that she laughed at him. It is only when he hears the cocked hammer of owner Skinny Dubois's (Anthony James) gun at the base of his skull that Mike stops his attack. The gun thus makes its first appearance in the film in a particularly dramatic way, functioning as it has in many other Eastwood films as an instrument that threatens violence but does so in the name of ending violence.

Skinny threatens to shoot Mike to settle the score, but Sheriff Bill Daggett (Gene Hackman) appears on the scene and decides that, since Skinny's property has been damaged, it is property he is owed: the men will need to return in the spring with ponies. Only Strawberry Alice (Frances Fisher) seems interested in considering what Delilah is owed. Alice leads the call for vengeance and gets the women to pool their limited financial resources in order to offer a reward for the deaths of Quick Mike and his friend Davey Bunting (Rob Campbell), despite the fact that it is not clear what Davey has done to deserve the death sentence he receives.

Interested in earning the reward, the Schofield Kid (Jaimz Woolvett) appears at Munny's farm in the hopes of taking him on as a partner in the bounty hunt. Claiming to be a killer himself, the Kid considers his gun to be central to his identity and attributes his nickname to the Schofield model Smith and Wesson pistol he carries.

Viewers first see Munny with his gun as he practices his marksmanship for the first time in years. Unable to hit his target, Munny soon trades his ineffectual revolver for a 10-gauge shotgun. Although he finally hits his mark, it appears that he is not the expert gunslinger he once was. But, needing the reward, he seeks out his old partner, Ned Logan (Morgan Freeman). Believing that the men to be killed have "got it coming," Logan and Munny decide that they might as well join the Schofield Kid in being the ones to give it to them.

When they begin their journey to Big Whiskey, the men do not know that the claims about the violence done to Delilah have been exaggerated. And, regardless of what Quick Mike deserves, it is far from clear that his friend Davey is culpable. Indeed, Davey is the only one of the men in Big Whiskey who thinks of compensating Delilah for the harm done to her and offers her his best pony.

Yet Davey is the first to die. Moreover, he dies a slow and painful death. Unlike the typical Western in which wounded men die almost instantaneously, Davey's protracted agony calls attention to the painful physical reality of being shot.

Where Davey's (arguably unjustified) death calls attention to the physical harm that guns can inflict on those who are shot, Quick Mike's death calls attention to the psychological harm that guns can inflict on the shooter. After the Schofield Kid kills Quick Mike, he breaks down, unable to come to terms with the life that he has taken. Admitting that the kill was his first, he seeks solace where Munny has found it in the past: in whiskey.

Despite being sober for ten years, Munny himself picks up the bottle and reclaims his violent past upon learning that Sheriff Bill Daggett has killed Logan. Munny continues to imbibe as he accepts the gun of the Schofield Kid (who claims that he isn't going to kill again) and rides into town to confront Little Bill. By the time he arrives he has finished the whiskey and started to become the gunslinger he once was. In the final showdown in Greely's, he shoots the sheriff. And, when Bill protests that he doesn't "deserve to die like this," Munny replies, "Deserve's got nothin' to do with it."

Indeed, the fact that desert has nothing to do with who lives and dies is an important theme in *Unforgiven*. Unlike the criminals in the *Dirty Harry* films, the townspeople of Lago in *High Plains Drifter*, Captain Terrill in *The Outlaw Josey Wales*, and LaHood, Stockburn, and his deputies in *Pale Rider*, it not clear that any of the people who are the victims of violence in *Unforgiven* fully deserve what happens to them. Delilah laughs at her customer (ridiculing his small penis) but doesn't deserve to be cut for it. Quick Mike cuts Delilah but doesn't necessarily deserve to die for it. Davey is Quick Mike's friend, and it is even less clear that he deserves an agonizing death. Ned Logan appears in town as a bounty hunter intent on killing Mike and Davey, but he doesn't deserve the excruciating death he suffers under Bill's whip. Skinny and the other men in Greely's don't deserve to die by Munny's gun. In fact, the only characters in the film that might arguably deserve to die are Little Bill, the very person who protests his death, and William Munny, who survives the shootout.

In separating the violence of the film from the dispensation of just deserts, the film implicitly calls attention to the problematic consequences of violence. As Munny admits when talking to the Schofield Kid after the youth's one and only kill, "It's a hell of a thing, killing a man. You take away all he's got, and all he's ever gonna have." And, even if the person seems guilty, seems like he "had it coming," Munny notes, "We all have it coming, Kid." None of us is without guilt. As a result, it is difficult to kill a man and to live with the realization that one has taken the life of another.

As Eastwood himself notes, *Unforgiven* depicts the escalating consequences of violence for the victims and for the individuals who wield the guns. Eastwood says that, in talking to Gene Hackman about the script, he noted that "we had a chance here to deal with the moral implications of violence. The consequences of the violent act affect the one who commits it as well as the one who is the victim of it."[21] In another interview, Eastwood elaborates: "in the past, there were a lot of people killed gratuitously in my pictures, and what I liked about this story was that people aren't killed, and acts of violence aren't perpetrated, without there being certain consequences."[22]

Unforgiven suggests several possible problematic consequences of violence. One is that violence can lead to unjustified pain and suffering, as it does in Davey's and Logan's deaths. Another problematic consequence is that violence can beget violence. Quick Mike's violence toward Delilah provokes the women to place a bounty on his head, which provokes Munny, Logan, and the Schofield Kid to kill Mike and Davey, which provokes Bill to whip Ned to death, which provokes Munny to revert to his violent past, to start drinking whiskey, and to kill Bill and his men. Finally, violence can brutalize the person who inflicts it. In addition to the physical harm done to the one who suffers the violence, there may be psychological harm done to the person who imposes it.

Unforgiven also seems to call into question the connection between honor and violence. According to the code of honor discussed earlier in this chapter, which requires injury as a response to insult, it could be argued that Quick Mike's initial act of cutting Delilah—the incident that initiates the subsequent violence in the film—is a justified response to the insult contained in her laughter. The sheriff's response to the situation supports that justification, since he aims to compensate Skinny for the damage to his "property" rather than Delilah for the cuts to her face and body.[23] Yet the film allows viewers to identify with Delilah—much more than with her attacker—and questions the justice of her treatment by Mike and by the sheriff. Moreover, the film shows how much violence and unnecessary pain and suffering result from Mike's decision to defend his honor by such a violent response to insult.

The ending of *Unforgiven* does not definitively reveal what happens to Munny in the years following the shootout at Greely's.[24] He may have succeeded in giving up his gun and returning to a peaceful and sober life on the farm. But he may not. At the beginning of the film Munny thinks that his gunslinging days are behind him; he protests that he is no longer that person. And the initial scenes support his claim. But the film makes it clear that he still harbors the psychological scars of the past and that he retains the violent potential to return to his weapon. Therefore, I question whether Munny has really given up his gun.

Giving up the Gun: *Gran Torino*

In *Gran Torino,* which Eastwood directed in 2008, he portrays a character that fully succeeds in giving up the gun. Sara Anson Vaux is right to note that the film "signals the thoughtful director's further reflection on 'what war does to men's souls,' as he told interviewer Terry Gross."[25]

In the film, Eastwood plays Walt Kowalski, a retired Ford autoworker who still lives in the house he shared with his wife, Dorothy, for most (if not all) of his married life. The film opens with Dorothy's funeral. Like Munny's wife in *Unforgiven,* Walt's wife has just died. And, like Munny's wife, it appears that Dorothy had been helping Walt be a better man. She held together his relationship with his sons, who express their concerns that he is going to "get in trouble, all by himself in the old neighborhood." She encouraged him to attend church regularly and made the young parish priest, Father Janovich (Christopher Carley), promise that he would "keep an extra-sharp eye" on Walt and try to get him to go to confession after she died—a promise that the priest works throughout the film to fulfill.

When viewers first see Walt, he appears to be a man more full of anger than he is of grief. He sheds no tears at the funeral and literally growls at his grandchildren. His sons talk about how it is impossible to make him happy, as Walt makes his disdain for his remaining family clear. Walt also has great disdain for his Hmong neighbors, whom he refers to in racist terms for much of the film. Calling them "swamp rats," "Chinks," and "gooks," Walt laments what has become of the houses on his street.[26]

As Roger Ebert notes in his review of *Gran Torino,* Walt is an aged Harry Callahan, "a cantankerous, racist, beer-chugging retired Detroit autoworker who keeps his rifle ready to lock and load. Dirty Harry on a pension, we're thinking, until we realize that only the autoworker retired; Dirty Harry is still on the job."[27] Manohla Dargis observes that "Dirty Harry is back, in a way . . . as a ghostly presence. He hovers in the film, in its themes and high-caliber imagery, and of course most obviously in Mr. Eastwood's face."[28]

Writing about Eastwood's characters in 1996, Lawrence Knapp rightly notes that "they are alienated from themselves and society. Isolated and besieged by the complexities of modern existence, the mid- to late twentieth-century antiheroes show little virtue: they are rude, selfish, self-destructive, rebellious, and stubborn. Each of them has a conspicuous character defect . . . that prevents them from being full-fledged heroes or healthy members of society. Invariably, they come into contact with people or events that force them to come to terms with their lack of conscience or ideals."[29] Though written twelve years before the release of *Gran Torino,* Knapp's comment provides an apt description of Walt and the arc that his character follows in the film.

The first gun appears just over fourteen minutes into the film. As Walt's young neighbor Thao (Bee Vang) walks down a deserted street reading a book, he is taunted by a car of Latino gangbangers. Thao's cousin Spider (Doua Moua) witnesses the scene and pulls up with his own rival gang. When one of the Latinos pulls a revolver, Spider's crew pulls a semi-automatic. Outmatched, the rival gang drives away, leaving Thao in the company of his cousin, who tries to convince him to get in the car. Thao refuses, prompting Spider to visit Thao at home and talk to him again about joining the gang and receiving its "protection."

Thao's reluctant initiation into the gang requires him to steal Walt's

1972 Gran Torino Sport. An inept thief, Thao makes too much noise. Realizing what is happening, Walt picks up his own gun for the first time in the film and confronts Thao, who manages to get away. Walt soon has another reason to pick up his rifle when Spider's gang comes to take Thao for what will most likely be his second attempted initiation. Thao resists and is in the process of being dragged to the car when Walt appears with his gun and saves the teen from being taken. The neighbors interpret Walt's action as a heroic gesture and begin bringing him gifts of thanks. He challenges this interpretation and suggests that he was merely defending his property and growls that he just wants everyone to stay off his lawn.

But it is not long before Walt once again picks up a gun—this time a Colt Model 1911 .45—to save one of his neighbors. This time it is Sue (Ahney Her), Thao's sister, who is being threatened by three men. Since she is not at his home, Walt cannot claim to be merely defending his property. Walt appears as an aged Dirty Harry as he steps out of his truck, calls the men "spooks," and intones, "Ever notice how you come across somebody once in a while that you shouldn't have fucked with? That's me." Making a gesture that he will repeat at several crucial moments in the film, he makes his hand into a representation of a gun, cocks the hammer of his thumb, and pulls the mock trigger. When that proves ineffective, he draws his weapon and tells Sue to get in the truck. As the film progresses, Walt befriends Thao and Sue and becomes increasingly concerned about protecting them from the violence of Spider's gang. Watching over their yard now as well as his own, Walt stands on his porch and uses his hand to mimic shooting several rounds at Spider's car as it cruises down the street.

Late in the film, Walt picks up his gun to confront Spider's gang after the hoodlums attack Thao on his way home from the construction job he acquired with Walt's help. Incensed that the gang used a cigarette to burn Thao's face, Walt goes to Spider's house and attacks the first man he sees. After pummeling the younger man with his fists, Walt draws his pistol. Using a shot highly reminiscent of the *Dirty Harry* films, the camera looks up at Walt from the perspective of the man on the ground. In the foreground of the shot is the barrel of Walt's gun. Behind it, he growls his warning to stay away from Thao because, if he has to come back, "it's gonna get fucking ugly." Walt ends up keeping his promise, though not in the way that Spider's gang expects.

It soon becomes clear that Walt's attempt to scare Spider does not work. The gang responds by using their fully automatic weapons to shoot many rounds into Thao's house. Walt grabs his own clearly ineffectual gun and runs to Thao's house, where he finds the teen superficially wounded. The real damage of the evening soon becomes clear, however, when Sue returns home beaten and bloody, having been assaulted and raped.

Thao wants vengeance, so Walt tells him to come over the next day and "what needs to be done will be done." Father Janovich pays Walt a visit, clearly worried about the escalating violence and fearful of what Walt plans to do to avenge Sue. Walt spends the day putting his affairs in order: he gets a haircut, gets fitted for a suit, entrusts his dog, Daisy, to the neighbors, and fulfills his wife's last wish by going to confession. When Thao arrives, Walt takes him to the basement to give him the medal Walt earned fighting in Korea, explaining that "we all knew the dangers that night, but we went anyway." Walt then proceeds to give his confession to Thao: he killed at least thirteen men in Korea, including at least one young soldier who was trying to surrender. Walt wants to protect Thao from having to live with the horror of having taken a life.[30] "It's goddamn awful, that's what it is. The only thing worse is getting a medal of valor for killing some poor kid that wanted to just give up, that's all. Yeah, some scared little gook just like you. I shot him right in the face with that rifle you were holding in there a while ago. Not a day goes by that I don't think about it. And you don't want that on your soul. Now, I got blood on my hands. I'm soiled. That's why I'm going it alone tonight."[31]

After locking Thao in the basement, Walt once again goes to Spider's house. Calling attention to the fact that, if the film were a Western, the final showdown would be about to occur, Walt tells the assembled gang members to "go ahead and pull those pistols like miniature cowboys." For the third and final time, Walt makes his hand into a simulated gun and pretends to shoot several rounds. But Walt's "gun" is merely symbolic; he is not actually carrying a weapon. The imaginary bullets will be the only ones he fires.

Spider's gang does not realize that Walt is not armed. So, when Walt reaches into his jacket for his lighter, the assembled men all fire at him.[32] Walt falls dead to the ground with his arms outstretched in a posture that recalls the crucified Christ. Clarifying that Walt did not draw a weapon, the camera focuses on the lighter in his hand—the lighter that bears the emblem of the 1st Cavalry Division, with which he fought in Korea. The police quickly respond to the shooting and are already arresting the gang members by the time Thao arrives on the scene wearing Walt's war medal. Officer Chang (Stephen Kue) tells him that, since the gang fired on an unarmed man in the presence of witnesses who will testify against them, the members will be sent to prison for a long time.[33]

In the end, Walt gives up his gun and sacrifices himself. In addition to saving Thao and Sue, the film suggests that, through his willingness to sacrifice himself, Walt saves himself. To see why, it is important to recall that Walt carries the burden of the terrible things he has done in Korea. He is not at peace. The Hmong shaman Kor Khue (Xia Soua Chang) notes this fact as part of his "reading" of Walt in which he claims that the retiree has "no happiness in life." His "food has no flavor." He "made a mistake in [his] past" that makes his current life difficult.

Walt's confession to Thao and his conversations with Father Janovich help viewers to understand the nature of that mistake. Recollecting his actions in Korea, Walt tells the priest, "I stabbed them with bayonets, hacked seventeen-year-olds to death with shovels. Stuff I'll remember 'til the day I die. Horrible things." Walt claims that these are horrors with which he lives.[34] But, as the priest astutely notes, Walt seems to "know a lot more about death than [he does about] living." The priest agrees with Kor Khue that, although Walt physically survived the war, he isn't really living in the fullest sense of the term.[35]

Indeed, it is only when Walt opens up to his neighbors and starts doing things to help others that he begins to come to life. Because he is not close to his sons or their families, Walt's only meaningful relationships in the film are those he cultivates with Thao and Sue. As he befriends them, he begins to care about their physical safety. He also begins to care that they not be damaged in the way that he has been by his actions in the war.

It is to save Thao from being both a victim and a perpetrator of violence that Walt confronts Spider's gang alone. Unlike Munny, who regretfully bears the scars of a violent past yet supports the Schofield Kid in making his first kill, Walt stops Thao from participating in the bloodshed. Unlike Mordecai and Hull Barret, who arrive at the end of the shootout just in time to save the hero, Thao arrives on the scene too late to save Walt from being killed. More important, as Walt intended, Thao arrives without a weapon. By giving up his gun, Walt saves Thao from using one.

Walt may be dead, but he has really won the shootout. Through his sacrifice, Walt helps to atone for his past misdeeds and makes himself into the hero that he would have liked to have been in the war. As a result, he saves Thao, Sue, and ultimately himself.[36]

Because he is not facing honorable opponents, Walt does not have

Wales's nonviolent option of mutual disarmament. Realizing that the gang will continue to wield its guns in the community until its incarceration, Walt decides to make himself the target of the gang's violence. Besides doing nothing to stop the violence or sacrificing himself, the only alternative arguably available to Walt would have been to get the police involved. That is the path for which Father Janovich argues. When the priest first hears that Walt has pulled his gun on Spider's gang, he insists that Walt should contact the authorities. Walt dismisses that option and maintains that there wasn't time for the police to arrive: "when things go wrong, you gotta act quickly." Toward the end of the film, Father Janovich contacts the authorities on his own and waits with them at Spider's house, anticipating the violence to come. But the police tell him that they have limited resources and leave the scene before Walt arrives. Ultimately, as is the case in many Westerns, the film seems to suggest that the powers of the law are limited in what they can do to prevent violence in the community.

Of course, it is also because of the existence of noncorrupt police officers that Walt is able to give up his gun and have his sacrifice force a cessation to the cycle of violence. Unlike the Stranger and the Preacher, who could not count on the presence of honest officers of the law to ensure that justice would be done, Walt counts on the police to arrest the gang for killing him.[37] Unlike Lieutenant Briggs, who worries that the courts fail to secure convictions and let guilty men go free, Walt trusts that the courts will send the gang to jail for a long time. So, even though he appears to sacrifice himself instead of turning to the law, Walt actually sacrifices himself in part because of his faith in the ability of the law to see that justice will be done.

The film's final scenes return viewers to the place the story began. This time the funeral is Walt's. This time Father Janovich does not proffer empty clichés but instead recounts what Walt taught him about life. At the reading of the will that follows, Walt leaves his Gran Torino, his most valued possession, to Thao. Having attempted to figuratively free Thao from the most malign influences in his neighborhood, Walt's final gesture renders that freedom literal, and the camera shows Thao driving away along Lake St. Clair in the company of Daisy.

The gun that is so prominent in Eastwood's early films and that becomes, throughout Eastwood's career, an emblem of masculinity, an instrument for courageous self-defense, and an apparatus for enacting retribution is in *Gran Torino* cast aside in favor of a heroic act of self-sacrifice. Honor is shown to be compatible with a nonviolent response. Eastwood's films, which begin with an emphasis on the use of the gun as a protection from physical violence, culminate in *Gran Torino* in the recognition that giving up the gun may be the best way to avoid the psychological damage that can come from wielding a weapon and ending a life.

Notes

I am grateful to Richard McClelland and Brian Clayton for their thoughtful editorial remarks and numerous helpful comments on earlier versions of this essay.

1. In what is perhaps intended as a further commentary on the problematic consequences of even the threat of violence, Walt's sacrifice relies on the gang's expectation that he has a gun and that he intends to use it against them. Having become so accustomed to a life of violence and to considering violence as their first and only response to confrontation, the gang does not consider that there may be a preferable response to Walt besides taking up arms against him. Once the gang's many guns are aimed at him, the fatal violence that follows seems almost inevitable—as Walt knows it will be. He knows that his act of retrieving his lighter—rather than the gun that the gang expects him to pull—will serve as the catalyst that sets in motion the violent scene waiting to be enacted.

2. It can be argued that Walt also sacrifices himself as part of an attempt to atone for his own violent past as a soldier in the Korean War and that he thereby attempts to save himself as well as others.

3. I thank Richard McClelland for calling this to my attention.

4. In the Encore documentary *Inside the "Dirty Harry" Movies* (2002), Eastwood comments on the shift in tone from the first to the second time Harry asks the criminal in question whether he feels lucky. Claiming that the first time Harry says the line, there is a "playful interaction" between the characters, Eastwood notes that "reprising it at the end, he'd become more bitter. But it was like his running routine, and he still knew all the words to it. But his attitude was totally different because he was at that time very disenchanted with the way things had gone." Perhaps, then, even in Eastwood's early films, there is a suggestion of a disillusionment with the consequences of violence.

5. Paul Smith, *Clint Eastwood: A Cultural Production* (Minneapolis: Univ. of Minnesota Press, 1993), 105.

6. Drucilla Cornell, *Clint Eastwood and Issues of American Masculinity* (New York: Fordham Univ. Press, 2009), 1.

7. It is interesting to consider whether Harry's use of the bomb to kill Briggs is indicative of the fact that his understanding of the role of violence is much closer to that of the vigilantes than the film seems to want to allow. Earlier in the film, Harry seems to reject the vigilante officer's claim that "it's not a question of whether or not to use violence. There simply is no other way." Yet he himself resorts to violence in killing Briggs, presumably out of belief that there is no viable alternative.

8. Pauline Kael, *For Keeps* (New York: Penguin, 1994), 421.

9. Ibid., 540.

10. Ibid., 524. While I am not convinced that the world over which Callahan's gun presides is a completely nihilistic one, I think Kael is right to be concerned about the utter ease and emotional abandon with which he dispatches judgment and brings about the deaths of those who are deemed unfit. Also troubling is the epistemic privilege he assumes in placing full confidence in his knowledge of who is guilty and who deserves to die. As I discuss in the latter sections of this chapter, I believe that Eastwood's later films indicate an awareness of these potential problems and evince a changing understanding of violence and its consequences.

11. In the film, Harry once again finds himself in pursuit of a vigilante killer, this time a woman, Jennifer Spencer (Sondra Locke), for whom he develops a personal interest before becoming aware of her responsibility for a series of murders. Spencer embodies the most sympathetic argument for vigilantism: gang-raped ten years ago along with her sister, who is now institutionalized in a vegetative state, she is certain of the identities of her rapists, who, as a result of the machinations of a lawman protecting his guilty son, have not been and will not be charged or serve time for their crimes. Since the law refuses to hold them accountable, she decides to take on this role herself. While Callahan claims that he doesn't approve of revenge when it breaks the law, his actions at the end of the film help Spencer to do away with her rapists, who are now threatening to rape her again, and help to ensure that Spencer will not face prosecution for her actions.

12. Richard Schickel quotes Eastwood as saying of the *Dirty Harry* series, "It's not about a man who stands for violence. It's about a man who can't understand society tolerating violence." Richard Schickel, *Clint: A Retrospective* (New York: Sterling, 2010), 99. Even so, the films portray an individual who uses violence to fight violence and who would not consider giving up his gun.

13. As Laurence Knapp notes, Eastwood uses "tracking shots, cross-in shots, and angle-reverse angles to make the Stranger the adhesive that holds the mise-en-scène and montage together" (Laurence F. Knapp, *Directed by Clint Eastwood* [Jefferson, N.C.: McFarland, 1996], 57). Knapp goes on to note that the Stranger "has no zeal for gunfights and bloodshed. It is his appointed task to engage in violence, a duty he performs perfunctorily without emotion or enthusiasm. Whenever possible, the Stranger gives his adversaries an opportunity to relent or repent" (*Directed by Clint Eastwood,* 59).

14. Commenting on the flashbacks of the whipping, Cornell notes that "standing up to such beatings becomes the hallmark of the hero's masculine self-restraint, the paradoxical power of not acting. But here we see a man prostrate, begging for help . . . stripped of humanity" (*Clint Eastwood and Issues of American Masculinity,* 11).

15. Because it is not clear whether Fletcher knew that Terrill planned to kill the men who surrendered or whether Fletcher was coerced into cooperating with Terrill, his guilt remains unclear.

16. Knapp, *Directed by Clint Eastwood,* 75.

17. Brett Westbrook, "Feminism and the Limits of the Genre in *Fistful of Dollars* and *The Outlaw Josey Wales*," in *Clint Eastwood, Actor and Director: New Perspectives*, ed. Leonard Engel (Salt Lake City: Univ. of Utah Press, 2007), 38–42.

18. Richard E. Nisbett and Dov Cohen, *Culture of Honor: The Psychology of Violence in the South* (Boulder, Colo.: Westview Press, 1996), xv. For additional discussion of the relationship between honor and violence, see Dickson D. Bruce Jr.'s *Violence and Culture in the Antebellum South* (Austin: Univ. of Texas Press, 1979), and Suzanne E. Hatty's *Masculinities, Violence, and Culture* (Thousand Oaks, Calif.: Sage Publications, 2000).

19. It is worth noting that the Psalm employs the language of tranquility and comfort, which contrasts with the reality of hostility, injustice, and loss that the miners continue to suffer from LaHood and his men.

20. Earlier in *Pale Rider* the Preacher is saved in a similar way by Club (Richard Kiel), who shoots Josh LaHood (Christopher Penn) as the young man prepares to shoot the Preacher in the back.

21. "Portrait of the Gunslinger as a Wise Old Man: Encounter with Clint Eastwood, Henri Behar/1992," in *Clint Eastwood: Interviews*, ed. Robert E. Kapsis and Kathie Coblentz (Jackson: Univ. Press of Mississippi, 1999), 187–192, 189. Brad Klypchak discusses this interview and Eastwood's shifting attitude toward violence in his essay "'*All on Accounta Pullin' a Trigger*': Violence, the Media, and the Historical Contextualization of Clint Eastwood's *Unforgiven*," in *Clint Eastwood, Actor and Director: New Perspectives*, ed. Leonard Engel (Salt Lake City: Univ. of Utah Press, 2007), 157–170. See also John C. Tibbetts's "The Machinery of Violence: Clint Eastwood Talks about *Unforgiven*," 171–180, in the same volume.

22. "Interview with Clint Eastwood, Thierry Jousse and Camille Nevers/1992," in *Clint Eastwood: Interviews*, ed. Robert E. Kapsis and Kathie Coblentz (Jackson: Univ. Press of Mississippi, 1999), 176–177.

23. *Unforgiven* thus seems to question the role of women in cultures with a code of honor that connects honor to violent response to insult and injury.

24. Speaking about Munny, Cornell notes that "only by forsaking the worst fantasies of the man with a gun can he ever hope to become a real man worthy of his gender" (*Clint Eastwood and Issues of American Masculinity*, 31). Maintaining that "Eastwood portrays Munny as a man undone throughout the film," Cornell notes that, in the final shootout, "he does not regain his manhood by completing what he considers a necessary act of vengeance for Logan, because that kind of violence can never restore the perpetrator to any kind of genuine wholeness—and Munny is well aware of that fact" (33).

25. Sara Anson Vaux, *The Ethical Vision of Clint Eastwood* (Grand Rapids, Mich.: Eerdmans, 2012), 168. She notes that the quote in her text comes from Eastwood's interview with Terry Gross on National Public Radio's *Fresh Air*, January 10, 2007.

26. Despite its frankness in showing Walt's racism, *Gran Torino* makes it clear that Walt has much in common with his neighbors, particularly the grandmother (Chee Thao), who sits on her porch and angrily mutters to herself about not knowing why

the old man doesn't leave the area just as he mutters to himself about why her family has come to the neighborhood. A little over twelve minutes into the film, the two are depicted spitting in sequence in a way that suggests their mutual contempt.

27. Roger Ebert, "Gran Torino," *Chicago Sun-Times,* December 17, 2008. The full text of the review is available at http://rogerebert.suntimes.com/apps/pbcs.dll/article?AID=/20081217/REVIEWS/812179989. It should be noted that Ebert mistakenly identifies Walt's weapon as a shotgun. It is, instead, a .30-caliber Garand semi-automatic rifle, which Walt brought back from the Korean War. I am grateful to the editors of this volume for calling this to my attention.

28. Manohla Dargis, "Hope for a Racist, and Maybe a Country," *New York Times,* December 12, 2008, as quoted in Vaux, *Ethical Vision,* 170.

29. Knapp, *Directed by Clint Eastwood,* 20.

30. The difficulty in taking a life is a theme in many of Eastwood's films. In addition to the films discussed throughout this essay, *Million Dollar Baby* (2004) addresses the burden involved in taking a life, even when one does so in order to fulfill the wishes of the person whose life is taken. When Frankie Dunn, the character Eastwood plays in the film, laments the fact that his paralyzed beloved fighter and friend Maggie Fitzgerald (Hilary Swank) has asked him to help her end her life, Father Horvak (Brían O'Byrne) tells him, "Whatever sins you're carrying, they're nothing compared to this. Forget about God or heaven and hell. If you do this thing [kill Maggie], you'll be lost somewhere so deep you'll never find yourself again." Because Frankie disappears after ending Maggie's life, it is possible that the priest was right. In any case, it appears that Frankie decides that he cannot return to his life at the gym after what he has done. The narrator, Eddie Dupris (Morgan Freeman), puts a positive spin on the possibility that Frankie has gone somewhere else to start over, but the film leaves it unclear whether he is really able to live with the role he played in ending Maggie's life.

31. In this speech Walt reveals both remorse and guilt. In a helpful discussion of these emotions, Robert C. Roberts notes that remorse pertains to a particular act that violates the moral standard that an agent believes to be right. In Walt's speech, he expresses remorse for killing the young man who was trying to surrender. The emotion of guilt, according to Roberts, pertains to the agent's self-assessment of his status as being guilty, of existing "as one who is morally spoiled" (Robert C. Roberts, *Emotions: An Essay in Aid of Moral Psychology* [New York: Cambridge Univ. Press, 2003], 223). Walt expresses guilt in discussing the blood on his hands and the way that it makes him "soiled." Although he is surely interested in saving Thao from remorse—from committing an act that the young man may later regard as blameworthy, Walt is particularly interested in saving Thao from the guilt that he might develop upon becoming a perpetrator of violence. For more discussion of the relationship between guilt and remorse, see Roberts, *Emotions,* 222–225. I thank Richard McClelland for bringing this source to my attention.

32. Walt's act of reaching for something in his pocket and having that gesture mistakenly interpreted as reaching for a gun parallels Butch Haynes's (Kevin Costner) act

of reaching for his wish list in *A Perfect World* (1993), one of Eastwood's earlier films. In the latter film, Butch's gesture is also misinterpreted—in this case by police—and he falls dead as the officers open fire.

33. Sara Vaux notes that "[i]n keeping with the earlier Eastwood films that emphasize witness (*High Plains Drifter, Unforgiven*), the innocent onlookers can no longer turn their faces away from the degraded condition of their neighborhood. They cannot save Walt, but they may be able to save others. The passivity of the nighttime crowd in *High Plains Drifter* has been reimagined in *Gran Torino,* not as vigilante justice but rather as the orderly investment of citizens, however diverse their background, in the stability of the rule of law and the health of their neighborhoods" (Vaux, *Ethical Vision,* 185).

34. The horrors of which Walt is guilty seem to extend beyond merely following orders in the war. At one point in the film, Father Janovich approaches Walt with arguments about the power of forgiveness to absolve a man of the violence he was commanded to perform—arguments that Walt refers to as "guns loaded." Walt admits that stronger men may have found salvation through forgiveness. But, he notes, "the thing that haunts a man the most is what he *isn't* ordered to do." He might have been ordered to kill the enemy in battle, but not to kill the young soldier who was trying to surrender.

35. The theme of living without being fully alive appears in several of Eastwood's films. The argument for killing Maggie in *Million Dollar Baby* is motivated by the sense that, although she is alive, she does not have a life that she believes to be worth living. The characters in *Flags of Our Fathers* (2006) struggle with the fact that they have lived through the war rather than having been killed in it. In *Hereafter* (2010) the character of George (Matt Damon) wrestles with his psychic connection to the world of the dead, reportedly telling his brother that "a life that's all about death is no life at all."

36. As Knapp rightly observes, "Eastwood's characters rarely initiate or salivate over violence; they respond to it with a weary, stoic stare. None of his characters walk away from a violent encounter unscathed. . . . On the whole, violence can be a source of redemption and/or damnation" (Knapp, *Directed by Clint Eastwood,* 14). The final shootout in Gran Torino appears to be both. Vaux also supports an interpretation of the film as redemptive, contending that healing and regeneration are central to the film (Vaux, *Ethical Vision,* 172).

37. Indeed, it is one of the weakest plot points of the film to ask viewers to believe that, having shot Walt, Spider and the other gang members would simply wait for the police to arrive to arrest them. Here the film seems to ask for a willing suspension of disbelief.

Eastwood, Romance, Tragedy

Deborah Knight and George McKnight

A significant group of Clint Eastwood's films fall within what we call, following Northrop Frye's *Anatomy of Criticism,* the master genre of romance.[1] With *Mystic River* (2003), Eastwood's films turn away from the genre of romance toward a focus on the tragic and on the master genre of tragedy. In this chapter we will examine the trajectory of Eastwood's films from romance to tragedy, focusing in particular on how both romance and tragedy are concretized by films that fall within familiar cinematic genres, such as the Western and the police procedural. We will examine how the generic form of Eastwood's films shapes their moral and philosophical concerns, including the relationship between the law and justice, the victimization of the innocent, and the role of the hero who, at least in the films that fall under the master genre of romance, is invariably compelled to help others, usually strangers.

First, let us consider the master genre of romance and its typical hero. The romance hero is superior in his skills and actions to those around him, and becomes involved in a quest—a journey or search—that ends in a confrontation with adversaries in order to defend an individual or to protect a community threatened by violence or criminal activity. The romance hero is drawn into the circumstances of others, and his actions involve undertaking a moral cause or commitment, often reluctantly. Our examples will be drawn from films dating from the formation of the Malpaso Company, including the Westerns *Hang 'Em High* (1968), *Joe Kidd* (1972), *High Plains Drifter* (1973), with brief references to *The Outlaw Josey Wales* (1976), through to *Pale Rider* (1985) and *Unforgiven* (1992).[2] Discussion of the police procedural will focus on *Dirty Harry* (1971), with references to *Magnum Force* (1973), *Sudden Impact* (1983), *In the Line of Fire* (1993), and *True Crime* (1999), which, while not strictly speaking a police procedural, features a protagonist who is an investigative reporter. Additionally, *True Crime* marks a transition between the master genre of romance and Eastwood's more recent tragic films.

There are two senses of the term "tragedy," both of which are relevant with regard to the Eastwood films we are considering. First, tragedy can refer to awful, devastating, catastrophic events that happen to essentially innocent characters. Between 2003 and 2008, Eastwood's work increasingly explores how characters respond emotionally and psychologically to injustices or when dealing with tragic events that befall themselves or others, events such as child abduction, rape, and murder. Examples include *Mystic River* (2003), *Million Dollar Baby* (2004), *Changeling* (2008), and *Gran Torino* (2008). But the term can also designate what Frye thinks of as the master genre of tragedy, where particular tragic events are incorporated into an overall narrative that leads the protagonist to discover how his or her actions have inadvertently brought about or contributed to the tragic events in question. With *Mystic River,* Eastwood's work as a director approaches the master genre of tragedy. Tragic events can certainly occur within the scope of the master genre of romance. It is in the three latter films that romance and tragedy most obviously intersect. While certain injustices may be righted in these films as a result of actions by Frankie Dunn (Eastwood) in *Million Dollar Baby,* Christine Collins (Angelina Jolie) and the Reverend Briegleb (John Malkovich) in *The Changeling,* and Walt Kowalski (Eastwood) in *Gran Torino,* there is, nevertheless, a lingering sense of loss about all four films. The central protagonist of a romance narrative is typically victorious, although that victory might be dark or ironic or, as we see in Eastwood's more tragic films, at a personal cost when he does what he believes is morally right. The protagonist of a tragic narrative is usually an antihero, who is morally liable for at least some of the tragic events that unfold, as we see in *Mystic River.*

Romance and the Romance Hero

In Eastwood's Westerns, the protagonist is an outsider located initially on the wilderness landscape, a lone individual who becomes involved with a community by force of circumstance. In his police procedurals, the protagonist is often reluctant to take on partners or is at odds with the institutional authority he serves. In *Hang 'Em High,* Jed Cooper (Eastwood) is seen first driving cattle across a river and rescuing a young calf. He is set upon by ranchers who mistake him for a rustler and murderer. Refusing to believe his story, they take the law into their own hands and lynch him. Rescued by a federal marshal and bearing the scar of the noose, Cooper initially wants revenge. The choice between revenge, on the one hand, and upholding the law on the other is posed directly to Cooper by Judge Fenton (Pat Hingle), who says he will hang Cooper if he goes outside the law to take revenge. Cooper becomes a marshal, and his search for those who hanged him now has the sanction of the law, although there is often a fine line in Westerns and police procedural films between the impartiality of the law and the partiality of personal involvement. Judge Fenton represents the stern upholding of the law when individuals commit crimes or when groups of men turn to vigilante justice. His decision to hang the two brothers despite Cooper's testimony on their behalf illustrates the often harsh nature of justice in the Western when establishing the authority of the law.

The foundational myth of the Western is to bring law and order to newly formed Western communities and the surrounding wilderness, especially to communities that face arbitrary violence or the threat of vigilante justice. Conventionally, in the master genre of romance, the protagonist's actions ultimately eliminate the threat to the community and symbolically reaffirm authority and establish or restore order. In the Western, the restoration of order occurs in a community where the institution of the law is often barely established. The law is threatened by groups that take vigilante action in *Hang 'Em High,* by a powerful land baron with hired gunmen who forces those with legitimate claims off their land in *Joe Kidd,* and by a weak sheriff in *High Plains Drifter.* In Eastwood's Westerns, it is the individual hero who must finally act to ensure some form of justice when the institution of the law has yet to be established or has failed. Eastwood's police procedural films locate the threat to the community in an urban setting where the institutions and apparatus of the law have become well established. Nevertheless, there is a clear discrepancy between the dictates of the law and ensuring justice.

Released between *Hang 'Em High* and *Joe Kidd, Dirty Harry* is perfectly positioned to illustrate the relationship between the need for law and justice on the Western frontier and the institutionalization of the law and the police in an urban setting. A recurring feature of the master genre of romance is the almost mystical nature of the hero's weaponry—which is why guns and rifles occupy such a prominent place in the iconography of the Western, and why it is wholly appropriate in a police procedural film that Harry (Eastwood) carries a .44 Magnum. The town of wooden buildings and the often picturesque prairie landscape stretching into the distance in Eastwood's Westerns have been replaced in *Dirty Harry* by the architecture and technology of the city with its skyscrapers, rooftop swimming pools, freeways, and frequent panoramic vistas of San Francisco, the Bay area, and the Golden Gate Bridge. Western expansion has reached the West Coast. The founding myth of the Western was to establish order on the frontier, institutionalize the law, and build communities that can nurture progress and culture. Implicit in the Western is the ideal of the law bringing justice and putting an end to vigilantism. Both justice and vigilantism, however, entail retribution that Kevin M. Carlsmith argues is the foundation of most forms of human punishment.[3] *Dirty Harry* offers a vision of urban moral decay and a profound division between the institutions of the law and the assurance of justice that will center finally around the issue of vigilante justice when those institutions cannot provide effective punishment for injustice.

Drawing on a convention of the Western, *Dirty Harry* begins with an act of arbitrary violence toward an innocent victim.[4] The villain Scorpio (Andrew Robinson) randomly shoots a woman with a high-powered rifle while she is swimming, suggesting a displaced form of the sexual violation. This is the film's initial representation of an increasingly sexually and socially permissive society. Scorpio's actions in the course of the film are put into the context of antiwar sentiments, nude dancers, and the exploitation of young college women in the strip clubs he frequents. Incidental to the action but not to the idea of permissiveness are shots of an adult bookstore and of sexual relations that violate traditional social and sexual norms seen through an apartment window, in Washington Square, and at the Mt. Davidson Cross, where Harry is approached by a young man looking for a casual sexual encounter. Scorpio's victimization of the innocent escalates when he shoots a ten-year-old black boy in the face, when he rapes and murders a fourteen-year-old girl, and when he hijacks a school bus and is violent toward the children. But *Dirty Harry* is not just about the injustices to innocent victims; it is also about the rights of the suspect. From the film's point of view, police procedures are now wholly subject to legal procedures that ensure the rights of the accused at the expense of the victims and the rights of their communities.

Dirty Harry combines features from the police procedural film with the figure of the outsider in the Western who is never finally a part of the community or institution he serves.[5] Harry Callahan prefers to act on his own and so inevitably comes into conflict with those in authority. While *Dirty*

Harry develops around the procedures involved in investigating a crime and pursuing a criminal, it also deals with the relationship between the nature of the job and the detective-protagonist's personal life. It is a film perfectly attuned to the Eastwood persona as a loner. In terms of his personal life, Harry's wife has been killed by a drunk driver. Professionally, he is reluctant to take on a partner. The detective's partner in police procedurals is often a means of objectifying the dangers of the job and the detrimental effect it has on personal relationships. Harry's partner, Chico Gonzalez (Reni Santoni), has been wounded by Scorpio and is considering changing professions. Gonzalez's wife fears for his safety every time he leaves the house.[6] The shooting of Gonzalez refers the viewer back to the film's opening shot of the memorial for police killed in the line of duty.

In *Dirty Harry,* the institutions of civic authority and the law are represented by the monumental façade of City Hall, with its imposing staircase, and the Hall of Justice, not to mention utilities, such as water services, garbage collection, and emergency services, such as fire and ambulance, along with a range of other social institutions, such as hospitals, or commercial institutions, such as banks—most of which appear only momentarily in *Dirty Harry* as part of the fabric of urban life. At a more personal level, the institutionalization of civic authority and the law are represented by the mayor, the district attorney, and the judge. If the police procedural film is grounded in the investigative procedures of gathering evidence, checking records, and identifying suspects, *Dirty Harry* extends this to include the procedures now demanded by the law to ensure a suspect's civil rights. References by the district attorney to the Miranda and Escobedo rulings indicate limitations on how the police can conduct their investigations. In a pivotal scene in the district attorney's office, Harry is positioned in a number of shots between the district attorney, the elected official of the law, and Judge Bannerman, who offers his legal opinion as a constitutional expert. Explaining the relationship between gathering evidence and the law, and why the evidence Harry has obtained is inadmissible in court, the DA finally says, "It is the law." It can be argued that, in the film's view, the law no longer guarantees justice. Indeed, in Book 5, chapter 10, of the *Nichomachean Ethics,* Aristotle recognized that the lawful and the just are not coterminous, otherwise it would not be possible to criticize the law on moral grounds. Since criminal offences are punished as offences against the state, any criminal justice system can create a division between it and the concerns of an individual victim of a crime that can lead to inequity. Additionally, if the law must protect the rights of the accused, the legal system can no longer necessarily ensure either a victim's rights or justice for innocent victims of crime. Harry finally kills Scorpio, then hurls his police badge into the quarry pond. Killing Scorpio is an example of retaliatory justice if not of urban vigilante justice.[7] Synonymous with the idea of revenge, retaliatory justice is the only form of justice available to Harry in the film's view. Throwing his badge away might initially suggest Harry is finished with the police, but it could also suggest that the law and its enforcement symbolized by the badge no longer provide any assurance of justice.

Eastwood's films released during 1972–1973 indicate a conflicted response to the relationship between the law and vigilante justice. Released on July 14, 1972, *Joe Kidd* continues Eastwood's concern with the law, justice, retribution, and the romance hero in relation to the myth of settlement and community. Released on August 22, 1973, *High Plains Drifter* quite clearly justifies retribution when the law fails to ensure justice in a Western that departs from the ideal of establishing the law-abiding community in the desert landscape. *Magnum Force,* released on December 25, 1973, calls for a need to maintain the law in a contemporaneous urban setting, although the film's plot is developed around those who take action when they believe the law cannot ensure justice. In *Joe Kidd,* the conflict is between Mexican peasants, whose land grants were signed either by the King of Spain or the Emperor of Mexico, American companies that have filed deeds and titles in the Territorial Court, and the land baron Frank Harlan (Robert Duvall), who takes the law into his own hands. As Harlan says, he is "not going to waste time arguing in court." Joe Kidd (Eastwood), a former bounty hunter and guide, is initially hired by Harlan to track the outlaw Luis Chama (John Saxon), who is supporting the peasants. Coincidentally, Chama has stolen horses from Kidd's ranch and wrapped Kidd's ranch hand in barbed wire. Harlan is prepared to kill innocent Mexican villagers to force Chama to surrender, and imprisons Kidd in the church with the villagers. Kidd escapes and seeks out Chama. He initially urges Chama to "give yourself up, take your chances in court," but is forced to pull his gun on him and escorts Chama back to town, where they face Harlan and his men. In the course of the film, Joe Kidd is transformed from a drunk and derelict character to a redemptive figure when he sees Harlan's violence, and Chama submits to the law and trusts in what the judge has earlier called "a court of justice." Faced with an ineffective town sheriff, however, Kidd takes his own form of justice in the courthouse while sitting in the judge's chair, killing Harlan. At this point, the law and a form of vigilante justice are bound together.

A consciousness of the generic antecedents of the Western and its foundational myth is clear in *High Plains Drifter* (1973), the first Western Eastwood directed. *High Plains Drifter* is a revenge drama. The Stranger (Eastwood) comes to the mining town of Lago, not to help ensure order and the safety of the community but to avenge the death of Marshal Duncan. Duncan is whipped to death by three gunmen working for the Lago Mining Company because he discovers that the mine is actually on government land. The Stranger emerges through a heat haze, across a dusty wilderness landscape, before entering the town. It is a classic Western opening sequence with a lone figure, his face not clearly visible or obscured by shadow, entering the small community along its only street with buildings of fresh-cut lumber, newly painted storefronts and signs, and new structures being framed. Everything here indicates settlement, expansion, and progress, with the church standing at the end of the street marking the boundary between town and wilderness. The Stranger, however, is not the idealized Western hero whose actions are necessarily bound to contribute to the well-being of the community.

High Plains Drifter employs familiar conventions of the Western to look at the violence, corruption, betrayals, and the absence of a moral ideal that are the darker underside of the Western myth. Sheriff Shaw is weak. The minister, who mouths platitudes, lacks both charity and courage.[8] The townspeople, particularly the mine owner, the former mayor, and the hotel owner, are driven by self-interest and, fearing the three gunmen who are returning to town, attempt to kill the Stranger. In the film's final scenes, the Stranger kills the three gunmen, who have taken over the town, and his retribution for the murder of Marshal Duncan is an appropriately violent justice. Unlike *Joe Kidd,* which is a more conventional Western that reaffirms the ideal of the court even though it is the individual who acts as the court's surrogate, *High Plains Drifter* is a revisionist Western that advocates retributive justice for past crimes when even lawful authority has failed. Following shortly after Don Siegel's *Dirty Harry* and iterating the idea of retribution, *High Plains Drifter* introduces into Eastwood's American Westerns the revisionist romance hero who acts when the community lacks the will or has lost its ideals, having been taken over by commercial self-interest.

Magnum Force presents a darker picture of urban vigilante justice when four young policemen take the law into their own hands and kill those they believe the law has been unable to bring to justice. They act because of the "failure of the courts" and with the sanction of Lieutenant Briggs (Hal Holbrook). Briggs tells Harry, in a manner that draws together the Western and the police procedural during the early 1970s, "A hundred years ago in this city people did the same thing. History justified the vigilantes. We're no different. Anyone who threatens the security of the people will be executed. Evil for evil, Harry. Retribution." Callahan's response is indicative of the ambivalence about the justice system at the time, "Briggs! I hate the goddamn system. But until someone comes along with some changes that make sense, I'll stick with it."

The relationship between the protagonist and the community in both Westerns and police procedural films is developed around a threat to the community that is invariably represented within the narrative not simply by violations of the law but by the victimization of innocent individuals or groups, particularly women, children, and those unable to defend themselves. Examples range from the threat to the Mexican villagers in *Joe Kidd,* to the shooting of Charlie McCoy (Mitch Ryan) in *Magnum Force,* to the killing of the bank clerk Pam Magnus (Patrika Darbo) and her roommate, Sally (Mary Van Arsdel), in *In the Line of Fire.* Many other examples could be cited. Consequently, the trajectory of these narratives is to redress such violations. In Westerns and police procedurals, this threat is often represented by violence toward women or the threat of sexual violation. In *Hang 'Em High,* Rachel Warren (Inger Stevens) continues her search for the man who victimized her. In *The Outlaw Josey Wales,* Laura Lee (Sondra Locke) is threatened with rape by bandits, while in *Pale Rider,* Megan (Sydney Penny) faces the threat of rape. In what may be Eastwood's final Western, *Unforgiven,* there is a graphic yet symbolic rape when the prostitute Delilah's (Anna Thomson) face is slashed with a knife by a drunken cowboy. The threat to innocent individuals is also evident in police procedurals, for instance the abduction and rape of the fourteen-year-old girl in *Dirty Harry* and the rape of Jennifer (Sondra Locke) in *Sudden Impact* (1983). The threat of violence and violation, particularly when it involves the innocent, is not limited to Eastwood's films within the master genre of romance. It is also central to his more tragic films, particularly the abduction and homosexual rape of Dave (Tim Robbins) in *Mystic River,* the beating of Danger (Jay Baruchel) in *Million Dollar Baby,* the abduction of Walter Collins (Gattlin Griffith) in *Changeling,* and the rape of Sue Lor (Ahney Her) in *Gran Torino.*

Because these narratives are constructed around the threat to or violation of innocence, viewers arguably experience a desire for retributive justice. The Western and the police procedural are constructed so that the hero's actions are ultimately precipitated and justified by the undeserved violence or threat of violence by lawless elements late in the narrative—violence that is frequently graphic in its representation. Examples range from the hijacking of the school bus in *Dirty Harry,* the killing of Callahan's partner, Inspector "Early" Smith (Felton Perry), in *Magnum Force,* the killing of Spider (Doug McGrath) in *Pale Rider,* the killing of Ned Logan (Morgan Freeman) in *Unforgiven,* the cold-blooded killing of Horrigan's (Eastwood) partner, Al (Dylan McDermott), after Al has been wounded in *In the Line of Fire,* and the sight of Sue Lor following her rape in *Gran Torino.* These are all instances of intentional violence by those who are seen to act without any regard for the individual, let alone due regard for the law. The master genre of romance typically fulfills the viewers' expectations through the actions of the hero on behalf of the community in the face of such violence. The romance hero embodies the viewers' desire for action to bring whatever form of justice or retribution is necessary. In Eastwood's films, the hero's actions often take extreme forms, although, arguably, it is the retributive character of the hero's actions within a particular narrative that makes these actions appropriate.

While *Unforgiven* arguably marks the end of Eastwood's Westerns, it also marks a recognition of the aging hero and an increasing concern with the emotions whose expression often take the form of action in Eastwood's films. In *High Plains Drifter,* the Stranger says at one point to Sarah, "What makes you think I care?" and that phrase is, in many ways, indicative of the persona initially developed around Eastwood, whose characters typically are reluctant to express their emotions or to commit themselves emotionally. Bill Munny (Eastwood) takes the job for cash to avenge the slashing of the prostitute in *Unforgiven.* Yet he avenges the death of Ned Logan—"I'm here to kill you, Little Bill, for what you did to Ned"—because of his friendship with Logan. *The Bridges of Madison County* (1995) is an uncharacteristic film for Eastwood since he is not typically identified with romantic dramas. His character in *Bridges* may initially appear to be in keeping with the Eastwood persona, as indicated when Francesca (Meryl Streep) tells Robert Kincaid (Eastwood), "You are not going to be made to feel anything, period," just before he leaves her. The next time we see him is when he stands in the pouring rain, his facial expression and posture suggesting sorrow and regret as he watches Francesca in her husband's truck. This silent expression of his feelings takes the form of action, however, when Kincaid's truck remains motionless in front of her husband's truck at the intersection, despite the green light, and when he places the cross on his truck mirror—actions that express his desire for her to join him. This initial reluctance to express personal feelings or to commit oneself emotionally followed by the expression of feeling through action will emerge with greater complexity in *Million Dollar Baby* and *Gran Torino.* It is also during the 1990s that Eastwood's characters deal more directly with age and the personal failures of the hero despite his willingness to act decisively when necessary in films such as *Unforgiven* and *In the Line of Fire.* This becomes most evident in *True Crime,* when the fate of an innocent man about to be executed finally rests in the hands of an alcoholic reporter and serial womanizer, or in *Blood Work* (2002), where an aging FBI agent is called upon to investigate the death of an innocent woman. Immediately after the critical and commercial failure of *Blood Work,* the Eastwood persona as a figure of romance action comes to an end and, with *Mystic River,* his more tragic work as a film director begins.

Romance and the Tragic

In Eastwood's more tragic films we see most clearly an essential aesthetic feature that has appeared throughout Eastwood's work: the inexorable convergence of storylines. Within the master genre of romance, story convergence is traditionally developed around conflict and a confrontation between the hero and the forces that threaten a community. In the more tragic films, the convergence is between past and present events where personal histories intersect with far greater emotional and psychological intensity than in Eastwood's previous work. Here, story convergence is set directly in relation to family although in each film families are fragmented or parent/child relationships are symptomatic of the failure of family relations. *Mystic River* is developed around the convergence of Dave Boyle's abduction in the past, the brutal murder of Jimmy Markum's (Sean Penn) daughter Katie (Emmy Rossum) in the present, and Sean Devine's (Kevin Bacon) investigation of the crime while he is separated from his wife. *Million Dollar Baby* is developed around the convergence of Maggie's (Hilary Swank) determination and ambition and Frank's failure as a father, his disagreement with a previous boxer about a title fight, and his initial unwillingness to train Maggie. *Changeling* is developed around Christine Collins's (Angelina Jolie) determination to find her son, the attempts of the L.A. police to cover up their failures in that investigation, the actions of a mass murderer, and the crusading actions of

Reverend Gustav Briegleb. *Gran Torino* is developed around the convergence of Walt Kowalski's racism, his sense of guilt for the unjustified killing of a young Korean soldier, and his new Hmong neighbors. These immigrant neighbors are themselves reminiscent of secondary characters in Eastwood's Westerns whose main wish is to settle and build their lives. In these more tragic films many of Eastwood's central thematic concerns reemerge, often in different configurations: the victimization of the innocent, justice and retribution, the omnipresent motif of the surrogate parent figure, and the need for individual action to help those who face injustice. In addition, we find a protagonist who is initially reluctant or unwilling to help others but who finally takes action because there is a need to speak out or to act.

Mystic River is an important exception at this point in his career because Eastwood does not appear in the film, and no character is cast to represent the Eastwood persona. *Mystic River* overturns the moral dynamic of the romance narrative because it presents us with a genuine antihero. Jimmy Markum, something of a working-class hoodlum whose associates include the appropriately named Savage brothers (Adam Nelson and Robert Wahlberg), sets out to find the person responsible for the brutal murder of his nineteen-year-old daughter. He embarks on this mission in the face of, and against the recommendation of, his childhood friend, Sean, now a detective in the Massachusetts State Police.

Caught between Jimmy and Sean is their childhood friend, Dave. While playing together on the street of their working-class neighborhood as boys, Dave was abducted by two pedophiles and raped over a period of several days before managing to escape.[9] It is clear that Dave has been permanently emotionally scarred as a result of the abduction and assault. That Dave was chosen rather than Jimmy or Sean is arbitrary—Dave's home happens to be farther away, while Jimmy's and Sean's families are too close to where the boys were playing to risk forcing either of them into the large black sedan. Jimmy, in particular, later talks about how everything would have been different if Dave were not the one who was abducted. Two paths of investigation into the murder of Jimmy's daughter go forward, one conducted by Sean and his partner, Whitey Powers (Laurence Fishburne), the other by Jimmy, who has threatened Sean that he will take action if the state detectives cannot resolve the murder quickly and to his satisfaction. A third path of investigation will be developed around Dave's wife, Celeste (Marcia Gay Harden). Celeste's uncertainty about Dave's behavior emerges as a plotline that will finally intersect with the investigations led by Sean and Jimmy.

In the present time of the narrative, Dave is having a beer in a bar where Jimmy's daughter is partying with girlfriends a few hours before she is killed. When Jimmy tries to solve the mystery of his daughter's murder, coincidences build up that cause him to suspect Dave. We know, but Jimmy does not, that after leaving the bar Dave brutally attacks a man. He returns home and confesses to Celeste that he thinks he may have killed a man, a robber, who confronted him. This story is partly true: Dave has killed a man. But the dead man was not a robber, he was a pedophile having sex with a young boy in a car.[10] Dave has a defensive injury across his right palm that he explains was caused by the knife the alleged robber wielded. The discovery of Jimmy's daughter's body, initially identified by Sean, who is working the case, brings all three men together as Sean investigates the murder and Dave and Celeste attend the wake for Jimmy's daughter.

As we might expect, a romance hero grappling with the murder of his daughter would vow to avenge her death, find her killers, and see justice done. Sean Penn's portrayal of Jimmy, as he suspects and then confirms that it is his daughter who has been murdered, is an intense study of profound, inconsolable paternal anguish. He swears over his daughter's dead body that he will find her killer and kill him. Jimmy commits himself to the quest for revenge, but he is not a romance hero. Working outside of the law, Jimmy persuades himself that Dave is guilty following Celeste's information about Dave on the night of the murder. She is both concerned and suspicious about Dave's account of that night, and her suspicions inadvertently lead her to betray Dave when she nods in agreement to Jimmy's question, "Do you think Dave killed my Katie?" After bringing Dave in the night to the side of the Mystic River, Jimmy brutally kills him.

The death of the romance hero's archenemy is a traditional feature of romance narratives, but in romance narratives the hero is right about who his enemy is and what the enemy has done to deserve retribution. Jimmy, by contrast, is wrong—a fact that eventually emerges when Sean's equally dramatic investigation of the facts reveals the identity of the actual killer. These two plotlines—Sean and his partner realizing who the actual killer is, and Jimmy's search for his daughter's murderer and his macabre execution of Dave by the river's edge—are presented in parallel, so that as audience we know unmistakably that, in his quest for revenge, Jimmy has killed his childhood friend who is innocent of the crime for which Jimmy holds him accountable. Traumatized and abused as a boy and trusting his friend Jimmy, who extracts from Dave a coerced "confession," he is led to his own murder at Jimmy's hands.

Despite his quest for retributive justice, Jimmy is not a romance hero. Rather, he bears a striking, although ironic, relationship to the hero of tragedy. As Aristotle indicates in his *Poetics,* the tragic protagonist acts without full knowledge of his own situation and its implications, initially believing he has acted correctly and then recognizing that his actions have been misconceived.[11] Thus, Oedipus kills his father and marries his mother, as his destiny was foretold, but of course does not kill the old man on the road *as* his father or marry the beautiful Jocasta *as* his mother. Jimmy kills Dave *as* his daughter's murderer, but is wrong. When Sean arrives the morning after the arrest of Katie's real murderer, "Silent Ray" (Spencer Treat Clark), and Jimmy's execution of Dave, it becomes clear to both what has happened. Sean realizes that Jimmy has killed Dave, and Jimmy realizes Dave was the wrong man. Hence the irony of Jimmy saying he wished Sean could have solved the crime "faster." In an extraordinary scene following Jimmy's recognition of his culpability in Dave's murder, he confesses to his wife, Annabeth (Laura Linney), that he has killed the wrong person. She praises him for his "heart," for his devotion to his children, his willingness to do anything to protect or avenge them. Annabeth's general approbation of Jimmy's actions indicates a kind of tribalism that runs right through *Mystic River* in its depiction of many of the families in this part of the city. The moment of the tragic protagonist's recognition of wrongdoing is translated into a moment of adoration if not celebration. *Mystic River* is distinguished from Eastwood's other tragically oriented films because the antihero Jimmy, whose wife calls him "a king," goes unpunished. Despite Sean's realization that Jimmy has murdered Dave, Jimmy will not be prosecuted now, although Sean's gesture could indicate that he will eventually get Jimmy. Jimmy has gone through the tragic protagonist's recognition of his own actions, but emerges with a gesture, which he shares with Sean, to suggest that nothing much matters—wrong things happen, life goes on.

What is most compelling about the later tragic films is the figure of the surrogate parent whose actions are tied directly to the role traditionally ascribed to the hero in the master genre of romance as the embodiment of either or both moral instruction or right moral action. *Mystic River* offers the bitterly ironic view of Jimmy as a surrogate father. Jimmy, who killed Just Ray, has provided money since the murder to Just Ray's widow. She raises her son, Silent Ray, who, as coincidence would have it, kills Jimmy's daughter. In *Million Dollar Baby,* Frankie, the lone, reticent trainer—who has failed both in his marriage and as a father to his daughter—becomes the surrogate parent as well as trainer and manager of Maggie, whose own family tries to exploit her when she is helpless. It is finally Frankie who must fulfill Maggie's wish to die. Reverend Briegleb takes on the role of surrogate parent in *Changeling,* providing direction and intervention on behalf of Christine—particularly when he confronts both the police and the mental facility where she has been wrongly confined. He also secures an attorney who will help bring some justice in her fight to find Walter. In *Gran Torino,* Walt is alienated from his own sons and their families who try to exploit him. Reluctantly, he agrees to enable the son of his Hmong neighbors, Thao (Bee Vang), to redeem their family's honor for attempting to steal his Gran Torino. Walt's involvement with the Vang Lor family leads increasingly to a surrogate role in the lives of both Thao and Sue. In *Million Dollar Baby, Changeling,* and *Gran Torino,* the surrogate parent provides instruction and support, acting on behalf of the individual who has been victimized regardless of his own safety. The injustices individuals face are balanced by the actions of those who assume a surrogate role because of a commitment to doing their civic duty, or doing what is just and right.

In the more tragic films, narrative closure is bittersweet if not ironic. These films end with an extended, contemplative time for the audience, as we are left to think about the relationships between characters and the moral issues in each film. The conclusion of *Mystic River* is set against the celebrations of a neighborhood parade with marching bands and sports teams. Consider: Jimmy's gesture to Sean, shrugging off his own actions; the exchange of looks between Sean and Dave's wife, Celeste; the defiant look of Jimmy's wife, Annabeth, who knows Jimmy has killed Dave; Celeste's futile attempts to get her son, Michael (Cayden Boyd), to respond as he sits disconsolately on a passing float; the exchange of looks between Sean and Jimmy, where Sean uses his hand to replicate cocking the hammer of a gun. This sequence is followed by the parade disappearing around the corner, the slow tracking shot to the pavement where Dave's name, which he was writing in wet cement, remains incomplete from the day of his boyhood abduction, and a final shot of the river with the camera moving steadily downward toward the water as its color changes from blue to black. In *Million Dollar Baby,* Frankie says goodbye to "mo cuishle" (my darling, my blood), disconnects Maggie's ventilator, gives her a shot of adrenaline, kisses her cheek again, then walks down the darkened hospital corridor and through the hospital doors. Then we see Eddie (Morgan Freeman), who has witnessed Frankie from the shadows. The final sequence returns us to the voice-over narrator, Eddie, in the gym waiting for Frankie to return. Eddie greets Danger, who still has blind faith in his desire to be a boxer. When Eddie returns to the office, we then understand that his narration is a letter to Frankie's estranged daughter, wondering if Frankie has asked for forgiveness. The film's final shot is a slow track toward the window of Ira's Roadside Diner, where—repeating an earlier shot when Maggie takes Frankie to the diner and tells him about going there with her father—we see a shot of Frankie now sitting alone eating lemon pie, just as Maggie's father once did. In *Changeling,* Christine tells Detective Ybarra (Michael Kelly) she has hope that Walter is still alive, then walks down the steps and across the intersection, becoming an increasingly smaller figure as she walks away, occasionally disappearing under the credits, before she disappears from the image. In *Gran Torino,* Thao is seen in the film's final extended shot driving Walt's Gran Torino along the quiet road beside the lake, Walt's dog in the passenger seat, with the film's theme song continuing well beyond the time the car rounds a bend and disappears from the image.

These final scenes and shots of Eastwood's tragic films serve two functions: First, they refer the audience back into the film and leave us to examine the moral implications of the actions we have witnessed—let alone to consider the need for individuals to act in unjust circumstances—rather than simply leaving us as passive viewers to observe the action. Second, they call upon the audience to examine characters such as Danger, Maggie, and Christine—as idealistic as they may be—who represent hope and determination in failed circumstances, as do Sean and Thao, who offer the promise of renewal. It is this vision of renewal that is carried into *Invictus,* with its themes of reconciliation and overcoming past injustices. Richard McClelland provides an incisive comment on Walt's death in *Gran Torino* that draws together the self-sufficiency of the romance protagonist and the role of the surrogate father, and suggests some of the implications the final scene asks the audience to think about: "Walt's death is a piece of brilliant problem solving on his part. He atones for and expiates his own life-long guilt; he prevents Thao from incurring similar blood-guilt; he brings his own suffering from disease to an end; he preserves his own autonomy (a fundamental value in his character); he protects his neighborhood; and he ensures justice against the gang. All in a single action. You don't get a better instance of the Aristotelian virtue of practical wisdom than that."[12]

Eastwood after Tragedy

Eastwood's films have, as we have argued, shifted from the master genre of romance into the mode of tragedy, but are arguably now shifting away from that mode. It is not that the philosophy of Clint Eastwood has changed; essential issues and concerns remain but are examined from different perspectives. Narrative elements evident in Eastwood's Westerns and police procedurals persist, but become darker in the more tragic films. The motif of the victimization of the innocent takes on a greater resonance in his later work. The victimized characters become more central and more individuated, as, for instance, Dave, Maggie, Christine, Thao, and Sue. Our empathy with these characters only increases our felt sense of their actions in the face of adversity or in how they deal with the circumstances that unjustly befall them. Eastwood's earlier Westerns and police procedurals featured Eastwood as a protagonist whose actions demonstrated both self-reliance and a clear moral sense. In these films there was always the expectation of a resolution where the protagonist triumphed and ensured some form of justice if not retaliatory justice. Eastwood's more tragic films, however, are characterized by an overarching vision that the circumstances that produce tragic events are invariably bitterly ironic while injustices are tempered only occasionally by some small measures of justice.

As we noted earlier, Eastwood does not appear in *Mystic River,* nor is there a character that embodies the values identified with the Eastwood persona. In his more recent films, such as *Invictus* (2009) and *Hereafter* (2010), one finds both tragic events and the renewal or regeneration associated with the master genre of romance. *Invictus* represents a shift away from these tragic films toward a vision of reconciliation and forgiveness despite past and present injustices. Nelson Mandela (Morgan Freeman) becomes the surrogate father of both a new South Africa and a surrogate son, Francois Pienaar (Matt Damon), whose actions and leadership of the Springboks are reminders of the hero from the master genre of romance. In *Hereafter,* George (Matt Damon) finally takes on a surrogate role by helping Marcus (Frankie McLaren and George McLaren) connect with his brother. The self-sufficiency and autonomy of the romance hero, along with a moral commitment to justice, have not been lost; they have been displaced into the figure of the surrogate father.

Both films also illustrate hope as a virtue in going forward despite tragic or unjust circumstances and the uncertainty of the future. As noted earlier, despite their determination, the hopes of Danger, Maggie, and Christine are not realized or are unlikely to be realized. Things change in *Invictus* and *Hereafter.* Nelson Mandela does not survive in prison for all those years without the hope that the most entrenched attitudes can be changed, that reconciliation is possible, and that a nation can be transformed. It is this shift in attitudes leading to reconciliation that we see individuated by Walt in *Gran Torino* now fulfilled in *Invictus,* where it takes on a national significance. In *Hereafter,* Marie's (Cécile de France) investigation into near-death experiences and her determination to write her book express a hope that there is something beyond the loss she incurs. Marcus's determination to communicate with his brother and George's insight into Marie's near-death experience lead to a positive affirmation of his psychic powers—that he previously described as "a curse"—when he helps Marcus, who in turn helps George to find Marie. The achievements of Mandela, the reunion of Marcus and his mother, and the possibility of a relationship forming between Marie and George in which there is the hope they will find together some healing for their hurt and loss all express the promise of renewal beyond tragic circumstances that was missing in many of Eastwood's earlier films.

Notes

We thank Richard McClelland and Brian Clayton for their always insightful comments and suggestions.

1. Northrop Frye, *Anatomy of Criticism* (Princeton, N.J.: Princeton Univ. Press, 1957).

2. The Malpaso Company was established by Eastwood in 1967 and is now known as Malpaso Productions. It is named after Malpaso Creek, which is just south of Eastwood's home in Carmel, California, on the northern border of Big Sur.

3. See, for example, Kevin M. Carlsmith, "The Roles of Retribution and Utility in Determining Punishment," *Journal of Experimental Social Psychology* 42 (July 2006): 437–451. See also Kevin M. Carlsmith and John M. Darley, "Psychological Aspects of Retributive Justice," in *Advances in Experimental Social Psychology,* vol. 40, ed. M. P. Zanna (San Diego, Calif.: Elsevier, 2008), 193–236.

4. Conventionally in a classic Western, arbitrary violence or the threat of violence to the innocent plays both a thematic and a structural role. Thematically, such action establishes the lawless conditions on the Western landscape and the precarious nature of Western expansion when establishing a community. Structurally, the narrative will develop around a resolution to this violence. For example, John Ford's *My Darling Clementine* (1946) develops around bringing the killers of Wyatt Earp's youngest brother,

James, to justice, while Ford's *The Searchers* (1956) concerns Ethan and Marty's search for the renegade Comanches who killed Ethan's brother Aaron's family and kidnapped his niece, Debbie.

5. Examples range from Wyatt Earp in *My Darling Clementine* and Shane in *Shane* (1953) to cavalry scouts such as Sam in *The Stalking Moon* (1968) and McIntosh in *Ulzana's Raid* (1972).

6. A recurring thematic concern in Eastwood's films is the killing of a policeman, often a partner or close colleague, at the hands of criminals. Examples include the killing of Charlie McCoy by a fellow policeman and the death of Smith in *Magnum Force* (1973), the death of Powell in *The Rookie* (1990), and the killing of Al in *In the Line of Fire* (1993). While such incidents may have a personal meaning for Eastwood, let alone for any law enforcement community, they are, nevertheless, structural elements in his films. Such incidents usually occur near the beginning of a film, establishing both the personal loss and the criminal's absolute disregard for the individual and the law, or toward its conclusion, reinforcing the need to bring the criminal to justice.

7. In "On Revenge" (1625), Francis Bacon calls revenge "a kind of wild justice; which the more man's nature runs to, the more ought the law to weed it out." While he recognizes that "the most tolerable sort of revenge is for those wrongs which there is no law to remedy," he again cautions, "but then let a man take heed the revenge be such as there is no law to punish; else a man's enemy is still beforehand, and it is two for one." See also Charles Barton, who argues in *Getting Even: Revenge as a Form of Justice* (Chicago: Open Court, 1999) that revenge is often the only form of justice available.

8. Eastwood's films, ranging from *High Plains Drifter* through to *Million Dollar Baby* and *Gran Torino,* often undermine the credibility of the church. In each film, it is the Eastwood protagonist who must act decisively in order to ensure justice or achieve the necessary resolution, most ironically in *Pale Rider* through the figure of the Preacher.

9. Masquerading as police officers, one of the pedophiles wears handcuffs at his belt while the other wears a crucifix and a ring with a cross. Implicit here is another recurring theme in Eastwood's films: the misuse of institutional authority and power.

10. The causal connection between Dave killing the pedophile and his own abduction by pedophiles is later made quite explicit when Dave describes the pedophile to Celeste as a "fucking wolf," recalling his description of his own abductors as "wolves." While recalling the killing to Celeste, Dave has a momentary flashback to his own flight from his abductors as he calls for the boy to "run."

11. Aristotle, *Poetics,* trans. Kenneth A. Telford. (Chicago: H. Regnery, 1961). See in particular II.3, "Plot as Functional Organization," which deals with the connection between tragic plot structure and the tragic protagonist's discovery of his or her role in the unfolding events.

12. Richard McClelland, editor's communication with the authors, citing Aristotle's account of *phronesis,* practical wisdom, in *Nichomachean Ethics VI*.5.

The Use of Silence in *Hereafter*

A Study in Neurocinematics

Richard T. McClelland

> But my words, like silent raindrops fell
> And echoed
> In the wells of silence.
> —Paul Simon and Art Garfunkel, "The Sound of Silence," 1964

Hereafter, directed by Clint Eastwood and released in the fall of 2010, is variously described as a supernatural drama or even "a spiritual thriller."[1] It raises a number of issues of interest to philosophers, most especially about the epistemic status of so-called near-death experiences, as well as attitudes toward death and the possibility of survival. Some of these issues are dealt with elsewhere in this volume (in McFarland's essay and in my own other essay). They are not, however, the focus of the present essay. Instead, I want to look at a very unusual feature of this film: its use of silence. My thesis is three-fold: first, that Eastwood has fashioned the use of silence on the model of his own preferred and very "spare" style of acting; second, that he has intuited elements of how silence functions at a neurobiological level; and third, that such uses of silence, when seen in the light of contemporary neuroscience, open up a rich set of possibilities for placing filmmaking itself on a scientific basis. I start with the phenomenology of silence in this very intriguing film.

Types of Silence in *Hereafter*

There are several kinds of silence that occur in this film. The first type involves at least four major episodes, each lasting from twenty to forty seconds, during which there is no sound of any kind in the film. These typically involve either a single major character: for example, Marie Lelay (Cécile de France), or George Lonegan (Matt Damon); or a distinctive couple: for example, the twins Jason and Marcus (Frankie McLaren and George McLaren), or Marie and George together (toward the end of the film). These episodes of silence occur at emotionally key moments in the film, moments which it is important for us to remember later on if we are to make sense of the entire film and its narrative arc. Thus, the earliest of these episodes occurs while Marie is undergoing her near-death experience during the tsunami, an experience that is pivotal for the whole film.[2] Another very poignant silent episode occurs just after Melanie (Bryce Dallas Howard) leaves George's apartment. We see him standing in the vestibule of his home, with a single overhead light in front him and with his back to us. We know at this point that he himself has despaired of ever forming a successful partnership precisely because of his psychic "gift" (which he regards as a curse in large part for this reason). He knows that what has transpired between Melanie and him that evening is probably the end of this possible partnership as well. He says nothing and does nothing. But his whole bodily posture radiates that sense of despair.[3] The precise function of the silence during this episode will concern us further below.

A second kind of silence in this film occurs when a particular actor might be expected to speak, but does not, these episodes lasting approximately two to five seconds. A third kind of silence, lasting for periods of five to ten seconds, occurs when an actor (often one of the main ones) is seen moving silently against a complex social background that involves ambient noise (opening and closing of doors, traffic sounds, footsteps, or the like), but without any sound coming from the actor. Fourth, there are ample instances of silence that function as rests during musical interludes. Eastwood, of course, is himself a notable musician and composer, and wrote the music for this film. He is especially fond of jazz and often writes pieces that start with very simple melodic lines (often in a minor key, played on piano or guitar) that contain rests typically lasting one to three seconds, followed by development of those simple melodies involving further instruments. There is nothing surprising about this, but such musical "gaps" acquire further significance in conjunction with the other types of silence that are found throughout this film.

So arresting are these uses of silence, especially in the four longest episodes, that some explanation for these practices is called for. I'm suggesting here that one part of this explanation lies in Eastwood's own distinctive acting style (considered later). The other has to do with the functions of silence in the human brain, and here we need contemporary neuroscience to help understand what is going on.[4]

Silence in the Human Brain

There are three discoveries made in recent neuroscientific studies of sound and silence in the human brain that are relevant to our subject. The first of these was made by Michael Wehr and his colleagues at the University of Oregon. They found that the primary auditory cortex (which lies along the top of the temporal lobe) contains two partially dissociable networks of neurons that are highly sensitive to the onset of sound and to the offset of sound (in other words, the beginning of silence). These networks partially overlap with one another, but their "tuning" and responsiveness to onset and offset of sounds are distinct from one another. The two networks, accordingly, generate two different signals in the primary auditory cortex for these two kinds of changes in our experience of sound. Such demarcation makes it possible for the brain to form a clearly delineated representation of sounds or silences (in other words, to represent auditory "objects"). Without such demarcation we would not have a coherent experience of sounds at all, but merely an auditory blur.[5] Moreover, it appears that this segregation of on and off pathways for sound processing runs right through from the basilar membrane to the auditory thalamus and the auditory cortex. Thus, the onset of sounds and the offset of sounds are processed in parallel but independent pathways all along the auditory hierarchy. Silence, then, carries with it distinctive neurobiological markers and boundaries, just as sound itself does. We may speak, then, of a neural representative of silence as itself an auditory object. As such, we might expect silence, at least in the brain, to have other surprising qualities. And such appears to be the case.

A team at Sheffield University presented experiment subjects with a single spoken phrase (emotionally neutral) made up of three to four words and lasting one to two seconds, followed by forty or more seconds of silence, watching brain activity by real-time fMRI and using noise-canceling earphones to screen out ambient and machine noises. What they found was the spontaneous appearance in the primary auditory cortex (PAC) of a pattern of spiking neural signals at roughly fifteen seconds (post silence), thirty seconds, and forty seconds. They occurred in the speech-sensitive area of the PAC and are believed to derive from auditory memory.[6] What is happening here is that the brain is filling the silence with auditory information generated by itself. Julien Voisin and his team in Lyon, France, also found fMRI evidence for spontaneous neural activation during silence, in this case in an experimental set-up in which the subjects were expecting sound to occur and were directed to detect it upon occurrence (being cued as to which side of the head the sound would appear to come from). In this case, silence lasted up to 7.5 seconds (between tones) and activity was relative to the resting state blood oxygenation level signal. Activation was found in the auditory areas, frontal cortical areas, and parietal areas, as well as the thalamus and caudate nucleus (both limbic structures). Activation was contralateral to the expected side of "hearing." The neuroscientists interpreted these signals as "anticipatory." The point for us is that here, too, the brain generated its own auditory signals during silence, in the complete absence of any relevant external stimulus.[7]

In a third, related series of experiments, David Kraemer and his team at Dartmouth College made up individual recordings of music, some of it familiar to the experimental subjects, some of it not, some of it involving lyrics, some of it purely instrumental. They extracted short segments (two to five seconds) and replaced those with silence. They then scanned the brains of subjects listening to these recordings. They found evidence for spontaneous activation of the primary auditory cortex specific to the silent periods in the recordings. Such activation was strongest for familiar music and especially familiar instrumental music. Curiously enough, no experimental subject reported being aware of those silent episodes during familiar music, only during unfamiliar music. It thus appears that the brain spontaneously "papers over the cracks," as it were, filling in the gaps especially where the occurrent sound is rich enough to evoke appropriate memories.[8]

These experiments establish several things about the nature of our neural experience of silence. The first is that the brain is designed to be responsive to silence in a fashion very similar to its responsiveness to sound. It is not difficult to see how possession of such sensitivity might be adaptive, especially in the early environment of adaptation for our species, when silence in an otherwise noisy environment might signal the presence of predators or of prey. We also learn that the brain is primed to pay attention to the onset or resumption of sound, following silence, and thereby also to pay attention to the boundaries of silence itself. Finally, we learn that the brain in some sense will not tolerate silence for very long without supplying its own spontaneous substitute for real sound, a kind of faux-sound that increases in strength as silence itself is prolonged. (This may account for our common experience of feeling anxious when silence sets in and endures.) We are often tempted to think of the brain as a passive instrument, waiting to respond to external stimuli, but instead it turns out that "the brain is a system intrinsically operating on its own and sensory information interacts with rather than determines the operation of the system," as one of our investigators has put it.[9] It is these attentional dynamics that concern me next. For with them we ascend from the level of neural behavior to that of psychological functions. It is here that silence acquires its uses in our film.

Silence, Attention, and Memory

So, silence is something that the human brain is designed to respond to in its own fashion. More particularly, silence serves to alert the brain, alerting being one element of attention and especially of attention shifting. The other elements are orienting and executive control (with respect to the stimulus attended to). These elements of attention are distinct and mutually dissociable, with their own neural networks supporting them and involving various neurotransmitters (notably dopamine, norepinephrine, and oxytocin). The alerting element of attention shifting is also part of what enables us to establish the salience of stimuli, and salience is a function of complex neural networks engaging areas of the frontal cortex, limbic system, and brain stem (of special importance here are the insular cortex, the anterior cingulate cortex, and dorsal lateral portion of the prefrontal cortex and the thalamus). Salience detection and determination serves as a *gating* function for both auditory and visual attention shifting: that is, "only changes that reached a certain salience threshold caused a switch of attention" in appropriate empirical experiments.[10] We do not attend to just any change in sound (or silence) and we do not attend on just any occasion. However, changes in the auditory environment can lead to involuntary and mandatory attention shifting. I posit that silence has similar functions, and thus that the deployment of significant episodes of silence in our film are well-designed to capture our attention and serve to alert us to what is going on in the film. Silence can be just as novel as sound can be, and the director can use silence to capture and focus our attention by taking advantage of automatic and reliable brain networks that control such functions.[11]

Attentional dynamics, in their turn, have important relationships with our short-term memory. This is the memory we use to observe something like a film and to hold enough of the information in our memory that we can shape the experience into something coherent and continuous (for example, a story). The various regions of the human brain that are responsible for these dynamics are further organized in two networks, each specialized for certain kinds of attentional problems (task-oriented or stimulus-oriented).[12] These networks interact such that as demands on short-term or working memory increase, the level of activation in one network increases while the level in the other decreases. And this kind of trade-off or competition applies for both visual and auditory working memory tasks. It thus appears also that the brain is wired such that attentional dynamics can enhance short-term memory efficiency.[13] Our director has intuited some of this, such that his major episodes of silence also limit the number of salient objects (namely, characters) that appear in them: either to a single person (Marie; George) or a couple (Marcus and Jason; Marie and George). By reducing sound to zero and limiting the number of salient objects in the visual scene, he enhances our ability to attend to the scene (and all of its affective and narrative associations) and to remember it. This includes, very probably, enhancing our capacity for "prospective memory," which is our ability to realize intentions after a delay caused by distracting intervening tasks. Such memory is needed to keep track of the multiple narrative lines in *Hereafter,* and to coordinate what we learn early in the film with what occurs later on, despite intervening material and our attention to it. All of these practices correspond very closely to what we now know about the underlying biological dynamics of attention and memory, as well as of their interactions with one another.[14]

Indeed, we may go further. Our attention (and with it our emotional reactions) can be *modulated* by silence just as much as by sound. Hence the *arresting* quality of the silences in *Hereafter,* I suggest. Modulation of attentional processes, in turn, suggests the idea that silence itself can function as a signal, a mode of control available to the director that communicates his intentions toward us, his audience. Here it is relevant to remind the reader that the predicaments of Marie, George, and Marcus, the three main characters in our film and three of the characters most often involved in periods of silence, are fundamentally similar to one another. All three are involved in relational predicaments involving their isolation from other people and the affective consequences of that isolation. For Marcus, it is isolation from his dead twin, Jason, and the terrible anxiety this causes him. George is cut off from the possibility for a durable intimate relationship with a woman and lives with the very kind of black despair that Dickens records in the novel George listens to (*David Copperfield*). And Marie is unable, until she meets George, to find anyone who fully enters into the reality of her own near-death experience and her wonderment about the visions she had during that experience. Even her own lover, Didier (Thierry Neuvic), has abandoned her, at least in part due to her obsession with figuring out what it was that happened to her during the tsunami and what might be its ultimate significance.[15] These predicaments are all solved in the course of our film (marking it firmly as a romantic drama, as opposed to a tragic one): Marcus learns, with George's help, that he can in fact live successfully "on his own" without his twin. In learning this, Marcus also learns that he can live successfully without the daily presence of his mother, Jackie (Lyndsey Marshal), who is a drug addict and has been removed to a treatment facility. We see this latter effect late in the film when Marcus is reunited temporarily with Jackie. The whole scene reflects his advanced emotional maturity and independence. That new capacity for independent living is what makes his joyous reunion with Jackie possible. George and Marie link up with one another (an event itself signaled by a significant period of silence of my first type). And in doing so, they resolve each other's relational/affective predicaments. Our attention to major episodes of silence enhances our ability to give appropriate weight to these changes by way both of enhanced attention and memory for important elements of their respective stories.

It is a fundamental rule of good storytelling that one must "show, don't tell." And Eastwood himself has said, "The story is king."[16] That is, he conceives his own role as director and actor primarily in terms of communicating the story and not of talking about it. What I suggest here is that in a film like *Hereafter,* which is dominated by three individual stories that eventually converge into a single coherent narrative, this aspect of "show, don't tell" is partially constituted by the director's use of silence. It is not so much that he tells us the story by means of silence as that he orchestrates our attention to, our memory for, and our emotional responsiveness to that story by means of silence. There is thus between the director and his audience a communication by means of silence. Silence, of course, is not a visual phenomenon, so we need some new version of "show, don't tell" that can encompass such silent communications: perhaps "speak but do not utter." They may well be akin to communicative gestures, a capacity for which very likely underlies our linguistic abilities (both ontogenetically and phylogenetically) and which is available to our closest primate relative.[17] Gesture, of course, is also a quintessential part of any actor's repertoire of communicative devices. And this brings us close to one other possible determinant for Eastwood's masterful use of communicative silence in *Hereafter.*

Silence in Eastwood's Acting Style and Compositional Practice

Clint Eastwood has always been noted for his laconic style of acting. He regularly portrays men of few words. Indeed, in some films, as James R. Couch has shown elsewhere in this volume, it is his nonverbal communications that are among the most effective. And we know from scientific studies that the human brain is well-adapted to receive such communications, especially affectively charged nonverbal communications conveyed by facial expressions or whole-body language. The human face is the most expressive part of the human body, in emotional terms, notably the region around the eyes, followed by the region around the mouth. Eastwood has learned or intuited the value of these expressive instruments and makes full use of them in his acting. He has become an icon of the verbally terse and minimalist style of acting. The neural substrata for our ability to take in such forms of communication are now well understood. Moreover, we also know that facial expressions and whole-body emotional language apprehension is relatively fast (supported by perhaps the fastest-responding part of the limbic system, the amygdala, which can process stimuli presented for as little as twenty-six milliseconds), largely reliable, and enhanced by the use of gestures.[18] There is a further study to be made, in my view, of Eastwood's acting style in terms of a more detailed analysis of these nonverbal dynamics and use of multimodal systems of communication. For the present, however, it is enough to note that his laconic style is well-suited to the exploitation of silence for communicative purposes. As Norman Mailer noted in his 1983 interview with Eastwood, "He is one actor who can put his soul into his eyes."[19] But not only so. Eastwood also has been known to project his preference for verbally minimal acting onto the scripts he acts from. Mailer records this in terms of the following anecdote told by Eastwood himself:

> I always was a different kind of person, even when I started acting. I guess I finally got to a point where I had enough nerve to do nothing. . . . My first film with Sergio Leone had a script with tons of dialogue, tremendously expository, and I just cut it all down. Leone thought I was crazy. Italians are used to much more vocalizing, and

> I was playing this guy who didn't say much of anything. I cut it all down. Leone didn't speak any English so he didn't know what the hell I was doing, but he got so he liked it after a while.[20]

Such reduction of verbal content in the film script makes perfect sense, given that Eastwood himself prefers a verbally minimal style of acting. Both his acting style, then, and this quasi-directorial minimalizing of the script already suggest very strongly a predilection for silence in communication with his audience.

Another possible influential factor has to do with the importance to Eastwood of music (especially jazz), both as a musician himself and as a composer. Here is his own comment (with reference to his 2002 film *Blood Work*: "Composing, especially, is very important to me. *Blood Work,* I felt, needed a real subtle score. Oftentimes today, the musical scores are so overwhelming. The scores were so wall-to-wall. I love music. When used properly, it can be very effective. Also, the lack of music can be very effective. I did not want a real grandiose score in *Blood Work.* Some films can be musical without having any music at all—the silences, the sounds."[21] As I noted earlier in this essay, the music Eastwood composed for *Hereafter* is marked especially by initial simple melodic lines, usually played by a single instrument, and with plenty of rests or silent periods marking out the tonal shifts in the melodies. It is a common aspect of musical education and training that the hardest things to get right in playing, for example, a Mozart piano concerto or even the works of more contemporary composers such as Satie or Bartok, are the *rests.* Beginning musicians are prone to rush them, not giving them their full values. But without playing the rests appropriately, the rhythm and tonal dynamics of the music will be misconstrued. And then the overall emotional and imaginative impact of the music can be compromised or lost. Eastwood knows this especially from his experience as a jazz pianist. And his musical scores reflect the same conviction: silence can be as emotionally eloquent as sound, especially when silence punctuates sound and thus modulates our emotional responses to it. What he probably did not know is that this creative and artistic intuition has a sound footing in the neurobiology of human cognitive responses to silence and sound both.

One reason, then, why the neuroscience matters to our understanding of Eastwood's work is that it vindicates his artistic intuition. What I think we see in the directing work of his maturity is a capacity, among other things, to control the affective responses of his audience by means of very subtle effects, including those of silence. This almost certainly represents an extension of his personal preferences by means of the direction that he gives to his films, perhaps most clearly and forcefully in *Hereafter.*[22] But there are further reasons why the science might matter to our understanding of a film like this, and of Eastwood's work as a natural philosopher.

Neurocinematics and Practical Realism in *Hereafter*

I have tried to argue that Eastwood uses silence in *Hereafter* to orchestrate and direct the affective, attentional, and memory capacities of his audience in such a way as to complement the acting, plotting, and cinematography of his film. Moreover, I have tried to suggest that his practice in this regard has a solid footing in the neurobiology of the human brain and its cognitive processes with respect to sound and silence, as well as their affective accompaniments. One reason for exploring the brain science, then, is to vindicate his artistic intuition. But there are further reasons for bringing our scientific knowledge of human cognition to bear on film techniques of this kind. And these reasons might serve as a further answer to the perfectly pertinent and insightful question "Why does this matter?"

One such reason is that the neuroscience opens up for us a perspective on the dynamics of sound and silence that is common to the members of our species and not merely specific to a particular cultural setting. It is, of course, a truism that cultural variations can and commonly do affect our cognitive processes and may be reflected in them. But the fundamental dynamics of neural processing are common to all biologically intact adult members of our species. We do not expect to find fundamental variations in such processing as we move from human group to human group. Culture, in this respect, does not trump biology. (Of course, such claims, about the neural representation of silence in particular, are easily subjected to empirical testing across cultural lines. Every neuroscientist worth her salt would be happy to do so.) A closely related gain of coordinating the neurobiology of silence with the phenomenology of silence in a film like *Hereafter* is to help us avoid a merely subjective response to those dynamics. Here, viewer response comes into contact with a more objective basis for that response. Murray Smith has put the same point in a recent essay: "we are latching onto real features of the world—of the embodied agents we refer to as people or character—rather than projecting or imposing 'assorted contemporary Western ideas . . . onto the experience of others,' as Catherine Lutz would have it."[23] It is this element of realism that undergirds the universality of grounding filmmaking practices in biological processes.

There are many variants of realism in philosophical discourse, to be sure. Here I want to take advantage of what some have called "practical realism"—that is, the realism that is grounded in our successful explanatory practices, whether the practices of common sense or of the natural sciences. Earmarks of such practices are that they are susceptible to error. Without the possibility of making mistakes, we are almost certainly not functioning in an objective realm or manner. "In objective matters, one stands subject to correction . . . objectivity is closely connected to the possibility of error."[24] Scientific practices are, of course, fallible and thus revisable and replaceable. Accordingly, so are the ontological commitments of scientific explanatory practices. A further aspect of such practical realism is that scientific explanations are publicly accessible to any suitably qualified observer. The combination of these features determines, in my view, the primary epistemic value of such explanations (as also those of common sense). To the extent that Eastwood's use of silence in *Hereafter* can be grounded scientifically, thus far we have reason to think that both he and we, his critical audience, have fastened upon aspects of reality and are not merely making a heuristically valuable contribution to film criticism.

Smith's 2008 essay referred to above explores mainly issues having to do with emerging neuroscience of human emotions, and their relevance to film interpretation (in his case applied specifically to the German film cycle *Heimat* [Edgar Reitz, 1984, 1992, 2004]). The scientific grounding, in his view, "provides us with a keener understanding of what an emotion is, and allows us to propose critical descriptions and interpretations that are sensitive to features of the emotions of characters and spectators that might otherwise go unnoticed."[25] I hope to have done the same with regard to elements of affect, attention, and memory connected to the uses of silence in *Hereafter*. A further value of the neuroscience, then, is to focus our critical attention on aspects of filmmaking and film viewing that we might otherwise overlook.

Finally, I hope to have given sufficient grounds for suggesting direct scientific investigation into the effects of silence in films in the brains of their viewers. That is, we may here have the basis for a new area of exploration in the emerging field of "neurocinematics." Here the work of Uri Hasson and his colleagues is of particular importance. Hasson has developed techniques for scanning simultaneously the brains of several viewers while they are watching films. He has used recent popular films, in particular, for this purpose (including *The Good, the Bad, and the Ugly*). He has thereby been able to show that viewers coordinate their neural responses to films, including visual scene analysis, with one another, such "inter-subject correlation analysis" generating a dynamic (and publicly accessible) view of how an audience interacts with the film at a neural level.[26] Hasson's team has also thereby demonstrated how the neural activity of film viewers is a function of film content, editing, and directing. My proposal here is that these techniques be adopted for similar empirical exploration of inter-subjective neural responses to silence in films. Related aspects of attention-shifting, visual scene analysis, and memory (including prospective memory) might be explored by means of similar techniques. Affective responses in all these areas could also be explored in an inter-subjective way, by means of physiological correlatives of stress (including heart rhythms, skin conductance, cortisol-generation), which belong to the autonomic nervous system, especially the parasympathetic branch of it. Correlative biochemistry of neurotransmitters, such as dopamine, norepinephrine, oxytocin, vasopressin, serotonin, and the like, could also be drawn into this project. In sum, there is nothing standing in the way of a full-fledged scientific program investigating further the objective correlatives of the psychological phenomena surrounding film silence. My prediction is that once that program reaches maturity, it will only further vindicate the native genius and practical realism of Clint Eastwood.

Notes

1. See blurb at Netflix: https://movies.netflix.com/WiMovie/Hereafter/70134615?locale=en-US. For "supernatural drama," see http://en.wikipedia.org/wiki/Hereafter_(film)/.

2. The salient real-world event reflected here is the tsunami that struck Indonesia and other areas of the region on December 26, 2004, killing over 160,000 people and leaving nearly 200,000 homeless. For a study of psychological resilience in children who survived the tsunami see Y. Hestyanti, "Children Survivors of the 2004 Tsunami in Ache, Indonesia," *Annals of the New York Academy of Sciences* 1094 (2006): 303–307. The issue of resilience and its significance for Eastwood's films will be treated at greater length in my other essay in this volume.

3. The emotional expressiveness of the whole human body is the subject of research by Beatrice de Gelder and her colleagues in the Netherlands: see, for example, B. de Gelder et al., "Standing Up for the Body: Recent Progress in Uncovering the Networks Involved in the Perception of Bodies and Bodily Expressions," *Neuroscience and BioBe-*

havioral Reviews 34 (2010): 513–527; and C. Sinke, M. Kret, and B. de Gelder, "Body Language: Embodied Perception of Emotion," in *Measurement with Persons: Theory, Methods and Implementation Areas,* ed. B. Berglund, G. Rossi, J. Townsend, and L. Pendrill (New York: Psychological Press, 2012), 335–352. For discussion of the neural regions (especially the amygdala and the insular cortex) and processing times involved, see R. McClelland, "A Naturalistic View of Human Dignity," *Journal of Mind and Behavior* 32 (2011): 24–29.

4. The issue of silence in Eastwood's music is a further and distinctive explanatory factor here, in my view. However, I am not competent to pursue the matter. It is only one aspect of Eastwood's musicianship that we regret not being able to treat in greater detail in this volume.

5. B. Scholl, X. Gao, and M. Wehr, "Non-Overlapping Sets of Synapses Drive On Responses and Off Responses in Auditory Cortex," *Neuron* 65 (2010): 412–421. Compare also K. Yasmashiro et al., "Automatic Auditory Off-Response in Humans: An MEG Study," *European Journal of Neuroscience* 30 (2009): 125–131; and K. Yamashiro, K. Inui, N. Otsuru, and R. Kakigi, "Change-Related Responses in the Human Auditory Cortex: An MEG Study," *Psychophysiology* 48 (2011): 23–30.

6. M. Hunter et al., "Neural Activity in Speech-Sensitive Auditory Cortex During Silence," *Proceedings of the National Academy of Sciences* 103 (2006): 189–194.

7. J. Voisin, A. Bidet-Caulet, O. Bertrand, and P. Fonlupt, "Listening in Silence Activates Auditory Areas: A Functional Magnetic Resonance Imaging Study," *Journal of Neuroscience* 26 (2006): 273–278.

8. D. Kramer, C. Macrae, A. Green, and W. Kelley, "Sound of Silence Activates Auditory Cortex," *Nature* 434 (2005): 158. For related phenomena in the primary visual cortex, and with related dynamics, wholly in the absence of visual stimulus, see K. Wang et al., "Spontaneous Activity Associated with Primary Visual Cortex: A Resting-State fMRI Study," *Cerebral Cortex* 18 (2008): 697–704. Hunter et al., "Neural Activity," suggest that such spontaneous activation of the auditory cortex may underlie the widespread experience among humans of auditory hallucinations.

9. Wang et al., "Spontaneous Activity," 702.

10. M. van Schouwenburg, H. den Ouden, and R. Cools, "The Human Basal Ganglia Modulate Frontal-Posterior Connectivity During Attention Shifting," *Journal of Neuroscience* 30 (2010): 9910–9918, here page 9916. For the role of the insular cortex and anterior cingulate cortex in salience detection, see V. Menon and L. Uddin, "Saliency, Switching, Attention and Control: A Network Model of Insula Function," *Brain Structure and Function* 214 (2010): 655–667; N. Medford and H. Critchley, "Conjoint Activity of Anterior Insular and Anterior Cingulate Cortex: Awareness and Response," *Brain Structure and Function* 214 (2010): 535–549; and M. Brass and P. Haggard, "The Hidden Side of Intentional Action: The Role of the Anterior Insular Cortex," *Brain Structure and Function* 214 (2010): 603–610. For neurotransmitters in these phenomena, see D. Tomasi et al., "Dopamine Transporters in Striatum Correlate with Deactivation in the

Default Mode Network During Visuospatial Attention," *PLOS One* 4 (2009): e6102; and S. Kähkönen et al., "Dopamine Modulates Involuntary Attention Shifting and Reorienting: An Electromagnetic Study," *Clinical Neurophysiology* 113 (2002): 1894–1902. The role of oxytocin is discussed in M. Ellenbogen et al., "The Acute Effects of Intranasal Oxytocin on Automatic and Effortful Attentional Shifting to Emotional Faces," *Psychophysiology* 49 (2012): 128–137. For dissociability of attention elements, see R. Cools, R. Ivry and M. D'Esposito, "The Human Striatum Is Necessary for Responding to Changes in Stimulus Relevance," *Journal of Cognitive Neuroscience* 18 (2006): 1973–1983; F. Mottaghy et al., "Systems Level Modeling of a Neuronal Network Subserving Intrinsic Alertness," *NeuroImage* 29 (2006): 225–233; C. Thiel, K. Zilles, and G. Fink, "Cerebral Correlates of Alerting, Orienting and Reorienting of Visuospatial Attention: An Event-Related fMRI Study," *NeuroImage* 21 (2004): 318–328.

11. Makers of thrillers and horror films may intuit this, often marking significant events by brief episodes of anticipatory silence. I owe this observation to Brian Clayton.

12. S. Majerus et al., "Attention Supports Verbal Short-Term Memory via Competition Between Dorsal and Ventral Attention Networks," *Cerebral Cortex* 22 (2012): 1086–1097. Compare also N. Cowan, "The Focus of Attention as Observed in Visual Working Memory Tasks: Making Sense of Competing Claims," *Neurophysiologia* 49 (2011): 1401–1406; and T. Kelley and N. Lavie, "Working Memory Load Modulates Distractor Competition in Primary Visual Cortex," *Cerebral Cortex* 21 (2011): 659–665.

13. E. Awh and J. Jonides, "Overlapping Mechanisms of Attention and Spatial Working Memory," *Trends in Cognitive Sciences* 5 (2001): 119–126; B. Postle et al., "The Where and How of Attention-Based Rehearsal in Spatial Working Memory," *Cognitive Brain Research* 20 (2004): 194–205; E. Awh, E. Vogel, and S.-H. Oh, "Interactions Between Attention and Working Memory," *Neuroscience* 139 (2006): 201–208; G. Woodman and S. Luck, "Visual Search Is Slowed When Visuospatial Working Memory Is Occupied," *Psychonomic Bulletin and Review* 11 (2004): 269–274. For limits on the capacity of working memory, see E. Ester et al., "Neural Measures Reveal a Fixed Limit in Subitizing," *Journal of Neuroscience* 32 (2012): 7169–7177. And for genetic factors that may influence storage capacity of short-term memory, see D. Anderson, T. Bell, and E. Awh, "Polymorphisms in the 5-HTTLPR Gene Mediate Storage Capacity of Visual Working Memory," *Journal of Cognitive Neuroscience* 24 (2012): 1069–1076. It is really not possible for humans to detect changes in something like a film image without using their short-term memory to do so: K. Inui et al., "Non-Linear Laws of Echoic Memory and Auditory Change Detection in Humans," *BMC Neuroscience* 11 (2010): 80.

14. There is here a whole area suitable for "neurocinematic" investigation which, so far as I can tell, has not yet been broached. The way forward, scientifically, may be laid down in R. Benoit et al., "Rostral Prefrontal Cortex and the Focus of Attention in Prospective Memory," *Cerebral Cortex* 22 (2012): 1876–1886.

15. Marie finds some relief by writing her book and presenting it at the London Book Fair, where evidently it receives a warm welcome, judging from the number of people

who buy copies and ask her to sign them. It is ironic, then, that George contacts Marie after his brief encounter with her at the book fair by means of a hand-written letter (the contents of which we do not learn). But these writing episodes are no substitute for real, warm, human relationships. Marcus meets George at the book fair, also; thus *writing* serves to mediate all these contacts and the solutions they afford.

16. D. Byrge, "Dialogue with Clint Eastwood," August 14, 2002 (with specific reference to the film *Blood Work*), http://business.highbeam.com/2012/article-1G1-90305622/dialogue-clint-eastwood. The interview was originally made for and reported in the August 2, 2002, *Hollywood Reporter.*

17. For a neurobiological perspective, see E. Bates and F. Dick, "Language, Gesture, and the Developing Brain," *Developmental Psychology* 40 (2002): 293–310; R. Willems and P. Hagoort, "Neural Evidence for the Interplay Between Language, Gesture, and Action: A Review," *Brain and Language* 101 (2007): 278–289. For the developmental perspective, see S. Özçalişkan and S. Goldin-Meadow, "Gesture Is at the Cutting Edge of Early Language Development," *Cognition* 96 (2005): B101–B113; J. Iverson and S. Goldin-Meadow, "Gesture Paves the Way for Language Development," *Psychological Science* 16 (2005): 367–371. And for communicative gesturing among chimpanzees, see A. Halloran, *The Song of the Ape: Understanding the Languages of Chimpanzees* (New York: St. Martin's Press, 2012). See also S. Goldin-Meadow, *Hearing Gesture: How Our Hands Help Us Think* (Cambridge, Mass.: Harvard University Press, 2003).

18. For some recent studies and reviews of these phenomena, see D. Sander et al., "Interaction Effects of Perceived Gaze Direction and Dynamic Facial Expression: Evidence for Appraisal Theories of Emotion," *European Journal of Cognitive Psychology* 19 (2007): 470–480; P. Vuilleumier and G. Pourtois, "Distributed and Interactive Brain Mechanisms During Emotion Face Perception: Evidence from Functional Neuroimaging," *Neuropsychologia* 45 (2007): 174–194. The early ontogeny of this ability in human infants is reviewed in T. Grossman, "The Development of Emotion Perception in Face and Voice During Infancy," *Restorative Neurology and Neuroscience* 28 (2010): 219–236. Unfortunately, Grossman's otherwise admirable study is marred by ignoring the work of A. N. Meltzoff and others on "cross-modal perception" in infants, which is almost certainly an innate cognitive capacity: see discussion in R. McClelland, "Autistic Space," *Psychoanalysis and Contemporary Thought* 16 (1993): 197–232. The importance of attention in these processes is considerable, and qualifies what is otherwise a largely automatic process: see L. Pessoa et al., "Neural Processing of Emotional Faces Requires Attention," *Proceedings of the National Academy of Sciences* 99 (2002): 11458–11463; A. Holmes, P. Vuilleumier, and M. Eimer, "The Processing of Emotional Facial Expression Is Gated by Spatial Attention: Evidence from Event-Related Brain Potentials," *Cognitive Brain Research* 16 (2003): 174–184; and L. Pessoa, "To What Extent Are Emotional Visual Stimuli Processed Without Attention and Awareness?," *Current Opinion in Neurobiology* 15 (2005): 188–196. The vital role of the amygdala in such emotional facial processing is revealed especially by lesion studies: see P. Vuilleumier et al., "Distant Influences of

Amygdala Lesion on Visual Cortical Activation During Emotional Face Processing," *Nature Neuroscience* 7 (2004): 1271–1278. Some genetic determinants are discussed in A. Brown et al., "Genetic Variants Affecting the Neural Processing of Human Facial Expressions: Evidence Using a Genome-Wide Functional Imaging Approach," *Translational Psychiatry* 2 (2012): e143, July 24, 2012, http://www.nature.com/tp/journal/v2/n7/full/tp201267a.html.

19. N. Mailer, "All the Pirates and People," *Parade Magazine,* October 23, 1983, 4–7, quotation from page 6.

20. Eastwood quoted in ibid., 6.

21. D. Byrge, "Dialogue with Clint Eastwood," August 14, 2002, http://business.highbeam.com/2012/article-1G1-90305622/dialogue-clint-eastwood.

22. Such effects are not limited to *Hereafter.* The emotionally climactic scene in *The Bridges of Madison County* (1995) involves Eastwood standing in the pouring rain, utterly silent but eloquently communicating by his whole bodily expression the despair and longing that his character feels. There is a wider study than the present one to be made of Eastwood's silences. There is likewise a further study to be made of his use and treatment of despair.

23. M. Smith, "What Difference Does It Make? Science, Sentiment, and Film," *Projections* 2 (2008): 60–77, here page 75. The focus on realism is, in my view, one of the most valuable aspects of this essay.

24. L. Baker, *Explaining Attitudes: A Practical Approach to the Mind* (Cambridge, U.K.: Cambridge Univ. Press, 1995), 233.

25. Smith, "What Difference Does It Make?," 75.

26. U. Hasson, R. Malach, and D. Heeger, "Reliability of Cortical Activity During Natural Stimulation," *Trends in Cognitive Sciences* 14 (2010): 40–48; U. Hasson et al., "Neurocinematics: The Neuroscience of Film," *Projections* 2 (2008): 1–26; and compare J. Cutting, J. DeLong, and C. Nothelfer, "Attention and the Evolution of Hollywood Film," *Psychological Science* 21 (2010): 432–439. It is a further matter to try to discover how very subtle interactions between film viewers themselves might affect the quality of the filmic experience for viewers.

The Mortal Hero

Two Inductions on the Meaning of Loss

Richard T. McClelland

The Buddha is reputed to have said that "all life is suffering," or perhaps that "the meaning of life is suffering." And there is little doubt that he was largely correct, for it is difficult to even imagine a realistic form of human life that does not entail some degree and kind of suffering. And, of course, for many of us, life has been or is likely to be filled with suffering.[1] The vast majority of humans who have ever lived have probably suffered more or less continuously throughout their lives in one form or another: hunger, cold, anxiety, disease, pain, loss. To be well-fed, securely housed, meaningfully employed, financially viable, socially well-supported, psychologically intact, and free of major diseases, while all highly desirable states and often considered the birthright of the affluent West, are the reliable possessions of only a fortunate few, at least from the point of view of our whole global species and its whole history. Most humans currently alive on the planet live in poverty, with high incidence of disease, shortened life spans (relative to the affluent industrial and postindustrial societies), and often with blighted prospects as regards education, employment, and the rest. Historically, human life for most of us has been lived on the margin, with average life expectancies exceeding forty years only in very modern times and in a limited range of modern cultures. Thus, for us humans a fundamental developmental task is to come to terms with our suffering. And the longer we survive the more urgent this task becomes, for the more evident it also becomes that suffering is our lot and cannot finally be avoided altogether, no matter how affluent we become individually or socially. One of the durable attractions of religion is its provision of transcendental varieties of meaning for suffering (an issue that will concern me further in the final section of this essay). It is a rare adult who has not suffered substantially and who does not feel the need for such meaning. Indeed, it is a rare child over the age of five years who is not similarly situated. For many adults, these issues are especially pressing after midlife. For by then we often know perfectly well that our bodies are failing us and that their dissolution is our ultimate fate (whatever, if anything, might come afterward). It seems to me that Eastwood meditates on this problem of the meaning of suffering in a variety of his films, especially those in which he has acted or which he has directed after he himself turned forty. Moreover, as he has passed through his forties, fifties, sixties, and seventies the meditation has grown more profound and perhaps more urgent. However, the results of this meditation are surprising, as I hope to show.

The Pessimistic Induction: Loss (and Death) Is Finally Irremediable

As early as *The Eiger Sanction* (1975), Eastwood plays a character (Dr. Jonathan Hemlock) who is starting to feel the ravages of age. Having laid off from mountain climbing for some time, Hemlock knows that his new undercover assignment to the team planning to climb the North Face of the Eiger (which has defeated him twice in the past) cannot succeed without a good deal of training and preparation. He has indeed "lost a step" or two, and so partners with his old climbing buddy Ben Bowman (George Kennedy) for that training. Eastwood himself, in real life, was just past his forty-fourth birthday when the filming was done and is reputed to have performed his own stunts. It is a rare adult male, even one as fit and athletic as Eastwood, who is not feeling his body starting to fail him by the time he reaches the mid-forties, so the dramatic situation of the character is curiously appropriate to the real-life situation of the actor.

The figure of the man of action in retirement reappears in *Firefox* (1982), a film directed by Eastwood. Major Mitchell Gant (USAF, retired) was a fighter pilot in Vietnam, where he was captured and where he witnessed the immolation of an entirely innocent young girl, images of which reoccur in his later flashbacks. Coerced by the government into a high-risk operation to steal a high-tech Russian fighter (a MiG-31, known as the Firefox), Gant undergoes appropriate retraining to fit him for his new role as spy and technological thief. As we expect, all of this succeeds wildly. But what is of interest here is the whole idea of retirement from the life of action, the inevitable slowing of reflexes and the loss of agility and strength that comes with such retirement and aging. Moreover, we have the new addition of psychological loss in the form of Gant's post-traumatic stress disorder, which almost debilitates him at vital moments during his training and mission. Here Eastwood plays a man who has not only suffered in the past, but whose suffering from that period has lasting effects into the present. Neither of these films is especially well-made, but both introduce us to a theme that will loom larger in Eastwood's later work: the aging hero who carries a variety of scars, physical and mental, mementoes of past and present losses, and who must compensate for those losses at the risk of losing his life absolutely.[2] Fast forward a further decade and we find the same theme writ larger, but with a twist.

In *Unforgiven* (1992), Eastwood both directs and acts. Here he is William Munny, once one of the most feared gunmen in the West, but when the film opens he is trying to farm and raise the two children left to him by his recently deceased wife (a victim of smallpox two years previous). Also coerced (by the promise of money, which he desperately needs) out of his "retirement," Munny shows us unmistakably that he has lost his gunfighting skills. Moreover, as the film advances, he does not get any better until fueled by both rage (over the torture death of his friend Ned Logan [Morgan Freeman]) and drink, when he reverts to the old Munny and slaughters his enemies ruthlessly and even wantonly, as he had done of old. The film is redolent of irredeemable losses. The prostitute Delilah (Anna Levine) is severely disfigured by Quick Mike (David Mucci), whose sexual adequacy she has insulted. Her knife cuts heal in due course, but leave her scarred and, in her own view, unattractive to men (a premise she tries out on Munny himself). Ned Logan is killed miserably, and this death cannot be redeemed even by Munny's successful revenge. Similarly, the evil sheriff "Little Bill" Daggett (Gene Hackman) suffers a squalid death at the hands of Munny. English Bob (Richard Harris) has been severely beaten by Daggett earlier in the film, and run out of town, his reputation in tatters and probably unrecoverable. The Schofield Kid (Jaimz Woolvett) belatedly comes to learn that killing is nothing like so easy as he had fantasized it to be, and is shattered psychologically by his one genuine act of killing (of a man helplessly sitting in an outhouse).[3] It is a great irony of the Kid's situation that not only has he never previously killed anyone, but that he is so short-sighted that he can only kill a man who is sitting perfectly still, who is unable to fire back, and to whom he can get close enough to see. The Kid thus proves to be short-sighted in more than one sense. Davey Bunting (Rob Campbell) we see die painfully and slowly from a rifle wound to the gut, giving the lie to every bland Hollywood Western death by gunfire in which the victim merely drops silently to the ground and is instantly and painlessly killed. Everywhere in this film there are losses, and many of those losses cannot be fully compensated for. In the case of the central character, Munny, it is clear that his losses are mainly due to the passage of time, which has also brought him a family and the enduring moral influence of his dead wife. Repeatedly he tells others that he is no longer the same man he once was. It is notable that Eastwood himself has said that he started thinking about making this film as early as 1976, but delayed until he would himself be old enough to play this character in a convincing fashion.[4] We get a strong hint at the end of the film that Munny's later life was more successful than what we have seen up to now (in other words, up to 1880), but it is only a hint and we are not shown how things turned out for him or for his children (a trope we will see again). Thus, whether or not Munny is able to compensate for the losses occurring during this period of his life remains unknown to us.

By the time Eastwood made *In the Line of Fire* (1993) he was well into his sixties. And despite his athleticism he was evidently feeling the press of time. Here again we find his character (Frank Horrigan) aging, others noting that he is the only active Secret Service agent remaining from the team that guarded President Kennedy in Dallas in 1963. Like Major Gant, Horrigan is haunted by a traumatic past in which he failed (as he sees it) in his duty to protect President John Kennedy from assassination. In one very moving scene, he stands in the window of the current president's hotel suite with his Secret Service partner Lilly Raines (Rene Russo) holding his hand while he weeps over the memory of that failure and loss. It is this past loss that has driven him to return to "standing post" to protect the president rather than continue in his more prosaic (but, as we see, nonetheless very dangerous) duties tracking down counterfeiters (also a vital task of the real Secret Service, which is a branch of the Treasury Department). The first time Horrigan has to keep pace with the president's limousine, however, we see just how out of shape he is and how much his advancing age has taken out of him physically. His fellow agents also play an elaborate practical joke on him, following this episode, pretending that a nap he takes in an office chair is the scene of a heart attack (even the paramedics are in on it). This whole subject is underscored by the fate of Horrigan's young partner, Al D'Andrea (Dylan McDermott), who is profoundly disturbed by his brush with death at the hands of those counterfeiters (enough to tender his resignation from the Service), and who is finally killed by Mitch Leary (John Malkovich), who, however, saves Horrigan's life in the same protracted chase sequence, only to torment him repeatedly on the telephone and about the Kennedy assassination in particular. At another point in the film, Horrigan's boss, Sam Campagna (John Mahoney), tells him, "You're too old for this shit." The film ends happily for Horrigan (and his unnamed president, played by Jim Curley), but with him actually retiring from the Service. He has successfully "taken a bullet" for the president and defeated Leary, thereby exorcizing his main demons from the past. But he cannot simply undo the past. Rather, he must come to terms with it, accepting its losses and their enduring effects, even those that are most unjust and undeserving.

Blood Work (2002) is also the product of both Eastwood's acting and directing. His character (Terry McCaleb) is once again the retired man of action, this time a former FBI agent and profiler who has been forced to retire because of a heart condition that almost kills him and requires a heart transplant to alleviate. We eventually see the long and robust scar that marks the sight of his open-chest surgery for the transplant. His condition is marginal throughout the film, and much is made of the fact that he is not supposed to drive (lest a deployed airbag strike him in the chest and kill him), and he risks infection due to over-fatigue when he starts investigating the murder of his transplant donor. All this is indicative of losses that must be compensated for but cannot be wholly erased or remedied. The other main characters, notably Graciella Rivers (Tina Lifford) and her nephew Raymond Torres (Mason Lucero) have also been scarred by the murder of Graciella's sister, whose heart McCaleb has. The whole idea is that he is able to live only because she has died (murdered, as we eventually learn, by Jasper Noone [Jeff Daniels], whose crimes are ultimately aimed at getting McCaleb to renew his hunt for the "Code" killer, a hunt interrupted by that earlier and nearly fatal heart attack). Raymond is a particularly interesting character, and one we will follow further later on.[5] But all the grievous losses in this film prove to be irreversible, though their final meaning is more plastic than one might expect.

This film was made in the spring of 2002 (released in December), when Eastwood himself was already seventy-two years old. He says of it in an interview: "At this particular stage of my maturity, I felt it was time to take on characters that have different obstacles to face than they would if I were playing a younger man of 30 or 40."[6] The statement is not a little disingenuous, as the really relevant contrast is not with a man of thirty or forty, but with a man of fifty or sixty (though any adult male envies Eastwood the physical condition he has apparently maintained in his eighth and ninth decades). Like some other leading male actors (for example, Robert De Niro, Sean Connery, Michael Caine, Jack Nicholson), Eastwood is aging very gracefully and powerfully. But he is aging nonetheless. And with age comes loss, and some losses cannot be compensated for, as aging adult humans often have to recognize. Indeed, this is the main aspect of their respective characters that binds Graciella Rivers and Terry McCaleb (and perhaps Raymond Torres) so closely together: shared and irremediable loss.[7] A decade further along, we see the irremediable character of some losses emphasized in Eastwood films even more strongly and characters who have been correspondingly more gravely damaged by those losses.

Eastwood directs but does not act in *Mystic River* (2003). Central to the story is the murder of young Katie Markum (Emmy Rossum). Revenge for her death becomes the all-consuming passion of her father, Jimmy Markum (Sean Penn). In the end, his "revenge" is visited on the wrong person, though the real killer is eventually caught by Jimmy's boyhood pal Sean Devine (Kevin Bacon), who has become a police detective in his adulthood. Jimmy and Sean had another boyhood friend, Dave Boyle (Tim Robbins), who was the victim of two pedophiles who kidnapped him and raped him repeatedly. The long shadow cast by this crime eventually falls on Dave himself as an adult, playing a key role in what leads to his false confession to Jimmy for having killed Katie. Even Dave's wife, Celeste (Marcia Gay Harden), is persuaded of his guilt, and Jimmy kills him in retaliation, only later to discover his error. The two pedophiles (who imitate police officers, kidnapping Dave under the pretense of arresting him for a minor bit of vandalism) are, so far as we learn, never caught and never punished. The innocents (Katie, Dave) are damaged permanently, and some of the guilty, at least, go free. Jimmy himself, despite his fatal error regarding Dave's guilt, is supported by his wife, Annabeth (Laura Linney), and remains, at the end of the film, unrepentant (though abashed) and a powerfully influential man in his neighborhood (an influence earned by his own earlier criminality and violence). One comes away from the film with a profound sense of loss and of the tragedy that plays out for Dave Boyle, in part because of the very psychological and cognitive damage that was done to him as a child. Indeed, we watch the intersections and collisions of past and present, character with character, social class with social class, like watching a complex series of slow train wrecks or the carefully orchestrated stages of an ancient Greek tragedy. Tragedies depend upon irreparable losses and our usually vain efforts to repair or prevent them. The same is true in this film. The precipitating event, the killing of Katie Markum, itself is almost random, depending as it does on her encounter with two other young boys and the oddities of her car. Her killer is Silent Ray Harris (Spencer Treat Clark), whose older brother Brendan (Tom Guiry) is in love with Katie and planning to elope with her. The Harris family thinks that their father abandoned them fourteen years earlier, but actually Jimmy Markum had killed him. Secretly, Markum sends $500 a month to the Harris family to compensate for his crime. Thus, layer after layer of loss, revenge, and violence are laid down and revealed to us as the film progresses. Katie's death is thus far from meaningless or pointless. On the contrary, its meaning is deeply written into the personalities that we meet and that have been shaped by their own shared and private pasts, including past traumas and losses. If anything, her death carries almost more meaning than the film can bear. Puzzles and mysteries connected with these interwoven losses are resolved, but the losses themselves only go on, causing pain and suffering for all the main characters in the film. In the next two films things get even more intense.

Eastwood both acted in and directed *Million Dollar Baby* (2004). He plays Frankie Dunn, who operates a gym devoted to training boxers, and he himself is an experienced and skilled trainer. When he finally becomes willing to do so, he trains Maggie Fitzgerald (Hilary Swank) and becomes her boxing mentor. Dunn is another wounded man of action, suffering from an on-going rupture in his relationship with his daughter, Kate, who returns his letters unopened. It is clear that he craves her forgiveness for some unspecified offenses in the distant past, but is unable to secure it. He is also weighed down by the way in which the boxing career of his friend Eddie "Scrap-Iron" Dupris (Morgan Freeman) ended. Allowing Scrap to fight one too many fights (his 109th), the result is a severe injury that effectively blinds Scrap in one eye and terminates his boxing career. Scrap lives at the gym and helps to run it. The two men have a relationship that is affectionate but also cantankerous. Frankie bears a considerable load of guilt with respect to Scrap's career, and this almost certainly conditions Frankie's reluctance to let Maggie push forward in her boxing career as rapidly as she wants. Failing to maintain Frankie's ironclad rule (the boxer must protect him or herself at all times in the ring), Maggie gets punched from behind by one of her opponents (who is losing the match and hits Maggie after the bell has rung) and crashes onto the stool that Frankie has in her corner, breaking her neck and paralyzing her from the neck down. The drama of Maggie's acceptance by Frankie as a real boxer is replaced by the drama of Maggie's desire to die and her repeated attempts to kill herself, given that she cannot tolerate her condition (exacerbated in due course by the amputation of one leg). Frankie is deeply unwilling to help her die, despite her request for assistance, and only acquiesces, in the end, in deep and bitter anguish. The issues (some of them discussed elsewhere in this volume) surrounding Maggie's assisted suicide are powerfully presented through the clashing emotions felt by herself and Frankie, and also through a very frank conversation he has with Father Horvath (Brían O'Byrne). After administering the fatal dose of adrenaline, Frankie disappears from our ken, though there is some reason to think that he has simply abandoned his gym and bought a diner that he and Maggie are seen in earlier in the film. There is much to explore in this film, not least failed family dynamics (itself a persistent theme in Eastwood's work, and one worthy of a separate investigation, especially in the light of his own complex web of partnerships and parenting). But here I emphasize just one prominent element of the film: irreversible and irremediable loss.

Maggie's injury ends all prospects of a continued boxing career, the thing she has desired passionately for many years, has worked amazingly hard to achieve, and has triumphed in only recently. She herself comes to regard her situation as intolerable. And she finally persuades Frankie that it really is intolerable. Her loss is far greater than the parallel losses of Scrap and Frankie himself, but those lesser losses prepared us for the greater one. Maggie's life, from her point of view, is effectively over, and holds no further prospects that she can value. In this light, ending her life is entirely intelligible, even though she is not, strictly speaking, in a terminal condition. Indeed, others have managed to live full and meaningful lives with injuries very similar to Maggie's. But the point in this film is that such is not a possible future that has any value for this character. Frankie's empathic connection with Maggie, as well as those past sins that haunt him, finally drive him to assist her to die. That is, he solves more than one problem by his action, giving Maggie what she now passionately desires, and also atoning for his past offenses against Kate and Scrap. He also (probably) brings his own involvement with boxing to an end in a way compatible with the best elements of his character: his honesty, directness, and compassion. Indeed, it is finally his own character (in the moral sense) and his deep emotional bond with Maggie that determines his actions. Given her request, her implacable will, her situation, and her repeated attempts to kill herself, no other action is really open to him. But we are also in no doubt that killing Maggie wounds Frankie Dunn deeply, certainly because he loses her thereby, but also because he acts against other elements of his conscience (his action is thus to some extent self-sacrificial). There is thus plenty of loss to go around, and those losses are irremediable.

The equifinality of a self-sacrificial action by a leading character is the same pattern that we find in *Gran Torino* (2008). Eastwood directs and also plays the central character, Walt Kowalski, a retired autoworker living in a Detroit neighborhood (Highland Park). Walt is also a man of action wounded by losses near and distant in time. His wife of many years has just died, as the film opens with her funeral (and will close with his). He is estranged from his two sons, Mitch (Brian Haley) and Steve (Brian Howe)—estrangement is almost a fixed feature in the dramatic landscape of Eastwood's most recent films. He also suffers from a tremendous sense of guilt over a killing he committed while serving in the U.S. Army in Korea. As we get to know Walt, we also discover that he is suffering from some very serious disease (perhaps lung cancer, as he is a regular smoker), coughing up blood repeatedly and passing out in his garage on one occasion. The suggestion, at least, is that his condition is terminal. Much of the action of this film is discussed in detail elsewhere in this volume. Here I want only to focus on the equifinality of Walt's sacrificial death late in the film. He arranges for that death himself, though it is at the hands of the Hmong gang whose depredations in his neighborhood he is out to frustrate and remedy. This death, by gunfire, achieves an array of goals. Because of his clever entrapment of his young protégé, Thao Lor (Bee Vang), he also manages to avenge the offenses that the gang has already committed against both Thao and his sister Sue (Ahney Her). Simultaneously, he remedies the whole neighborhood's problem of this pestilential gang. He also achieves an autonomous death for himself, thereby solving the problem posed by his disease while upholding one of his most important values. By means of his will, the provisions of which are enacted because of his death, Walt also frustrates the greedy aims of his own children and makes provision for the ongoing care of his dog, Daisy, and both ironic and vengeful disposition of his own property, notably the bequest of his beloved Gran Torino automobile to Thao himself. The slow smile that appears on Thao's face as the will is read is rich indeed, and will be shared by most film viewers. The closing sequence, of Thao driving the Gran Torino with Daisy seated beside him along the shore of Lake St. Clair, carries with it a sense of completion and satisfaction that mirrors our own sense of satisfaction in the final outcome of the film. That satisfaction hinges on our sense that Walt's death, and all that leads up to it, not only solves an array of problems all at once, but also indicates one way in which the loss that is death can be given meaning: by making that death serve the real needs of others and also making it an act of autonomy. It remains the case, however, that the losses are real and, though meaningful, are finally irremediable.

My claim, then, is this: in these films Eastwood lays the groundwork for a pessimistic induction on the meaning of loss, and especially the meaning of death. What we see in these films is that some losses cannot be remediated, some wounds cannot be healed, and some damaged relationships cannot be restored. Similarly, some actions by key characters wound the very actors themselves, and wound them irremediably. It is rather like watching the tide go out: waves keep coming in and in, but slowly and inexorably the tide nonetheless goes out. Multiplication of such patterns of events, whether in the characters of these films or in the lives of their viewers, leads to this conclusion with regard to our greatest loss: death is probably itself an irremediable loss. Having said this, there is another dynamic to be found in these films. To consider it in all its richness requires first, however, an exploration of the concept of psychological resilience in the face of traumatic experience.

Interlude: Resilience in Contemporary Scientific Perspective

I began this essay with some very general remarks, even commonplace statements, regarding the prevalence of suffering in human affairs. And it is true that most human lives are marked by various kinds of suffering and the losses that they entail. Moreover, we know that traumatic loss can leave indelible scars and debilities in the sufferers. There are also many forms of suffering that simply result in mental and/or physiological death of the organism. And, finally, all of us will die. It remains the case, however, that humans are also remarkably resilient in their responses to even traumatic injury or loss. Indeed, there is in the human species a truly astonishing capacity for such resilience, such that almost any form of human suffering has been made good use of by someone. This matter of psychological resilience, especially, has become the target of concerted scientific investigation in recent decades. The scientific literature is now vast and only a few parts of it will be noted below. But the notion of resilience is also present, in my view, in Eastwood's films, including those considered in the previous section. The scientific work can help us to focus more clearly than we otherwise would be able to do on the earmarks of resilience that appear in these films. As I hope to show, Eastwood has intuited some very important aspects of resilience as a natural phenomenon. Major characteristics of that phenomenon follow.

Several researchers have stressed that resilience is itself far more common than we used to think. George Bonanno, for example, has argued that in most cases of even traumatic events (for example, terrorist attacks, criminal assaults, and the like) about 50 percent of victims are likely to respond resiliently to those events. Even children exposed to traumatic events prove to be resilient in a high percentage of cases. Such resilience does not mean that the individuals do not suffer, but rather that they are able to cope with the events in such a way as to recover their ability to function normally and usually within a reasonably short period of time. So marked is this capacity that some researchers have taken to referring to adverse events as "potentially traumatic events" (PTEs). Moreover, such a capacity for resilient coping is not due to exceptional qualities of the individual personality. It is also true, of course, that a substantial percentage of groups exposed to potentially traumatic events respond with various forms of pathological functioning, up to and including PTSD (in some populations and in some cases as much as one-third of samples). But most victims prove to be resilient. Speaking, then, of PTEs, Bonanno concludes: "There is now compelling evidence . . . that genuine resilience to PTE's is not rare but common and not a sign of exceptional strength or psychopathology but rather a fundamental feature of normal coping skills. Moreover, several studies have demonstrated that resilience and recovery can be mapped as discrete and empirically separable outcome trajectories."[8] Resilient persons (whether adults or children) present with a variety of coping skills and practices. Some are very active, such as problem solving and executive functioning (for example, planning), as well as openness to social support and ability to make use of such support. Resilient individuals avoid denial or other avoidance of the facts and significance of PTEs, and resist behavioral disengagement from others. They tend also to be disposed toward optimism and high degrees of positive emotionality—dispositional characteristics that tend to reenforce the coping power of social networks and support. These dispositional properties are based on distinctive neurobiological circuits that we are beginning to understand well. There is thus ample room for a wide variety of specific coping strategies among the resilient.[9] There is not room here to rehearse even the broad outline of the underlying neurobiology, but it ranges from phenomena involving neural plasticity of the prefrontal cortex, to flexible capacity to cope with the physiological results of stress (especially in the dynamics of the hippocampus-pituitary-adrenal axis, the main stress-regulating system of the human body), to distinctive patterns of neurotransmitter deployment and metabolism (including dopamine, norepinephrine, serotonin, vasopressin, glutamate, and oxytocin).[10] We also now know that the capacity for resilience shows marked effects of gender. Some of these effects are due to the fact that stress affects male humans primarily through networks in the right prefrontal cortex and left orbitofrontal cortex, while stress in females activates networks in the limbic system (including ventral striatum, insular cortex, and cingulate cortex). Thus, both the neural footprints and the patterns of functioning of stress-regulation systems in humans differ according to gender (which may explain further distinctive differences in the manner by which males and females cope with PTEs). Gender effects have also been found in nonhuman animals that furnish valuable models for human regulation of stress and response to stress.[11]

A further layer of complexity in explaining resilience (as also vulnerability) in the face of PTEs has to do with genetics. More particularly, recent research suggests very strongly that individual capacity for coping with potential trauma (and thus whether trauma actually occurs) depends not merely on genetic heritage at the genomic level, but also on the complex manner in which individual genomes are expressed in their particular environments. DNA in cells can be altered by virtue of changes in the complex proteins that surround that DNA and which interact with it as it functions to govern generation and distribution of vital proteins in the cell during development and between cells during later functioning. Moreover, such changes can be quite durable and transmissible across generations (in other words, inherited). Many of them are also reversible. Their influence does not depend on alterations of the underlying DNA itself at all. This is the subject of *epigenetics,* and the epigenetic turn in the study of resilience is very marked in recent scientific literature. This is one way in which environmental influences take effect in humans (and nonhuman animals, and even plants). A full understanding of these mechanisms at the molecular level is beginning to appear and to affect our further understanding of the material substratum of resilience. Resilience itself, then, even at this very basic level is not simply a property of the individual's bodily resources, but also very much a product of their interaction with environmental factors.[12]

This emphasis on the interaction of biological and environmental factors, in the generation of psychological resilience and/or vulnerability, has begun to loom very large in the research literature. Resilience is thus not merely a function of our biology, complex as that may be. It is also a function of how the animal interacts with its environment, and how environment and biology interact with one another. Environmental factors influence biological factors, and vice versa. Thus, understanding resilience demands multiple levels of analysis and a view of the animal as a complex developmental system. This new perspective leads very rapidly to a view of resilience as a function of the *ecology* of the individual and of the manner in which individuals take advantage of environmental resources (including social and cultural resources), which in turn make resilience possible: "biological factors can predict positive developmental outcomes in stressful environments, but only to the degree that the environment triggers developmental gains or helps the child [and mutatis mutandis, adults] avoid overburdening his or her physiology."[13] Resilience, on this view, is a function of a complex negotiation between individuals and their environment whereby the individual is able to use environmental provisions in a resilient fashion. These may include, for example, socioeconomic status, parental support and expectations, peer relationships, community cohesiveness, availability of good schools, alternative networks of social support, such as churches, and the like. There is thus also an irreducibly probabilitistic aspect to resilience: resilient children and resilient adults (and also their vulnerable counterparts) are partially the product of favorable social and cultural milieus. Individuals, of course, have to be motivated and able to take advantage of such environmental provisions for resilient outcomes to emerge.

The upshot of all this is an essentially ecological understanding of resilience, a view which is increasingly dominant in the scientific discussion and investigation of this complex human phenomenon: "In the context of exposure to significant adversity, resilience is both the capacity of the individuals to *navigate* their way to the psychological, social, cultural, and physical resources that sustain their well being, and their capacity individually and collectively to *negotiate* for these resources to be provided and experienced in culturally meaningful ways."[14] It is this ecological view of resilience, in my view, that is reflected in the same films that grounded the pessimistic induction on the meaning of loss and death discussed earlier in this essay. And hereby Eastwood gives substantial evidence of having intuited aspects of psychological resilience that are not only now given a solid empirical basis in science, but also furnish us with a very different kind of induction on the meaning of death.

The Optimistic Induction: All Losses Are Remediable

In an entirely expectable way, the heroic figures in *The Eiger Sanction* and *Firefox* manage to surmount their problems and deficits, both mental and physical, to vanquish their enemies and triumph in the end. And thus the usual comic (in the classical sense) ending ensues. For thrillers made in this period, during the Cold War, such endings are no surprise, and they pretty much dictate how things will stand at the end of the film with their main characters. Moreover, at least to some extent, both heroes manage their victories with the help of others. Indeed, Major Gant in *Firefox* achieves a vital refueling and rearmament of his aircraft only with the aid of a U.S. submarine and its crew (and thus with the further aid of the complex military organization that sent them to help him), and at the end of the film is en route to a NATO airbase where he is assured of a friendly reception. The focus of the film is on the hero, to be sure, however, and these very substantial social networks that enable his success remain largely out of view. In *The Eiger Sanction* it is Ben Bowman (George Kennedy), Hemlock's old friend and climbing partner, who both trains Hemlock and finally saves his life, though his own status as a friend turns out to be more complicated and dubious than we knew previously. In both films, then, we see one important aspect of the modern scientific understanding of resilience: the importance of the social environment of the resilient individual in providing needed resources. But the point is merely tangential to the main action of both films.

In sharp contrast, *Unforgiven* contains very little in the way of resilience. Most of the losses are irremediable, since the sufferers die—and in such fashions as to prevent even elementary forms of resilience. That said, however, we see that Delilah recovers from her wounds (as we also see Munny recover from his illness), and we see the Schofield Kid abandon his attempt to be a gunman, and presumably take up some more socially acceptable form of life. We also get a strong hint at the end of the film that Munny himself has left his gunfighting ways once again and made a better life for himself and his children in San Francisco. These are adumbrations of resilience, but not much more. As far as they go, however, we also see the ecological perspective appear, for none of these recoveries and reformations takes place without the aid of environmental supports from concerned others. Indeed, Munny himself is one of the vital instruments of the Kid's reformation. The film is otherwise littered with persons who have died in squalid and miserable ways.

The same hero-positive resolution is evident in *In the Line of Fire*, which as I noted earlier ends with Horrigan actually retiring from the Secret Service, and evidently making a success of his relationship with Raines. He has finally accepted his boss's advice. But surely this is the point: Horrigan's success is dependent upon his relationships with both of these characters. It is also dependent on his capacity to come to terms with the past, and especially with his failure at the Kennedy assassination. This further point is made visually: Horrigan "takes a bullet" for his president, but has prepared for this eventuality by wearing a bulletproof vest. In the climactic confrontation with the villain, Mitch Leary, Horrigan signals to Lilly to order the sharpshooters to open fire on the elevator cage containing both men. And in the scene where he weeps in Lilly's presence, it is she who takes his hand. Both times we see a character successfully *navigate* his way to and *negotiate* with (to return to Ungar's definition of resilience) environmental provisions. The principal environmental resources in question are friends and/or lovers, and this pattern is, if anything, intensified in later films. However, there is a notable role in *Line of Fire* for music. Horrigan is repeatedly shown playing the piano in his favorite bar (his predictability in this regard is also dangerous), and we know, of course how very influential music and especially jazz has been in the real life of Clint Eastwood. But here we see it worked out in the film itself, and it is clear that those evenings spent at the piano in the bar are an important mechanism that promotes his character's resilience in the face of suffering, trauma, and loss. The film thus shows us a number of features characteristic of resilient persons, including individual dispositions and effective engagement with environmental resources.

In *Blood Work* our hero is especially dependent on his friends for his eventual success in the face of adversity. His doctor, Bonnie Fox, is perhaps the most vital of these friends. But the deputy sheriff, Jaye Winston, is also a good friend and gives repeated support to McCaleb's efforts. Even the pseudo-friend, Jasper Noone, starts out as a key element in McCaleb's support network. Perhaps the most telling image, however, of an ecological perspective on resilience comes at the end of the film. We see McCaleb motoring off in his boat in the happy company of Graciela Rivers (Wanda De Jesus), who has become his lover, and of Raymond Torres, her young nephew. They have formed an alternative family-like unit, and the recovery of each of them from their respective traumatic losses is once again a matter of successfully navigating to and negotiating with environmental resources. We fully expect them to continue to thrive. (It should be noted, once again, that institutional resources are not entirely invisible—for example, the sheriff's department that supports Jaye's work and the hospital network that contains the vital information about blood groups that ensures success in McCaleb's investigation and eventual unmasking of the villain. But these are relatively silent partners in the resilience of the main characters.)

Mystic River is a much darker film, its stage finally strewn with the unredeemed dead, but is also not without indications of a rich human capacity for resilience. Even the tragedies of Dave Boyle's and Katie Markum's deaths do not entirely overshadow the resilience displayed by Jimmy Markum. At the end of the film we see Jimmy standing outside the building in which he lives, watching the parade. We have already learned that his wife supports his actions entirely, that his family is intact, despite its dreadful loss of Katie, and that his position in his community is secure, despite his own dreadful crimes. Even his friendship with Sean Devine is largely intact, though Sean knows that Dave Boyle was not guilty of Katie's death, and Jimmy knows that Sean knows this. There is about all this a kind of tribalism, whereby family and old neighborhood ties are the deepest and most durable. Jimmy Markum is the strongman, the chief, of his local tribe, and he remains firmly in that position throughout the film. It is perhaps most ironic in the form of the help he gets from the Savage brothers, Val and Nick (Kevin Chapman and Adam Nelson, respectively), themselves minor criminals but fiercely loyal to Jimmy, like medieval retainers. His strongest supporter is his wife, Annabeth, who, all the more in the light of her own loyalty to Jimmy, despises Celeste Boyle's betrayal of her husband as a failure of loyalty. Stressed to the breaking point by the death of Katie, the Markum tribe responds to that trauma resiliently and does not actually break. The ecological perspective on resilience is clearly evident. We also see here that the value of resilience is not dependent on the moral value of the actions that instantiate it. Jimmy Markum is a poster boy for psychological resilience in the face of adversity, but he is not a morally good man.

This latter point is perhaps most sharply made in *Million Dollar Baby* and *Gran Torino.* Both films hinge on what amount to suicides: Maggie's at the hands of Frankie Dunn, and Walt Kowalski's at the hands of the Hmong gang he is seeking thereby decisively to undermine. The assisted suicide of Maggie Fitzgerald is the more controversial, to be sure, given the state of discussion of the related issue of physician-assisted suicide in contemporary American culture, and indeed the culture of the West generally. Father Horvath speaks eloquently of the more traditional moral condemnation of such actions, and even Frankie Dunn himself is horrified by what it is that

Maggie has asked him to do. But he does it nonetheless, and clearly he does it because he loves Maggie and wants what is best for her. (From the point of view of recent laws in Oregon and Washington governing the right to assisted suicide, however, Maggie's death would be unlawful, since she was not in an imminently terminal condition.) We do not finally get a clear verdict about the effects of his actions on Frankie, but the hint that when he leaves his gym he may have gone on to purchase the diner and carry on his life that way is at least a suggestion that he has not simply been undone by those actions. We are clearly intended by the film to share Frankie's point of view: horrified by the prospect of helping Maggie to die, but finally willing to do so. The moral status of the action remains contested. Less contested, in terms of the interior narrative of the film, is the death of Walt Kowalski. I have noted elsewhere (as have others in this volume) the equifinality of Walt's last act: he achieves a variety of good outcomes by means of it. Among those, I contend, is the preservation of a value that has been absolutely central to his own life, and which establishes the moral ground on which his integrity rests: his autonomy. He hereby chooses the means, manner, and timing of his own death (which is otherwise, we believe, not far off, given his health problems).[15] And in doing so, he himself constructs the meaning not only of that death but also of the whole life that precedes it and leads up to it. This is a kind of resilience: resilience in the making of meaning. We have also seen that Walt has acquired a new "family" in the extended neighborhood circle of Hmong, new and more rewarding children in Thao and Sue Lor, and even a friend almost as crusty and curmudgeonly as himself in Grandma Lor. He has, in sum, acquired a new tribe, and it is not without significance that Sue, in particular, is dressed in traditional Hmong clothing at Walt's funeral. The cases of Thao and Sue themselves are also full of resilience, in their cases dependent on family resources and the vital friendship of Walt Kowalski. All three characters have had to navigate and negotiate their ways to appropriate resources in order to respond resiliently to their losses.[16]

There is thus in these films the groundwork for another kind of induction on the meaning of loss. This is the optimistic induction: losses can be remediated at the hands of resilient individuals placed in resilience-promoting environments. We even see some of the interior pathways by which resilient individuals navigate and negotiate their ways to those environmental resources to resilient ends. If we think of death, then, as the final loss, the suggestion here is that even death might not be final and might not be irremediable. That possibility is the subject of the final film to be considered here.

Counterbalanced Inductions and Agnosticism about Loss and Death

The films considered thus far in this essay seem to me to give evidence of two inductions regarding the final meaning of loss. One suggests that loss is often irremediable and thus that the greatest of personal losses, our own deaths, are probably irremediable also. This would further suggest that death brings dissolution of the person together with their body, the view that was defended in antiquity by Aristotle. On this view, the destruction of the body terminates the person's causal powers and thus any prospect of continued personal existence.[17] So runs the pessimistic induction on loss and its further consequences for our attitude toward death. But I have also argued that there is present in Eastwood's films, and notably so in his most recent ones, a counterinduction that is much more optimistic about our capacities for resilience in the face of even very grave adversity. On this view, perhaps even our own bodily death is something that we may be resilient toward. If so, then the ecological element of resilience will come to the fore, it being highly unlikely that we can survive our bodily deaths without the powerful assistance of others (and finally perhaps of divine intervention). However, if I am right that there are the ingredients in Eastwood's films for two such counterbalanced inductions, then it may well be that his own answer to the question "Can we survive our own death?" is simply "I don't know." This agnostic solution finds some support in one of his most recent films.

Hereafter (2010) is discussed at length elsewhere in this volume. Here I note only two further aspects of the film. The first is that it is redolent of the notion of resilience, notably in the final outcomes for Marcus, Marie, and George, all of whom solve the problems posed by their potentially traumatic losses, and solve them in highly resilient fashion. (The ecological perspective on resilience is also readily evident in their cases, not least in the overarching narrative arc by which their three lives are entangled with one another.) But there is also an agnostic aspect to this film. Marie has what appears to be a near-death experience during the tsunami. Indeed, Dr. Rousseau tells her that she probably actually died in this incident. And this experience, of course, sparks her restless search for the truth about what has apparently occurred to her. We see and hear her read at the London Book Fair the closing segment of her book on this topic. What is remarkable about this passage, however, is that she does not claim to know what near-death experiences are about and goes so far as to say that perhaps we will never know what they are actually about, and thus that we may never know whether survival is really possible. The conclusion of her investigation, then, is markedly agnostic. She remains open, in true agnostic fashion, to the possibility that survival is possible, but claims to lack the requisite knowledge to settle the issue one way or the other. In his scene with Marcus, when George finally consents to "do a reading" for him, we find a similar note struck. Losing touch with Jason (the dead twin), George evidently makes up some further comments to give to Marcus, whose predicament he understands very well: whether or not Marcus can live successfully without his twin. Marcus responds by asking George where Jason has gone. And George confesses that he does not know. This is perhaps the most surprising agnosticism in the film, given that George's whole "gift" (or curse) has to do, it appears, with the ongoing lives of the dead. (I say "appears" because it is possible, at least, that he is not communicating with the dead at all, but rather with something in the minds of those living persons to whom he gives those readings.)[18] It is these expressions, by the two leading characters in the film, that are most surprising, in my view. I take it that they cannot be merely accidental or the product of ad-libbing, but rather are due to deliberate decisions by the director. And if so, then we have further reason to think that Eastwood's own view about the possibility for surviving death is similarly agnostic. It is an entirely respectable view to have on such a difficult and persistent metaphysical problem. It is also, in my view, entirely in keeping with the practical nature of Eastwood's philosophical bent, avoiding grand explicit speculations in favor of showing us visually and in terms of the story how we might approach such problems and something of what might be at stake if we adopt either of two competing solutions.

Notes

1. Nothing in my argument hinges on this, but I do regard the Buddha as a historical figure, probably dating from the fifth century BCE. See discussion of this in K. Armstrong, *Buddha* (New York: Penguin Books, 2004), and M. Carrithers, *The Buddha: A Very Short Introduction* (New York: Oxford Univ. Press, 2001). I doubt, however, that we know very much in detail about the life of the Buddha.

2. H. Hughes, *Aim for the Heart* (London: I. B. Tauris, 2009), 200, puts the point this way: "Watch the trailer, read the book [by Craig Thomas, 1977], play the game—just avoid the film, it's another *Eiger Sanction.* Less a 'Firefox' than a damp squib, or at best a smoldering turkey."

3. For a very knowledgeable and insightful study of just such psychological effects in real life, see D. Grossman, *On Killing: The Psychological Cost of Learning to Kill in War and Society* (New York: Back Bay Books, 2009). For the underlying psychology and biology of killing, see D. Buss, *The Murderer Next Door: Why the Mind Is Designed to Kill* (New York: Penguin Press, 2005).

4. See http://en.wikipedia.org/wiki/Unforgiven.

5. For a treatment of the psychological issues for young children arising from the death of a parent, see S. Dunning, "As a Young Child's Parent Dies: Conceptualizing and Constructing Preventive Interventions," *Clinical Social Work Journal* 34 (2006): 499–514. Raymond remains largely underdeveloped in this regard.

6. http://www.writingstudio.co.za/page287.html.

7. That Graciela Rivers and Terry McCaleb are linked by loss is underscored by the actress playing Graciela, Wanda De Jesus: http://www.clinteastwood.net/filmography/bloodwork.

8. G. Bonanno and A. Mancini, "The Human Capacity to Thrive in the Face of Potential Trauma," *Pediatrics* 121 (2008): 369–375 (quotation is from page 371). Compare G. Bonanno, "Resilience in the Face of Potential Trauma," *Current Directions in Psychological Science* 14 (2005): 135–138; G. Bonanno, "Loss, Trauma, and Human Resilience," *American Psychologist* 59 (2004): 20–28; and A. Masten, "Ordinary Magic: Resilience Processes in Development," *American Psychologist* 56 (2001): 227–238.

9. A. Feder, E. Nestler, and D. Charney, "Psychobiology and Molecular Genetics of Resilience," *Nature Reviews Neuroscience* 10 (2009): 446–457. Compare G. Bonanno, R. Pat-Horenczyk, and J. Noll, "Coping Flexibility and Trauma: The Perceived Ability to Cope with Trauma (PACT) Scale," *Psychological Trauma: Theory, Research, Practice, and Policy* 3 (2011): 117–129. On the importance of positive emotions, see A. Ong, T. Bisconti, and K. Wallace, "Psychological Resilience, Positive Emotions, and Successful Adaptation to Stress in Later Life," *Journal of Personality and Social Psychology* 91 (2006): 730–749; and M. Tugade, "Positive Emotions and Coping: Examining Dual-Process Models of Resilience," in *Oxford Handbook of Stress, Health, and Coping*, ed. S. Folkman (New York: Oxford Univ. Press, 2011), 186–199. The neurobiology is examined in E. McCrory, S. De Brito, and E. Viding, "Research Review: The Neurobiology and Genetics of Maltreatment and Adversity," *Journal of Child Psychology and Psychiatry* 51 (2010): 1079–1095; and M. Haglund et al., "Psychobiological Mechanisms of Resilience: Relevance to Prevention and Treatment of Stress-Related Psychopathology," *Development and Psychopathology* 19 (2007): 889–920.

10. In addition to the papers mentioned in note 8, see also M. Katz et al., "Prefrontal Plasticity and Stress Inoculation-Induced Resilience," *Developmental Neuroscience* 31 (2009): 293–299; J. Cao et al., "Mesolimbic Dopamine Neurons in the Brain Reward Circuit Mediate Susceptibility to Social Defeat and Antidepressant Action," *Journal of Neuroscience* 30 (2010): 16453–16458; and C. Waugh et al., "The Neural Correlates of

Trait Resilience When Anticipating and Recovering from Threat," *Social Cognitive and Affective Neuroscience* 3 (2008): 322–332.

11. J. Wang et al., "Gender Differences in Neural Response to Psychological Stress," *Social Cognitive and Affective Neuroscience* 2 (2007): 227–239. For animal studies, see B. Mueller and T. Bale, "Sex-Specific Programming of Offspring Emotionality after Stress Early in Pregnancy," *Journal of Neuroscience* 28 (2008): 9055–9065; N. Goel and T. Bale, "Examining the Intersection of Sex and Stress in Modeling Neuropsychiatric Disorders," *Journal of Neuroendocrinology* 21 (2009): 415–420; M. Weinstock, "Sex-Dependent Changes Induced by Prenatal Stress in Cortical and Hippocampal Morphology and Behavior in Rats: An Update," *Stress* 14 (2011): 604–613.

12. K. Dudley et al., "Epigenetic Mechanisms Mediating Vulnerability and Resilience to Psychiatric Disorders," *Neuroscience and Biobehavioral Reviews* 35 (2011): 1544–1551; C. Bountra, U. Opperman, and T. Heightman, "Animal Models of Epigenetic Regulation of Neuropsychiatric Disorders," in *Molecular and Functional Models in Neuropsychiatry,* ed. J. Hagen (Berlin: Springer-Verlag, 2011), 281–322; T. Bale et al., "Early Life Programming and Neurodevelopmental Disorders," *Biological Psychiatry* 68 (2010): 314–319; P. McGowan et al., "Epigenetic Regulation of the Glucocorticoid Receptor in Human Brain Associates with Childhood Abuse," *Nature Neuroscience* 12 (2009): 342–348; T. Franklin et al., "Epigenetic Transmission of the Impact of Early Stress Across Generations," *Biological Psychiatry* 68 (2010): 408–415.

13. M. Ungar, "The Social Ecology of Resilience: Addressing Contextual and Cultural Ambiguity of a Nascent Construct," *American Journal of Orthopsychiatry* 81 (2011): 1–17 (quotation from page 3). Compare also D. Cicchetti, "Resilience Under Conditions of Extreme Stress: A Multilevel Perspective," *World Psychiatry* 9 (2010): 145–154; B. Ganzel, P. Morris, and E. Wethington, "Allostasis and the Human Brain: Integrating Models of Stress from the Social and Life Sciences," *Psychological Review* 117 (2010): 134–174.

14. M. Ungar, "Resilience Across Cultures," *British Journal of Social Work* 38 (2008): 218–235 (quotation is from page 1225). Emphasis is in the original.

15. For an eloquent and persuasive defense of the right of the terminally ill to make such decisions, see R. Dworkin, T. Nagel, R. Nozick, J. Rawls, T. Scanlon, and J. Thomson, "Assisted Suicide: The Philosophers' Brief," *New York Review of Books,* March 27, 1997, 41–47.

16. Even Walt's dog, the faithful Daisy, proves resilient early in the company of Grandma Lor, and late in the company of Thao, as we see in the final scene of the film.

17. Of course, were a suitable body to be reconstituted or substituted, and were there some way to instill the personality in that body, both perhaps to be accomplished by means of a divine action, continued personal existence might be possible. See Thomas Aquinas, *Summa Contra Gentiles,* trans. Charles O'Neil (Notre Dame, Ind.: Univ. of Notre Dame Press, 1989), 4:79, 81–89, for discussion. And for the view that theists need not be dualistic about mind and body, see L. Baker, "Need a Christian Be a Mind/

Body Dualist?," *Faith and Philosophy* 12 (1995): 489–504; and L. Baker, "Persons and the Metaphysics of Resurrection," *Religious Studies* 43 (2007): 333–348. There is a useful general discussion in J. Green, "Resurrection," *Internet Encyclopedia of Philosophy* (2008), http://www.iep.utm.edu/resurrec/#SH4a. My own view is that even if survival of death is possible, it is not due to the natural immortality of possessing a Cartesian soul, the existence of which is wholly independent of the body.

18. This view is fully compatible, I take it, with the perspective offered by Doug McFarland in his contribution to this volume.

Eastwood's Dream

The Philosophy of Absence in *Hereafter*

Douglas McFarland

> I was privileged to see ghosts and spirits.
>
> —David Copperfield, in Charles Dickens's *David Copperfield*

Hereafter (2010) begins with a relentless and indifferent surge of destruction and death. A tsunami sweeps over the landscape of a tropical resort, and the near-death experience of a vacationing journalist (Cécile de France) provides the ostensible thematic context for the film. Her narrative parallels and eventually converges with those of a San Francisco psychic (Matt Damon) and a boy whose twin brother (Frankie McLaren and George McLaren) was killed when he was hit by a truck. The existence and characteristics of a life after death will prove of less importance, however, than the profound sense of abandonment that death necessarily brings to the living and the struggle to discover meaning in a world intrinsically mutable. Quite appropriately, images of the afterlife provide the least imaginative visual elements in the film. The "hereafter" of the title refers less to a realm beyond the phenomenal, a promised land that awaits the living after death, than to the life that lies ahead in this world and the responsibility of the living to fashion meaning and authenticity in the face of absence and abandonment.

Hereafter as Philosophy

One can easily imagine the wry grin that would form on the face of Clint Eastwood upon being told a volume of essays devoted to his "philosophy" was about to be published. Eastwood has cultivated a laconic persona characterized by plain speaking and an insistence upon his being a storyteller, not an abstract thinker. In discussing *Hereafter*, Eastwood has commented, "the story is everything, the story is the king."[1] One could argue that *Hereafter* is effective precisely because it avoids being philosophical, if one means by philosophical a process of abstract thought. I will argue, however, that telling the stories of individual characters who struggle emotionally to discover answers to difficult questions concerning the human condition does constitute a form of philosophical inquiry. Moreover, storytelling is itself a medium within the film to which one of the central characters turns when confronted by the problems of life. George, the San Francisco psychic, finds solace at moments of despair or confusion in listening to recordings of *David Copperfield*. Near the end of the film he makes a pilgrimage to Dickens's residence in London and correctly identifies a painting entitled *Dickens' Dream* in which the author is depicted sleeping with the figures of his imagination floating above him. *Hereafter* is Eastwood's dream. I do not mean to associate the medium of film with the landscape of dream images, but rather to argue that, like Dickens, Eastwood is intimately bound to the characters of his imagination. And it is through their struggles in coming to terms with the conditions of life, especially its ephemeral and transitory nature, that he explores philosophical issues. We care about the lives of Eastwood's characters not simply because we feel empathy for them or are curious about how their narratives will be resolved in the unfolding of the plot. We care about them because they have been forced to discover ways to live meaningful lives in a world that is not of their making. Facing his own personal loss, George listens to a recording of David Copperfield's expression of despair. In a chapter appropriately entitled "Absence," Dickens's hero confesses, "From the accumulated sadness into which I fell, I had at length no hope of ever issuing . . . I felt its own weight now; and I drooped beneath it, and I said in my heart that it could never be lightened."[2] It is fitting that *David Copperfield* should have a significant presence in the film. Dickens's novel is filled with moments of abandonment not only in this passage but throughout its narrative. Until the very end of the novel, David repeatedly finds himself leaving someone or someplace behind. His struggle to find a way forward in the face of loss mirrors the struggles of the central characters in *Hereafter*.

This understanding of philosophy as a process not of arriving at universal truths through logical analysis, but of discovering a way to live is described by Alexander Nehamas in *The Art of Living*: "But apart from philosophy as we most often conceive of it—as an effort to offer systematically connected answers to a set of independently given problems—another tradition, equally philosophical, is concerned with what I have called the art of living, the care of the self, or self-fashioning."[3] Nehamas is in part trying to place so-called continental philosophy within a humanist tradition. He therefore begins his book with Socrates and concludes with Foucault. But he ultimately is less concerned with rescuing post-structuralist thought than he is with affirming the intrinsic philosophical value of constructing a mode of being in this world "through the investigation, the criticism, and the production of philosophical views."[4]

Although the three protagonists in *Hereafter* are not aware of themselves as philosophers per se and do not ask and investigate questions in the manner that Nehamas may envision, they are, nevertheless, searching for meaning to fundamental questions concerning the human condition. As I said earlier, these questions have less to do with the existence of an afterlife than they do with the here and now. Near the beginning of the film George is beset by a woman who has lost her child. She pleads with him to use his psychic powers to communicate with her daughter. She hysterically sobs, "I lost everything I had." Although this character is on-screen for only a few minutes, her sense of loss spreads out over the entire film. She offers in a viscerally intense and emotional way the central question of the film: How does one find enduring meaning amid the ephemeral and transitory impermanence of the world?

Augustine and the Philosophy of Absence

Nehamas identifies several figures who practice what he calls an "art of living," ranging from Socrates and Montaigne to Kierkegaard and Nietzsche. It is perhaps understandable that he would avoid mentioning Augustine, since this church father was ostensibly concerned with arriving at universal theological truths of Christianity. But in *The Confessions* Augustine places his philosophical inquiries into the context of an autobiographical narrative. Near the end of *The Confessions,* in book 9, Augustine finds himself in the same position as the bereaved mother in *Hereafter.* The person most dear to him in life, his mother, has been snatched away by death. Prior to this traumatic event, Augustine had found a way to reconcile the material nature of the phenomenal world with the immaterial essence of its creator, or to put it simply, between becoming and being. In book 7, Augustine recounts how he first thought he had discovered an answer to his problem in Platonic reasoning. But the light of rational intelligence through which he moves step by step from "bodies to the soul" proves dissatisfying. He is still beset by a hunger that reason cannot relieve.[5]

In book 8 Augustine experiences what he believes will be his final conversion. He finds himself sitting in a garden still struggling with his problem when he hears a child chanting "pick up and read, pick up and read."[6] He opens the Bible and reads a passage from Paul: "make no provision for the flesh" (Romans 13:14). This conversion or turning away from the world is achieved not through willful reasoning. Instead of a moment of rational insight he experiences an emotional revelation. "At once," Augustine recounts, "with the last words of the sentence, it was as if a light of relief from all anxiety flooded my heart."[7] All the shadows of doubt have been dispelled as the absent creator enters his heart rather than his head. At this moment Augustine achieves his goal of shaping his own personal narrative into an idealized Christian model.

This moment is, however, short-lived. Augustine is almost immediately thrown from the universal back into the particular with the death of his mother. This response is foreshadowed in book 4 with the death of a young man to whom Augustine was extremely close. After his death, Augustine is consumed by an unrelenting despair: "everything on which I set my gaze was death. . . . My eyes looked for him everywhere, and he was not there."[8] Similarly, upon the death of Monica, Augustine is overcome by an "overwhelming grief." It is only by an act of "mental control" that he can stabilize himself. He rationally understands that his mother does not "suffer extinction." And yet he experiences a "fresh wound caused by a break in habit formed by our living together . . . a bond suddenly torn asunder." He feels as if he himself had been "torn to pieces."[9] His faith in an immaterial creator to whom one returns in the hereafter cannot sustain him in his time of grief.

Augustine's traumatic fall from grace, his fall from being an idealized Christian sustained by faith to a particular Christian beset by doubt, necessitates a renewal in his struggle to fashion an art of living in the context of absence. This moment becomes critical for the kind of philosophizing that Nehamas describes. I would argue, for instance, that both Montaigne and Sartre in their autobiographical works of philosophy struggle, at least in part, with the same set of issues concerning the impermanence of the material world with which Augustine struggles in *The Confessions*. For Montaigne and for Sartre, however, the struggle shifts from the need to achieve a transcendence over the transient nature of the world to the need to fashion an authentic way of living in this world. In *On Repentance,* Montaigne succinctly asserts, "I am not portraying being but becoming."[10] In another essay he expresses this somewhat differently: "To practice death is to practice freedom."[11] Here Montaigne is responding to the argument made by Socrates in the *Phaedo* when he attempts to explain how it seems natural "that a man who really devoted his life to philosophy should be cheerful in the face of death."[12] Socrates argues that death is itself nothing more than the separation of the soul from the body and that with death the soul is able to exist unencumbered by physical needs. Since the philosopher seeks to free his soul from "association with the body," death is merely the fulfillment of that endeavor.[13] The acquisition of pure knowledge is, in short, "only possible after death."[14] To avoid the detractions and impediments of the body and to focus instead on the pursuit of knowledge is the business of philosophy. "True philosophers," therefore, "make dying their profession."[15]

Montaigne, however, deviates from his Socratic starting point in a manner that speaks to the characters in *Hereafter.* The essayist is ultimately less concerned with how the soul might escape the body than how soul and body exist together. The formal characteristics of *The Essays* differ significantly from those of the Socratic dialogue. The latter reflects a process of question and answer that would lead to truth, however limited. The former offers a medium perpetually in motion and perpetually under revision, one in which Montaigne seeks no conclusions but rather probes the conjunction of the material and immaterial. Near the end of his final essay, *On Experience,* he modifies the Socratic position that the soul should be separated as far as possible from the demands of the body when engaged in the pursuit of the truth. Montaigne asserts, "As for me, then, I love life and cultivate it as it has pleased God to vouchsafe it to us. I do not go yearning that it should be without the need to eat and drink."[16] His point is not simply that we need to attend to our physical well-being with a degree of pleasure, but that the truth is itself inseparable from our material existence. In his own version of Socratic irony, he concludes, "Upon the highest throne in the world, we are seated, still, upon our arses."[17]

Sartre will take this further when he argues that philosophy begins not simply with the recognition of death but also with the acknowledgment that there are no universal truths to which one might aspire. Absence, to put it differently, provides the freedom to philosophize. "Everything is permissible," asserts Sartre, "if God does not exist, and man is consequently abandoned."[18] In *The Words* he puts this in a way that speaks directly to an art of living: "never have I thought that I was the happy possessor of a 'talent'; my sole concern has been to save myself by work."[19] The lifetime work undertaken by Sartre is the task of investigating the human condition and formulating tentative views about it. In Sartre's case these are the tasks of philosophy and literature.

Finally, the modernist filmmaker Paolo Pasolini brings these ideas together in a compelling narrative fiction. His *Teorema* (1968) is both an attack on bourgeois values and a fictional engagement with the idea of Christian abandonment. The film begins with the arrival of a charismatic young man into a typical bourgeois household. Each member of the family falls in love with his physical and spiritual beauty. Then one morning at dawn before anyone in the household has risen he leaves the house and disappears down the street, not to be seen again. His sudden absence throws each member of the family into confusion. The void left in their lives precipitates a crisis of identity and meaning. Each individual in the household reacts in his or her own way. The son obsessively paints, the mother becomes excessively devout, and the father quite simply goes mad. The emotional and psychological struggles of these characters are grounded in abiding philosophical questions concerning the material conditions of the world and the immaterial aspirations of its inhabitants. *Hereafter* is philosophical in just this way. In a world beset by absence, Eastwood's characters seek to maintain the tenuous bonds that bind the living both to one another and to the departed.

Ghosts

Although the story of Marcus, whose twin brother is killed in a traffic accident, unfolds after the first two narratives have been established, his experience lies at the heart of the film. Marcus and Jason are the children of a single mother (Lyndsey Marshal) who, because of her addictions, seems incapable of properly caring for her children. Although the responsibility that they demonstrate to one another and to their mother suggests that at an earlier age they had been taught a certain set of values, they nevertheless must now construct and maintain their world by themselves. They have, as a result, become disproportionately dependent on one another. Marcus seems more vulnerable to separation than Jason. This is hinted at when Marcus asks Jason for help on his math homework. And when agents of Social Services arrive, Jason tells Marcus how they should handle the situation. Their relationship is symbolically suggested by their birth order. Jason was born a few minutes before Marcus and is technically the older brother. The dependency of Marcus on his brother will become even clearer near the end of the film, when Jason tells Marcus through George that he knows his brother had relied upon him, but that he cannot do so anymore.

When Jason is suddenly struck by a lorry and killed, Marcus is thrown into a crisis similar to the one experienced by Augustine with the death of his close friend. Augustine laments, "My eyes looked for him everywhere, and he was not there. I hated everything because they did not have him, nor could they now tell me 'look he is on the way,' as used to be the case when he was alive and absent from me."[20] Marcus also knows that Jason is not on his way home and that the absence he now experiences is an enduring one.

The circumstances in which Jason has been killed are, in addition, if not deeply ironic, then most certainly poignant. Their mother, apparently moved by the near loss of her children to a government agency, sends Jason to the chemist to pick up a prescription for a drug that counters the effects of drug addiction. It is on this errand, one that would quite possibly change their lives, that he is killed. The irony of this may not be readily apparent to Marcus, but it is to the audience of the film. Moreover, the death of Jason indirectly causes Marcus to suffer a second devastating loss. His mother recognizes that she must enter a treatment facility. She tells Marcus, "I'm not running away," but she also acknowledges, "it must feel like the worst thing in the world." The "normal family" that Marcus and Jason thought was just ahead has now for Marcus become a foster family.

Marcus has been cast into a region of absence and confronted with the precariousness of human life. Through the remainder of the film, Eastwood will chart Marcus's frustrating attempts to communicate with Jason through a series of psychics rather than fashioning a way of living without Jason. His struggles and their tentative resolution reflect the struggles of the other principal characters in the film and provide, as I pointed out earlier, the basis for the film's philosophical inquiry.

Authenticity

The vision of the afterlife that Marie experiences at the beginning of the film is itself of less interest to Eastwood than how she responds to her traumatic encounter with death and her vision of an afterlife. In the days and months that follow, largely because of her overriding concern with her experience, she will lose what has defined her professionally and personally. Before the tsunami hits, Marie and Didier (Thierry Neuvic), her producer and lover, have come to the end of their vacation together in Indonesia. They plan to return to Paris on that day, and she asks her companion if he has bought gifts for his children. He suggests that they buy them at the airport. She is amused and forgiving of his seemingly uncaring attitude and declares that she will take care of it herself. On her way to the shops in the village, she calls a colleague in Paris to ask how many posters promoting her television program have been put up in the city. Prior to the tsunami, she seems unaware of the shallowness of her lover and the superficiality of her celebrity status. She has not yet undertaken a critical self-examination of her life in order to determine its authenticity. After her return to Paris her public and private personae will collapse in a relatively short amount of time.

Because her return to television proves to be premature, Marie signs a contract to write a hard-hitting book on Mitterrand. The project, which she had first considered prior to her accident, is soon replaced, however, by a plan to write a book based on her own experience of the hereafter. She pitches the book as if it were an exposé of a plot to suppress discussion of an afterlife. When told by the publisher that he had commissioned a political biography of Mitterrand, she asserts, "this is political." She then asks, "Why are you all against this . . . why are you so afraid of this?" She then points out, "There is scientific evidence from well-known researchers forced to work in secret," and then adds, "a Nobel prize winner, hounded by the religious lobby. That's a story." And finally, the subtitle of her book is *A Conspiracy of Silence,* suggesting that there is some sort of cover-up. She approaches her subject as the investigative reporter she has been trained to be. While she has this exchange with her publisher, news of the bombing of the Underground in London plays on a monitor. At one point she looks up and sees her replacement report the story on the television, perhaps putting pressure on her to spin her project as hard-hitting. She is still trying to authenticate a former version of herself by authenticating the existence of an afterlife.

As part of her research for the book, Marie travels to a hospice in the Swiss Alps. After the receptionist has gone off to tell the director of the hospice (Marthe Keller) that the journalist from Paris has arrived, Marie looks around the clinic. She stops in the doorway of a room in which a patient, surrounded by loved ones, is on the verge of passing away. It is a troubling and complex moment in the film. After a point of view shot is established, the camera moves slowly in on the face of the dying woman. It keeps moving, however, until it rests on the face of the sobbing husband, who is being comforted by what appears to be his mother. Eastwood makes it clear that the focus of the scene is not on the woman who is passing away and what she might soon experience, but on the living who are left behind and who must discover a way to go on in the face of a wrenchingly painful loss. It is unclear if Marie, symbolically standing on the other side of the threshold of the room, shares in this sense of loss or is still concerned with her own vision of the afterlife. At this moment the hospice director appears and makes a remark to Marie that dramatically misses the point: "What we wouldn't give to know exactly where she has gone." She then directly addresses Marie: "But from what you wrote in the letter perhaps you know already." The director overlooks the loss that the survivors of the deceased woman are experiencing and instead focuses on the possibility of an afterlife. Marie and the director move into a garden, where they have tea and discuss the general skepticism of the public over the existence of life after death. The director asserts that "the evidence is irrefutable," and encourages Marie to use her status as a journalist to convince others of the validity of her vision. Marie literally takes away an armful of evidence but has not yet, I would argue, faced the important problem of how one might fashion a meaningful way of life in a world where loss is inevitable.

Marie's fall from grace reaches its climax at a dinner with Didier. She tells him that she wishes to resume her career on television. She tellingly laments, "Today they even took down my posters." When Didier tells her that she cannot return, she accusingly asks him if he is sleeping with her replacement. When he evades the question, the camera moves slowly closer to Marie's face to record her recognition of what has happened. At this moment she suffers a second death experience. The personal and professional world she had constructed for herself proves an ephemeral edifice. It will be the process of writing and sharing her book that will ultimately lead her into a future life.

Communion with the Living and the Dead

The lynchpin of *Hereafter* is the psychic, George. His role in the lives of the other two protagonists is critical. He not only directly encounters both Marcus and Marie at the London Book Fair but also has access to the afterlife in a way that they both lack. But his psychic gift ironically denies him access to the living. As he tells his brother, Billy (Jay Mohr), his power is really a "curse." Earlier in the film, Billy explains George's reluctance to use his psychic powers to a business associate whom George has agreed to help. George has told Billy, "A life about death is no life at all." It is not simply that George's gift requires him to visit the dead instead of the living; it prevents him from establishing meaningful relationships with the living. Although he can cross the boundary between this world and the next, he cannot cross the boundary between self and other. When George communicates the words of the dead, he becomes privy to the secrets of strangers. The intimacy he achieves is perhaps too powerful and yet concurrently distancing. His situation is dramatically portrayed in his encounter with Melanie (Bryce Dallas Howard). After taking the first steps in creating a relationship, Melanie becomes aware of George's psychic gift. She persistently implores him to use his abilities and connect her with those who have passed from her life. After a vision of her mother appears, George tells her that a man seeks forgiveness for what "he had done to her." We infer from her reaction that she has been the victim of her father's sexual abuse. George has unintentionally uncovered a dark and damaging secret from her past. A curtain descends, dramatically and irrevocably separating them. It is ironic that when the couple physically touch, when George takes hold of the young woman's hands as an aid in calling up the dead, it almost immediately closes off the future. Clearly this is not the first time George has had this experience. As soon as Melanie becomes aware of his powers, George sees what is coming. His gift provides an intense, immediate, and deeply ironic intimacy that forms a barrier between him and those he helps. This talent envelops him in the absence that others experience, as well as the absence he feels in his own life.

Denied this and other intimacies, George seeks solace in the imaginative landscapes of fiction. In a darkness that cuts him off from the imperfections of the world and safely substitutes for the darkness of the underworld, he listens at night to the voice of Derek Jacobi reading *David Copperfield.* As I mentioned earlier, Dickens's novel provides a particularly apt narrative. David's life is informed by loss, abandonment, and death. The three passages that George listens to in the film all pertain to absence or its possibility. In the first, David recalls how his nurse, Peggotty, runs out to give him cakes and three shillings as he begins his traumatic journey away from his home and his mother. In the second, Micawber is mixing punch for what appears to be a festive occasion. But it has come after the unwavering loyalty of Mrs. Micawber seems about to break under pressure of yet another financial crisis. The punch is intended to relieve the "despondency, if not to say despair," caused by Mrs. Micawber's condition. And finally, after Melanie has left him,

George listens to David's accounting of the deep despair with which he is overcome with the deaths of Dora and Emily. George has moved from the voices of the dead to the voices of Dickens's imagination. But George does not yet utter his own words, nor reveal his own secrets.

Dissatisfied and seeking a way to care for himself rather than others, George undertakes a pilgrimage to Dickens's home in London. When George arrives at the very desk on which Dickens probably wrote *David Copperfield,* he reaches out his hand and touches its surface. This touching differs significantly from the touch of those who come to him for help. From the look on his face, George feels a powerful and personal connection to the past. He experiences how physical space can hold memories. This remains, however, still an encounter with the dead. He has not yet established a relationship to the living.

This changes for George in the final scenes of the film. Before leaving London, George attends a reading of *Little Dorrit* by Derek Jacobi at the London Book Fair. It is tempting to argue that this reading marks a symbolic change in George. Of course he did not choose the reading, but its contents differ from those moments of loss and absence to which he was drawn in Copperfield's narrative. A plasterer, Plornish, has come to Marshalsea Prison to deliver a message to Little Dorrit. When he leaves the debtors' prison, where he himself had once resided, he ponders whether he might at some future date be sent there again. He is in some sense still a prisoner of the Marshalsea workhouse, still not fully released from its psychological hold. George occupies a similar position. He has left the problems of San Francisco but has yet to be released into the future.

At the reading, George is recognized by Marcus as the psychic whom he had seen on the Internet. He follows George to his hotel and stages a vigil on into the night until George agrees to contact Jason. Through George, Jason tells Marcus that he knows he has relied on him but now he must be on his own. When George tells Marcus that Jason is leaving, Marcus pleads, "Don't leave me," and begins to cry. A fundamental reorientation of George now occurs. Until this moment his head had been turned away from Marcus as he concentrated on the words of Jason. Now, however, he looks directly at Marcus and sees in his face the intense moment of loss and abandonment that lies at the heart of the film. Throughout the film whenever George listens to the dead he has turned his head away from the bereaved so as to concentrate on what he sees and hears. Now, however, he holds his eyes on the face of Marcus when he tells him Jason is returning. Eastwood means for the audience to sense that George is himself delivering the message, that he has looked into the face of Marcus and absorbed his intense sense of abandonment before telling Marcus what he himself believes he must hear in order to proceed with his life without Jason. "If you are worried about being on your own, don't be." Jason and Marcus are "one cell, one person," and cannot be apart. When George tells Marcus that Jason is again leaving, Marcus asks where he is going. George quite simply responds that he does not know. This is perhaps further evidence that Eastwood's concern is not the nature of the afterlife but rather the conditions of the living. Regardless, this is an extraordinary moment for George. He may still be able to see and hear the dead and convey their words back to the living, but he now also can hear the living. One senses that he has a new way of seeing, a new way to penetrate into the lives of others that can release George himself into the future. George takes Marcus back to his foster family in a cab. When Marcus leaves the cab, he walks straight to the door in a manner that has become typical with him. He has made little acknowledgment of others, and his gait and posture has reflected his single-minded interest in his brother. But as he reaches the door, he turns and waves goodbye to George, and George lifts his hand in return. The camera slowly moves first to Marcus's face and then to George's, alternating as it moves closer to each face. As I will point out later, this is a technique used throughout the film to convey an intensity of emotion. For this one moment it is not the dead who are important but the living.

The second transformative encounter at the end of the film is between George and Marie at the same book fair where George meets Marcus. George hears Marie reading from her recently published book and approaches her booth. Based on her reading, we get some indication that Marie has changed since she began her project on the hereafter. In the conclusion to her book, she admits that she will probably never know if her glimpse of the afterlife was genuine or merely a fantasy and that she has been left with as many questions as she had when she started. She seems much less intent on exposing the "conspiracy of silence" than on pondering how the possibility of an afterlife might affect the living. At her book signing, Marie and George touch hands and he momentarily has a vision of her encounter with death. Clearly a strong mutual connection is made between them. But when George later returns to the booth where she had been signing books, Marie has already left. It will be Marcus who tells George where Marie is staying in London. Despite George's denials, Marcus sees that George does in fact want to find Marie. This offers yet another example of how "seeing" has become in the final act of the film an activity shared by the living. It is not simply George who has looked into the eyes of Marcus, but Marcus also who has seen into George.

Acting on the information Marcus has provided, George does go to the hotel where Marie is staying. When she does not answer her telephone, George decides after some hesitation to leave a message. We are never privy to the precise contents of the letter, but because of its length and the expressive look on the face of Marie when she reads it, we can infer that George has communicated more than a mere suggestion to meet for coffee. While in the past George has been a conduit for the voices of the dead, he now communicates in a very personal way. Let us go so far as to say that he speaks not from the hereafter but from the heart.

The final scene in the film takes place at Leadenhall Market, where George has invited Marie to meet him. We see Marie arrive in a point of view shot that is through George's eyes. Eastwood then cuts to a reaction shot of George's face, and the camera moves slowly and fluidly toward him. He then cuts to Marie's face with the camera still moving slowly. Once again, this is the signature camera movement of the film. Now George has his final vision in the film. George experiences an unaccustomed type of vision. Instead of calling up the voices of the dead, he foresees himself and Marie embracing and looking into each other's eyes. When their hands touch, George does not see the dead souls who reside in Marie's past as he had done with the woman he had met earlier in the film. He simply sees her face in the here and now. It is a moment of imagined intimacy suggestive of *A Midsummer Night's Dream,* in which when Helena is told by her father that she must marry the man of his choosing she laments, "I would my father looked but with my eyes" (1.1.56). This is the quintessential statement of Shakespeare's understanding of his own art. The theater is a place where one enters the imaginative realm of another and this somehow changes one, expands one's understanding of self and world. At this moment in the film, Shakespeare's art of living becomes Eastwood's, an art informed by imagination and the capacity to see the world through the eyes of another. The film ends with the couple prepared to enter the land of the living and the hereafter of their meeting.

Although *Hereafter* is relatively traditional and unassuming in its formal manner of storytelling, the film nevertheless probes a fundamental and profound question, one that figures such as Augustine, Montaigne, and Sartre also address: Is there an authentic way of life that acknowledges the problems of vulnerability and solitude? Each of the three principal characters in *Hereafter* struggles to achieve such authenticity. As their paths intersect at the end of the film, they seem to have discovered tentative solutions.

Ceremony

Although Peter Morgan wrote the script for *Hereafter,* Clint Eastwood is ultimately responsible for the telling of the tale. As I pointed out earlier, Eastwood sees himself primarily as a storyteller, and this modest assessment of himself is reflected in what I would call a certain nonchalance or *sprezzatura* that seemingly characterizes his demeanor in life as well as on the set. Although many of his films are informed by violent outbursts and aggressive male assertion, it is forbearance that stands out as the salient authorial characteristic of *Hereafter.* If the overriding theme of the film is communion among the living, Eastwood's camera creates its own type of communal ceremony. Moments of intimacy between subject and audience periodically surface in the narrative flow and establish the underlying tonal character of the film. The camera does not function as a voyeur, moving stealthily closer in order to spy upon the privacy of an individual, as Hitchcock's camera might do. Nor is it the camera of Bergman that will simply stay on its subject, relentlessly refusing to move and creating an intensity of emotional and psychological contact. At the beginning of the film, when Marie loses consciousness and is carried along underwater, the camera moves slowly closer to her face until it hovers over a single eye. This sets the stage thematically and formally for the remainder of the film. It announces that the subject of the film is the passing into the interior of another consciousness, not entering the landscape of the afterlife. This camera gesture will be repeated in more subtle movements throughout the film. When Marie returns to consciousness on the dock, the camera makes an almost imperceptible movement toward her face. At the first psychic reading, after a series of 180-degree shots of George and a man seeking to hear from his deceased wife, the camera advances slowly closer to the man's face. After George has closed the door on the woman imploring him to use his gift, an unhurried camera moves in on the face of George. Several variations of this technique occur later in the film. In the scene at the hospice in which Marie looks into the room of the dying woman, Eastwood cuts from the camera patiently approaching the bed to the reverse motion at the same pace toward the face of Marie. In a telling shot of George eating alone at his kitchen table, the camera begins to move forward but then slowly moves back across the threshold of the room, abandoning George just as he has been abandoned in life. This tone of forbearance and intimacy, as I have suggested, has been largely overlooked in Eastwood's work, but it occurs again and again, from the lyrical and elegiac frame of *Unforgiven* (1992) to the quiet solemnity of Butch Haynes (Kevin Costner) as he stares up into the sky in *A Perfect World* (1993).

In the final scene of the film, when Marie and George meet at the market in London, the camera pulls up and away, again with the same smooth and effortless pacing. In this instance, rather than abandoning the couple, it releases them into the world. *Hereafter* concludes, therefore, with its focus on the life to come in this world. Our protagonists have ceased to look for the dead and instead look for and then step into the future world that they will create. But this is not simply a happy ending. One is reminded of another play by Shakespeare. Near the end of *The Tempest,* when Miranda sees the men whom her father has brought to their island, she feels wonderment and senses the possibilities that maturity will bring. She calls what she sees a "brave new world" (5.1.183). But we know, as does Prospero, that it is a precarious future that she is about to enter and no amount of magic will rid it of the risks entailed in life. There will be love and birth, but there will also be betrayals and loss. As Augustine realized and then experienced, everything in this world passes away, and although one might very well believe in a hereafter which awaits in the next world, it is in this world where faith is tested and meaning forged. We do not know what awaits Marcus and his mother or George and Marie. But we do sense that they are willing to forego thoughts of the hereafter for the trials and tribulations of the here and now.

Notes

1. Clint Eastwood, "The Eastwood Experience," *Hereafter* DVD, 2011.

2. Charles Dickens, *David Copperfield* (Oxford: Oxford Univ. Press, 1981), 793.

3. Alexander Nehamas, *The Art of Living* (Berkeley: Univ. of California Press, 1998), 104.

4. Ibid., 4.

5. Saint Augustine, *The Confessions,* trans. Henry Chadwick (Oxford: Oxford Univ. Press, 1991), 127. All translations are from this edition.

6. Ibid., 152.

7. Ibid.

8. Ibid., 57

9. Ibid., 174–175.

10. Michel de Montaigne, *The Essays,* trans. M. A. Screech (New York: Penguin, 1991), 907. All translations are from this edition.

11. Ibid., 96.

12. Plato, *Phaedo,* trans. Hugh Tredennick (Princeton: Princeton Univ. Press, 1961), 63e–64a. All translations are from this edition.

13. Ibid., 64c.

14. Ibid., 67c

15. Ibid., 67e.

16. Montaigne, *Essays,* 1264.

17. Ibid., 1269.

18. Jean Paul Sartre, *Existentialism Is a Humanism,* trans. Carl Macomber (New Haven: Yale Univ. Press, 2007), 29.

19. Jean Paul Sartre, *The Words,* trans. Bernard Frechtman (New York: George Braziler, 1964).

20. Augustine, *Confessions,* 57.

Desperate Times Call for Existential Heroes

Eastwood's *Gran Torino* and Camus's *The Plague*

Jennifer L. McMahon

Albert Camus's novel *The Plague* (1947) depicts a town under siege. It describes the Algerian city of Oran as its inhabitants confront a devastating outbreak of the bubonic plague. Though their scourge is different, the occupants of Highland Park, Michigan, the setting of Clint Eastwood's *Gran Torino* (2008), are likewise under assault. Whereas the citizens of Oran face death at the hands of an impersonal microbe, the residents of Highland Park confront the more palpable threat of gang violence. Though different in many respects, *The Plague* and *Gran Torino* invite comparison by virtue of the fact that both works depict communities in desperate times, communities whose salvation depends on the action of extraordinary individuals, individuals who can be classified as existential heroes.

Anyone familiar with Clint Eastwood's film *Gran Torino* knows that the character Eastwood plays in the film, Walt Kowalski, is its hero. Though aging, ill, and grappling with the recent loss of Dorothy, his wife, Kowalski overcomes his own racial prejudice as well as the anger and self-absorption associated with his grief in order to aid his community, a community threatened by gang violence. Indeed, at the end of the film Kowalski heroically gives his life to eliminate the threat to his community, particularly to his neighbors. What may not be clear, however, is why Kowalski should be classified as an existential hero. In order to understand that, one must familiarize oneself with some of the tenets of existential philosophy, and more specifically, the characteristics of Camus's rebel, or man of revolt.

Rebel with a Cause

Existential philosophy finds its roots in the works of a number of philosophers, among others, Søren Kierkegaard (1813–1855), Friedrich Nietzsche (1844–1900), Martin Heidegger (1889–1976), Jean-Paul Sartre (1905–1980), and Albert Camus (1913–1960). Though Camus is known for denying his classification as an existentialist, his theory of the absurd nonetheless articulates one of the main tenets (if not the central premise) of atheistic existentialism—namely, the meaninglessness of the world.[1] Though this theory is articulated throughout Camus's corpus, it is conveyed succinctly in *The Myth of Sisyphus and Other Essays* in an essay titled "An Absurd Reasoning," where he boldly asserts, "the world is absurd," then corrects himself by stating, "I was too hasty. This world in itself is not reasonable, that is all that can be said."[2] As Camus explains, while frequently regarded as such, absurdity is not a state of affairs but a "feeling," namely, the feeling that emerges when an individual apprehends the "impossibility of reducing the world to a rational . . . principle" and the "absence of any profound reason for living." Ultimately, the absurd results from a "divorce" between "the mind that desires and the world that disappoints." As such, the absurd depends as much on humans as on the world. It stems, quite simply, from the tension that emerges when the individual's "wild longing for [reason and] clarity" confronts the seemingly "unreasonable" nature of the world.[3]

According to Camus, the feeling of absurdity can strike anyone at any moment; it can do so because it represents the normal affective response to reason's lucid recognition of the human condition. As Cecil Eubanks and Peter Petrakis state in their essay "Reconstructing the World: Albert Camus and the Symbolization of Experience," virtually every "human being comes into conflict with the absurd at one time or another . . . [and] most [people] turn away."[4] Most people turn away from absurdity because its impact is so unsettling.[5] Camus describes the encounter with the absurd not merely as "dizzying," but also "crushing," and sometimes so psychologically debilitating that it inspires a "longing for death." Indeed, Camus asserts there are but three responses to the absurd: "plain suicide," "philosophical suicide," and "revolt."[6] According to Camus, whereas actual and philosophical suicide represent evasions of absurdity, revolt alone preserves lucid recognition of the absurd, and as such, while rare, is the response he recommends. It is the response taken by the individual he elevates to the status of an existential hero: the rebel or man of revolt.

Camus's rebel represents the individual who refuses to succumb to the feeling of absurdity and instead makes meaning in the face of meaninglessness. She is not only able to survive the encounter with absurdity, but to retain her intellectual integrity and ability to act. As Camus indicates, most people do not openly acknowledge absurdity, let alone revolt against it, and therefore cannot be classified as rebels. Instead, they solve the problem of absurdity through some form of denial or escape. Unlike Camus's rebel, most people "sacrifice . . . [their] reason" by committing philosophical suicide. Philosophical suicide takes many forms, religion being one of the more obvious examples. According to Camus, regardless of one's religious affiliation, if one's religion supports either the belief that the world is invested with transcendent reason and divine purpose or that individuals will be delivered from suffering and death, then one has "mask[ed] the evidence . . . of the absurd" and fallen prey to the "fatal game that leads from lucidity in the face of existence to flight from the light."[7]

As the former passage suggests, Camus recognizes that the encounter with absurdity can be fatal. While uncommon, some people take their own lives in order to avoid the absurd. While one might think that actual suicide represents the ultimate form of revolt against absurdity, Camus sees it as the ultimate expression of surrender to it. As John Cruickshank states in *Albert Camus and the Literature of Revolt,* suicide represents "collusion with the absurd and not a solution of it. . . . [F]ar from negating the absurd, [it] actually confirms and intensifies it."[8] Suicide confirms and intensifies the absurd by virtue of the submission to death it represents and the effects it engenders. Absurdity emerges from the encounter or "confrontation" between reason and the world. When an individual commits suicide she surrenders her being in order to "den[y] one of the terms" necessary to sustain the feeling of the absurd. As such, suicide represents not victory over absurdity, but the victory of absurdity over the individual. It marks the individual's decision to forfeit her being and any future opportunity to create meaning in order to escape an unpalatable feeling. Camus rightly indicates that "the absurd ends with death" to the extent the eradication of the subject who experienced the absurd renders her continued perception of that feeling impossible; however, for those who remain, her suicide operates as a powerful catalyst for their experience of absurdity. As Camus makes clear, while absurdity reveals there is no inherent reason for living, it does not necessarily imply that one cannot (or should not) live. Rather, Camus emphasizes that without certainty in anything beyond this existence, "the point is to live."[9]

Camus's statement here may perhaps shed light on his reluctance to align himself formally with the atheistic existentialism associated with his contemporary, Jean-Paul Sartre. Whereas Sartre maintained that the world is absurd, Camus is clear that the individual merely perceives it as such. Thus, for Camus, though it is possible that the world lacks intrinsic purpose, we cannot be certain that it is absurd because we cannot dissociate from our subjective position sufficiently to determine that statement to be objectively true. What is certain, however, is that most individuals at some point feel that their existence is absurd. For Camus, though this feeling is powerful, it should not be taken as a legitimate cause for suicide. Rather, his statement that "the point is to live" and his assertion that it is "a matter of persisting" suggest he assigns some value to life, a maneuver contrary to the radical existentialist assertion that life is inherently meaningless. For Camus, life has worth because it is the necessary condition for the creation of values and because we tend to desire it more than the alternative. Indeed, his goal in "An Absurd Reasoning" is to show that while some people believe that "refusing to grant a meaning to life necessarily [means] . . . it is not worth living . . . [in] truth, there is no common measure between these two judgments."[10] In his estimation, even if we could know that life was objectively meaningless, it would not necessarily mean that we should not go on living, since we can make meaning for ourselves. Indeed, the fact that humans experience the feeling of absurdity suggests that life does mean something to them and they are struggling with the fact that it is not giving them exactly the meaning they want from it.

Rather than lay down arms to the absurd, Camus asserts that the rebel engages in an "unceasing struggle," indeed "permanent revolution" against it.[11] In *The Rebel,* Camus writes, "What is a rebel? A [person] who says no, but whose refusal does not imply renunciation. [A rebel] is also a [person] who says yes."[12] In this passage, Camus clarifies his definition of his existential hero through an allusion to the work of Friedrich Nietzsche, specifically an allusion to Nietzsche's higher man. As Nietzsche makes clear in works such as *Thus Spoke Zarathustra, The Gay Science,* and *Beyond Good and Evil,* the higher man is "the ideal . . . most high-spirited, alive, world-affirming human being"[13] who says "Yes" to existence even though it is fraught with hardship and frequently monotonous repetition.[14] Camus and Nietzsche agree that regardless of what life throws at the ideal individual, she remains affirmative. The existential hero does not say "No" to life. She does not gnash her teeth at existence resentfully. She does not surrender when faced with adversity. Instead, as exemplified by Camus's Sisyphus, the rebel perseveres, "combin[ing] lucidity with courage," bravely determining values and making decisions while simultaneously recognizing the perennial nature of the struggle and "the irreducibility of the world to . . . rational categories."[15] "Revolt gives life value" because it is only through lucid human action that authentic meaning can be made, namely meaning that does not rely on illusion. Rather than relieve the burden of absurdity by abandoning herself to consoling but ultimately deceptive narratives regarding the human condition, the rebel "takes on the weight of [her] own life," thereby "restor[ing] its majesty" and demonstrating her dignity. And as Camus states, "there is no finer sight than that of the intelligence at grips with a reality that transcends it."[16]

Rough Justice: Revolt Personified

One of Camus's most complete and compelling portraits of his rebel or man of revolt is found in *The Plague.* Here Camus offers several characters that epitomize revolt and therefore qualify as existential heroes. The most obvious is the main character and narrator of the chronicle, Dr. Bernard Rieux. As critics attest, while the novel presents us with a number of heroes, Camus gives "special authority to Rieux."[17] Consequently, there is little debate that "Rieux [is] the central hero of *The Plague.*"[18] Readers of *The Plague* are introduced to Rieux almost immediately as he describes the "unusual," indeed "extraordinary," events affecting the ordinary city of Oran—namely, the unnerving emergence of thousands of rats from the sewers and their subsequent and rather grisly death in the streets.[19] As our narrator, Rieux, explains, while the populace initially regards the appearance of the rats as a strange and "disgusting nuisance," their "perplexity . . . [gives] way to panic" when the city is quarantined and the authorities announce that the rats herald a more menacing "adversary": plague.[20]

As Rieux states, while "everybody knows that pestilences have a way of recurring in the world . . . somehow we find it hard to believe in [them]." Consistent with Rieux's remark, most of Oran's citizenry are "caught off guard" by the arrival of the plague. To them, it is inconceivable, "absurd" in fact, that something so terrible could come "out of the blue" and shake their unsuspecting little city "to its core." Effectively illustrating both absurdity and the prevalence of philosophical suicide, most of the citizens of Oran engage in some sort of denial rather than immediately confront the threat that lies at (and sometimes on) their doorstep. When it would seem as if "they had no choice but to come to terms" with their predicament, they instead drown their concern with liquor and distract themselves with sex. They tell themselves that "it'll pass" and work feverishly to convince themselves of the efficacy of makeshift remedies.[21] They also run in droves to religion. Rieux, however, responds differently. In doing so he illustrates what it means to revolt.

As the principal physician in the city, Rieux must tend to those who suffer from the plague. Amid rampant suffering and stationed in what Camus describes as a "huge necropolis," Rieux represents the one possible defense the citizenry of Oran have against premature death. Though he cannot save all—or even most—of his patients, he fights the fight nonetheless. Initially, he battles with authorities who are reluctant to take action. As the story progresses, he struggles with patients who refuse to take precautions and later resist treatment. And most obviously, he wages war with an elusive enemy that is too small to be seen by the naked eye and yet kills with horrifying efficiency. When his friend and colleague Jean Tarrou reminds him that his "victories [over illness and death] will never be lasting," he responds forcefully, "that's no reason for giving up the struggle." Instead, Rieux asserts that he intends to "fight creation as [he] finds it" as long as there is illness and suffering that he might alleviate or altogether allay.[22]

Throughout the text, Camus establishes Rieux as a rebel. He emphasizes Rieux's heroic stature by portraying his character, in effect, as a soldier in a "battle," a battle not only with disease and death, but also with absurdity. Using the language and imagery of warfare, Camus portrays Rieux as a hero on the front lines of a critical conflict. Rieux is described, alongside his compatriots, as "mak[ing] a stand," and "fighting" a "war" against "a shrewd [and] unflagging adversary." Rieux epitomizes revolt not simply because he acts courageously, but because he displays the lucidity that is also required of the rebel. He acknowledges that the odds are against him and that despite his best efforts thousands will die. He admits that he is faced with "an absurd situation," but nonetheless commits himself to the "struggle." Admittedly, one might question, at this point, what makes the situation in Oran absurd as opposed to merely tragic. It is important to remember two things. First, Camus defines the absurd as a feeling, not a state of affairs, and the feeling of absurdity occurs when the individual confronts a situation that doesn't conform to his or her existential expectations. Camus is clear that these expectations are held intellectually, but are also shaped by desire, particularly our desire for order and security. Second, to say that something is absurd is not to say that it defies understanding in the sense of causation, but rather that it is the feeling that results when an individual's sense of the proper order of things is challenged.[23] Clearly, Rieux and his colleagues understand that the epidemic that affects Oran has a definitive physical cause. It is not senseless in that respect. Indeed, it is described in logical terms as having a "terrible cogency."[24] However, the plague is felt to be absurd because the populace, by virtue of their apathy or ignorance, did not imagine that something this terrible could happen to them. Their situation is analogous to the one described in Leo Tolstoy's *The Death of Ivan Ilych*, where Ivan recognizes that while "the syllogism from Kiezewetter's Logic: 'Caius is a man, men are mortal, therefore Caius is mortal,' had always seemed correct as it applied to Caius . . . [it] certainly [did] not as applied to himself."[25]

Most importantly, though others might see Rieux's effort as "futil[e]," he does not quit. Instead, he "do[es] what needs to be done." For Rieux, doing what needs to be done means working around the clock, day after day, night after night, treating hundreds of patients, observing an almost intolerable volume of suffering, and witnessing thousands of deaths. He acknowledges that the work takes its toll on him both physically and emotionally. Yet he does not relent. He does not surrender. He cannot. For Rieux, doing his part is "a matter of common decency," in fact a moral imperative, because "everybody's in the same boat" and everyone needs defense. While Rieux denies that he is acting heroically, the contrast between his action and that of the hundreds who try to escape or otherwise evade the situation makes it clear that whether Rieux accepts the title or not, he represents an ideal figure in Camus's eyes.[26] Indeed, Rieux's refusal to be considered heroic betokens a humility that effectively reinforces, indeed amplifies, his status as an existential hero.

Gran Torino's Kowalski bears a resemblance to Camus's Rieux. As such he serves as an effective contemporary illustration of Camus's rebel. Importantly, the similarity between Kowalski and Rieux lies not in their profession. Kowalski is a retired automobile worker and Korean War veteran, not a physician. Neither does their similarity lie in their demeanor. Kowalski is cantankerous and intolerant whereas Rieux is reserved and broadminded. Instead, the similarity between the two characters lies in the function they serve relative to their communities. Both Kowalski and Rieux find themselves in communities that are subject to a threat that defies human sensibility and that the authorities in their community ignore, but from which each community desperately needs "deliverance."[27]

Though he does not display the same immediate sense of duty, Kowalski, like Rieux, acts lucidly, courageously, and at personal risk when he comes to the aid of his neighbors, and by extension his community. Over the years, from the front porch of his home, Kowalski has watched the slow decline of his community, a decline accelerated by the presence, and increasing prevalence, of gang activity, most recently from the local Hmong gang. This threat hits home shortly after Kowalski's wife's death when his young Hmong neighbor, Thao (Bee Vang), is pressured into joining his cousin Spider's (Doua Moua) gang and is compelled to steal Kowalski's mint-condition 1972 Gran Torino to complete his gang initiation. Fortunately, Thao's attempt to steal Kowalski's car is foiled by Kowalski himself, and rather than steal the car Thao instead has his first conversation with the man who redirects him to a more productive way of life and eventually saves his life. As viewers of the film are aware, Kowalski not only saves Thao, he also secures the safety of his sister, Sue (Ahney Her), and that of the rest of the community. He does so by intervening after Thao is beaten, Thao's family's home is attacked, and Sue is kidnapped, beaten, and raped—all as retribution for Thao's decision to not join the gang. In a manner analogous to *The Plague,* the aforementioned events establish the environment in Highland Park as one "charged with menace," where members of the community feel that their lives are "imperiled." Like their counterparts in Oran, the threat in Highland Park leaves the citizens of this community feeling "abandoned" and as if they have been "cheated of the future." This despondency is nowhere more evident than in the scene where Sue returns to her home subsequent to her beating and rape. Her bloodstained figure and vacant expression articulate the profound extent of her victimization and hyperbolically illustrate the generalized defeat of her community in the wake of gang violence. Collectively, their state of "dereliction" contributes to a general feeling of "listlessness" and malaise, one that the ailing Kowalski helps remedy.[28] Forging a solution that prevents Thao himself from engaging in illegal retributive violence and thereby jeopardizing his newfound job and future, Kowalski lures Spider and the members of Spider's gang to commit a crime the authorities cannot ignore and the law cannot forgive, the shooting of an unarmed decorated military veteran: himself. The closing scenes imply that Kowalski's sacrifice leads to the arrest, prosecution, and conviction of all of the members of the Hmong gang. Thus, through Kowalski's individual action the threat to his community is removed and Thao and his family, among others, are given the opportunity to move toward the futures they desire, rather than be forced to subsist in fear. Importantly, Kowalski's death also affords him the opportunity to atone for past crimes, namely, unjustly killing a young Korean soldier in the war, and to avoid the anticipated suffering and physical decline associated with his cancer diagnosis.

An important parallel between Rieux and Kowalski is that both characters illustrate an important philosophical point: revolt against absurdity is not an abstract conceptual exercise, but a concrete effort. As indicated previously, the absurd is not an object against which the rebel wages war. Instead, it is a subjective feeling that the rebel combats when confronted with a specific situation that defies her understanding and/or offends her sense of what is right and just. To combat the absurd means to act to promote change. As Camus states, revolt is primarily a "reaction [to] an intrusion that is considered intolerable." Considered together, *Gran Torino* and *The Plague* illustrate that rebellion is a concrete response to an intolerable situation, whether brought about by human agency or a natural process. Regardless of the cause, Camus states, "rebellion . . . protests, it demands, it insists that [this] outrage be brought to an end," and as such "the preoccupation [of revolt] is to transform." Its goal is to minimize "suffering," eradicate "humiliation," and eliminate "oppression." Revolt is simultaneously born of and seeks to establish a "sense of solidarity" between individuals. It strives "to preserv[e] common existence" and establish "the common good." This desire is motivated by the rebel's recognition not only of the common lot of humans, but their "natural community," namely, their connection as social beings who are subject to a common fate.[29] As Eubanks and Petrakis state, revolt "begins in solitude and progresses into an act of solidarity in the name of all men and women."[30] Cruickshank echoes this point, stating that the rebel's goal is to remedy injustice and establish "freedom for each and justice for all."[31] Importantly, a true rebel is not under the naïve impression that the successes she achieves are permanent. Rather, the rebel acknowledges that the struggle is unceasing and "victories will never be lasting."[32] Both Rieux and Kowalski have lived long enough to know that plagues return and people are prone to intolerance and violence; however, neither one thinks that this is sufficient cause to give up the fight.

Faith Is Not Enough: The Revolt Against Religion

Another important parallel between Kowalski and Rieux lies in their skepticism concerning religion, skepticism that is expressed concretely in the tension between the two protagonists and the religious representative present in each work, Father Janovich (Christopher Carley) in *Gran Torino* and Father Paneloux in *The Plague.* As mentioned previously, Camus maintains that religious conviction represents one of the most prevalent forms of philosophical suicide. Rather than encourage individuals to admit that existence defies reason, religion often tends to promote the notion that life possesses it—namely, that life either has a higher purpose that can be understood by humans or that it has a purpose that transcends human comprehension. Indeed, Paneloux's two sermons illustrate these two types of philosophical suicide.

Introduced just prior to his first sermon, Paneloux is characterized as a "fiery" individual who has become "a local celebrity" in Oran due to the renewed interest in religion brought about by the arrival of the plague. Paneloux's "passionate" nature is made evident in his stormy first sermon. Indeed, his thunderous voice is echoed by thunder itself. As rain pours down unsympathetically from the sky, the congregation seeks solace under the roof of the church; however, they find no absolution. Paneloux's words rain down on his parishioners as relentlessly as the "downpour" outdoors. Speaking of the plague he states, "Calamity has come down on you my brethren, and . . . you deserved it." According to Paneloux, the plague is not a senseless atrocity. It has not come without reason as a manifestation of indifferent Nature. Instead, its reason is clear and should be evident to everyone in the congregation: God has sent the plague as punishment for sin. And in Paneloux's estimation, the citizenry of Oran need to accept their punishment and "repen[t]."[33]

Rieux, however, does not accept this explanation. When Tarrou asks him what he thinks of Paneloux's sermon, he states, "if [I] believed in an all-powerful God [I] would cease curing the sick and leave that to Him. But no one believe[s] in a God of that sort; no, not even Paneloux . . . and this [is] proved by the fact that no one [not even him] thr[ows] himself on Providence completely." And Rieux is right. Despite Paneloux's forceful condemnation of the congregation and his assertion that their punishment is deserved, he ministers to the sick alongside Rieux. Later in the novel, after the horrific death of M. Othon's young son, Jacques, Rieux confronts Paneloux with his own inconsistency. Here, rather than refer to the hypocritical character of Paneloux's action, Rieux fastens upon an even more powerful counterexample to Paneloux's argument that the plague is punishment for sin. Specifically, Rieux cites the death of the innocent boy, Jacques, as evidence that the plague is not justified as punishment for sin. Barely able to control his contempt when Paneloux encourages him to accept the boy's death as a necessary event in the divine scheme of things, Rieux responds to Paneloux "fiercely," shouting, "that child . . . was innocent, and you know it as well as I do!" Rieux's point, of course, is that the boy's innocence is logically incompatible with Paneloux's prior assertion that the plague was designed to punish sin. Admittedly, Paneloux's position is logically incompatible only if the boy is taken as wholly innocent. The doctrine of original sin affords the priest an escape from the charge of inconsistency. However, Paneloux does not utilize this way of escape. Rather, Paneloux, like Rieux, is profoundly affected by the loss of the child. Indeed, as the child suffers acutely in the last moments of his life, Paneloux drops to his knees and cries: "My God, spare this child!" Presumably, Paneloux would not appeal to God for a reprieve if he felt the child was sinful and deserved punishment. Paneloux also does not refute Rieux's indictment subsequent to Jacques's death, "That [the] child . . . was innocent."[34] Rieux's comments force Paneloux to revise his position and serve as the inspiration for his second sermon, a sermon Rieux finds even more troubling than the last.

Both the atmosphere surrounding the second sermon and its content are less volatile than the first. Whereas the first sermon depicts Paneloux as a commanding force thundering spiritual judgment in the midst of an actual storm, in the second both the atmosphere and homily are more sedate. Paneloux displays a more contrite demeanor and "instead of saying 'you' he now said 'we.'" As important, Paneloux now explains the plague not as a punishment designed to single out sinners as "wheat is separated from the chaff," but as a test of faith for all. As Paneloux tells his congregation, the death of an innocent child and other instances of "apparently needless pain" provide the individual who confronts such disturbing events the opportunity to recognize that divine purposes transcend human understanding. For Paneloux it would be an act of hubris to refuse to accept God's will. He states, "the [good] Christian must yield himself wholly to divine will, even though it passed his understanding." He asserts that faith demands "total self-surrender"—indeed, "humiliation" before God. This explanation and its mandate inspire a sense of "mad revolt" in Rieux.[35] Rieux refuses to take the "leap [of faith]" that Paneloux implores him to take not only because it requires that he abandon his reason, but more so because it requires that he embrace something he regards as a moral "outrage" as necessary.[36] He rebukes Paneloux, shouting, "until my dying day I refuse to love a scheme of things in which children are put to torture." As Rieux suggests to Tarrou, given the prevalence of suffering and death, and with no assurance that either has purpose, "mightn't it be better . . . if we refuse to believe in [God] and struggle with all our might . . . without raising our eyes toward the heaven where He sits in silence?"[37]

Like Rieux, Kowalski has a conflicted relationship with his local priest, Father Janovich. Thus, in a manner analogous to *The Plague, Gran Torino* illustrates the tension between the life of revolt and the life of faith by placing the representatives of those lifestyles in conflict with one another. In *Gran Torino,* the tension between Kowalski and Janovich is initially established by their contrasting physical appearance. Whereas Kowalski is old and hardened, Janovich has a boyish appearance. His red hair and cherubic cheeks contrast sharply with Kowalski's weathered countenance and perpetual scowl. Likewise, Kowalski's cynical growl is juxtaposed to Janovich's youthful chirp. Though Kowalski does seem to appreciate the support the priest offered his devout Catholic wife prior to her death, he is not favorably inclined toward the Church. Indeed, he expresses his disdain for religion consistently from the onset of the film. In the opening scenes at Kowalski's wife's funeral, Kowalski grimaces and angrily mutters, "Jesus Christ!" when Father Janovich blithely refers to death as something the good Christian regards as "sweet." This exclamation recurs in the film, and on each occasion Kowalski's ironic use of the Lord's name effectively reinforces his negative opinion of the Christian faith. His skepticism is also shown in his repeated refusal of Janovich's invitation to come to confession and in the conversation he has with the priest in which the two men debate who is more qualified to offer advice regarding "life and death." As a war veteran, father of two, and someone with over sixty years of life experience, Kowalski sees himself as infinitely more educated on issues of life and death than the young priest. When Father Janovich disagrees, citing his seminary experience and spiritual status as evidence of his acuity, Kowalski openly mocks him, characterizing the priest as a charlatan of sorts: "You're a twenty-seven-year-old virgin who likes to hold the hands of superstitious old ladies and make them promises [you] cannot keep." In Kowalski's estimation, while Father Janovich might have good intentions, he has no authority to offer advice because he is unstudied in the ways of the world. He not only has too little experience, he has too much faith in the goodness of humans and too little knowledge of their capacity for evil. Consequently, the solutions he proposes are naïve, impotent, incapable of engendering real change.

Interestingly, though *Gran Torino* and *The Plague* convey profound skepticism regarding the value of religion by juxtaposing the potency and lucidity of the protagonist to the inexperience or inconsistency of the priest, neither work vilifies religion generally.[38] Instead, specific religious positions are depicted as erroneous ideologies. The religion's assertions are criticized, but its representatives are portrayed sympathetically as well intentioned. For example, Rieux declares Paneloux a brother in arms. He states, "we're allies" and takes Paneloux's hand.[39] Similarly, Kowalski and Janovich eventually commune together over a beer. In addition, Janovich eventually shows his respect for, and deference to, Kowalski at the end of the film by referring to him as Mr. Kowalski, instead of Walt, and by taking direction from him. Ultimately, Paneloux and Janovich are portrayed as sincere but misguided insofar as they endorse belief systems that are not "faithful to the evidence . . . [of] the absurd" and encourage apathy and acquiescence rather than decisive action aimed at the improvement of the human condition.[40] Through their celebration of Kowalski and Rieux, *Gran Torino* and *The Plague* elevate the rebel over the representative of religion, establishing the former as the true existential hero and the more viable agent for change. Ultimately, neither Kowalski nor Rieux is interested in taking a leap of faith and letting "God . . . see to the rest."[41] Instead, both characters exhibit the features Camus attributes to the rebel when faced with religion: "He is asked to leap. All he can reply is that he does not fully understand . . . [and] he does not want to do anything but what he fully understands. He is assured that this is the sin of pride . . . [and] perhaps hell is in store . . . but that seems to him an idle consideration. An attempt is made to get him to admit his guilt. He feels innocent . . . what he demands of himself is to live solely on what he knows . . . and bring in nothing that is not certain."[42] For example, though Kowalski develops tolerance for the young priest and eventually concedes to his repeated requests that he attend confession, Kowalski's critical view of religion is confirmed in the ironic scene in the confessional. Rather than admit his guilt for the murder he committed in the war, his shortcomings as a father, or the crimes his action is about to engender, Kowalski instead confesses to an adulterous kiss stolen years ago at an office Christmas party and his failure to pay taxes on the sale of a boat. Ultimately, both Kowalski's superficial confession and Janovich's peremptory remedy of Hail Marys cast suspicion on the value of a system that can absolve sins so easily.

Same Symbols, Different Savior

Though *Gran Torino* and *The Plague* exhibit skepticism regarding the existential efficacy of religious belief, both works utilize conventional religious symbolism to make their case for an alternative savior: the rebel. Their use of religious imagery and diction invite comparison between Kowalski and two additional characters: Tarrou (Rieux's friend and ally) and Jacques (the child who died). Whereas Rieux survives the plague and lives to tell the story of the siege that almost annihilated his community, neither Kowalski nor Tarrou nor Jacques survives. Instead, each falls prey to the threat that the community faces, and each figure is portrayed in sacrificial terms.

Both Kowalski and Tarrou are outsiders in certain respects. Though Kowalski has lived in his house in Highland Park for decades, he has become an outsider in his community due to the fact that the neighborhood has changed over time. Rather than housing predominantly white automobile workers, the neighborhood is now home primarily to Asian and Hispanic immigrants. Indeed, Kowalski is presented as the last holdout when, in a scene midway through the film, Thao's grandmother (Chee Thao) mutters to herself, "Why doesn't that old rooster leave?" Unlike Kowalski, Tarrou literally comes from the outside. He comes to Oran to escape his past and to try to find out if he can live in a manner consistent with his morals. As Tarrou explains to Rieux, he is trying to see if he can live without being a party to death. Here we see the first similarity between Kowalski and Tarrou. Though their demeanors are notably different, both men report having seen enough death. Tarrou cannot reconcile himself to the fact that his father played an integral role in state-sanctioned public executions. Kowalski cannot shake the guilt he experiences as a result of the fact that he put men to death in the war, and most specifically that he killed a young Korean soldier after he had surrendered. Both men admit having been agents of death, and both men now seek to "bring relief" and establish justice. Both struggle earnestly to "attai[n] peace."[43] In the end, both characters give their lives, and in their final portrayal are depicted like Christ.

In *The Plague,* Tarrou's death comes at an especially painful and ironic point, namely, during the final weeks of the quarantine after a "serum" has been created that cures most cases. Tragically, as the situation in Oran seems to be improving, Tarrou contracts the plague. Indeed, he exhibits the characteristics of the two most pernicious strains of the disease. Despite the severity of his symptoms and the failure of the serum to engender positive effects, he vows to "put up a fight." With his "eyes . . . glowing with courage" Tarrou stoically struggles not to "lose the match," and to become "a saint" while his body is mercilessly "ravaged" with fever and "lacerated" with pain. Though his resistance is described as glorious, even "superhuman," Tarrou succumbs.[44]

Like Tarrou, Kowalski meets his end bravely and with his eyes wide open. Though both anticipate their imminent death, Kowalski actually orchestrates his demise. Just as Tarrou's body is ravaged mercilessly by the plague, the bullets from the gang members' guns lacerate Kowalski's body repeatedly. Though he is unarmed on this occasion, Kowalksi intentionally draws this fire by reaching into his coat in the same manner as he had previously in the film when he drew a gun. While Tarrou's visage in death bears similarity to descriptions of Christ on the cross in its simultaneous strength and peace, when Kowalski falls to his death he falls in the form of a cross.

This incorporation of the cross invites another comparison, namely, between Kowalski and Jacques. While different in virtually every other respect, the boy who epitomizes innocence and the old man who suffers so much guilt bear resemblance to one another in their final moments. Like Kowalski, when Jacques finally succumbs to the plague he is depicted in cruciform position. When Jacques dies he is described as lying "spread X-wise," "wasted . . . [and] racked on the tumbled bed, a grotesque parody of crucifixion." Similarly, Kowalski not only dies in the form of the cross, his death brings salvation to his community. Thus, not only in form, but also in function, Kowalski's death is redemptive. He is a savior. In a less obvious fashion, Jacques too saves his community. Specifically, it is through his protracted survival that Rieux is able to confirm the efficacy of the serum that he later uses to save hundreds. The serum made the boy "suffe[r] longer," but his suffering also enabled him to put up a "figh[t]," a fight that made it obvious that the treatment had a therapeutic effect.[45]

Though Kowalski, Tarrou, and Jacques are all portrayed in sacrificial terms, there is an important difference between Kowalski and the other two characters. Unlike Tarrou and Jacques, Kowalski knowingly incites the events that lead to his own demise. While it is true that Tarrou may have neglected to take appropriate "precautions" against the contagion, precautions he knew could save his life, his oversight can easily be attributed to fatigue or the desire to expedite the delivery of aid to waiting patients.[46] He doesn't neglect hygienic practices in order to catch the disease. In contrast, Kowalski deliberately orchestrates the scenario that leads to his death. He sets up the situation in which Spider and the other members of his gang not only anticipate his arrival, they also expect him to attempt violent retribution due to Kowalski's earlier beating of one of the members of their gang. As Kowalski anticipates, they come out like "miniature cowboys" with guns blazing, firing into the unarmed Kowalski, the willing victim of their execution, as he reaches into his coat.

The difference between Kowalski and the characters Tarrou and Jacques is critical not only because his intentional self-sacrifice distinguishes him from them, but also because it serves to elevate him in the eyes of the audience. It is also important to consider his sacrifice because it could compromise his stature as an existential hero. As mentioned previously, Camus adamantly opposes suicide as a solution to the absurd. Far from being heroic, Camus maintains that committing suicide amounts to "confessing that life is too much for you."[47] As such, suicide is indicative of defeat, not revolt. Thus, to the extent Kowalski intentionally incites the events that lead to his death, it can be argued that he commits suicide and in doing so cannot qualify as a man of revolt.

Careful consideration of Camus's corpus and Kowalski's action proves otherwise. While it is true that the rebel cannot kill himself as a means to escape absurdity, Kowalski does not do this. Kowalski has no illusions about his own death. He knows he is dying. The blood he coughs up throughout the film and his physician's sober countenance confirm it. He knows he has a limited amount of time left. His death is imminent. When he engages the gunfire of the gang, he acts not on the hope that his death will bring him consolation or transport him to a more perfect world. He acts because he knows that his death has the potential to benefit his neighbors, a family for whom he cares deeply, and by extension his community. Kowalski's action is oriented toward the achievement of that end. His death is a means to the desired end of increased security for his community and greater opportunity for those in the community to determine the course and meaning of their lives. As the principle of double effect suggests, an action that is normally considered immoral by virtue of the fact that it produces a harmful effect can be justified if the intent of the action is not to bring about that effect, but some other effect which is good.[48] Kowalski's death clearly meets this standard. Rather than represent a standard case of suicide that Camus would oppose, Kowalski's death instead exhibits the features of revolt. His action is designed to promote life, not to escape the absurd. As Camus states, the rebel acts on the basis of a "feeling of revulsion at [an] infringement . . . and [out of] complete and spontaneous loyalty to certain aspects of himself . . . he implicitly brings into play a standard of values that he is willing to support no matter what the risk." Clearly, Kowalksi demonstrates this willingness to accept risk. In fact, Camus asserts that the rebel is willing not only to "accept pain" and risk, but also "to sacrifice himself for the sake of the common good which he considers more important than his own destiny."[49] Clearly, Kowalski's death exemplifies this sort of willing sacrifice, sacrifice that Camus celebrates rather than criticizes.

Rather than disqualify him as an existential hero, Kowalski's action decisively establishes him as one. Indeed, he serves as a particularly good example of what it means to revolt because he illustrates that revolt is a course of action available to ordinary people; he demonstrates that normal—even profoundly imperfect—people can revolt. While characters like Rieux and Tarrou are inspiring figures, both are so ideal that audiences may have a difficult time identifying with them. After all, Tarrou is not only highly idiosyncratic, he is trying to be "a saint."[50] To be sure, while he isn't as strange as Camus's most famous protagonist, Meursault, he isn't an ordinary Joe either. Likewise, while Rieux's position as a physician effectively amplifies his heroic status, it also gives him special authority. Most importantly, it makes him professionally obliged to act, an obligation most ordinary individuals lack. As one critic states, "Rieux and Tarrou are . . . the least interesting" characters in the novel from a moral standpoint because "they have no real decisions to make . . . [and] because they do not give much indication that decision-making is difficult."[51]

Unlike Rieux and Tarrou, Kowalski initially has neither an obligation nor a strong inclination to act heroically on behalf of his community. He is concerned about his community, yes. He sees the decline that is evident, the deterioration of the homes adjacent to his own, the decline in property values, the joblessness and poverty, and he wrongly attributes these conditions to the influx of immigrants in the neighborhood. He keeps his property in pristine shape, but beyond that he initially does little else to improve his community. Granted, grappling with the loss of his wife and his failing health, he's working hard just to keep his own life afloat. However, through a twist of fate he meets Thao, a boy whom his bias compels him to disregard, yet in whom he nonetheless comes to see goodness and a future worth saving. Though he has no formal obligation to act on Thao's behalf, Kowalski sees the threat facing Thao and he wants to help. And the threat facing Thao is a threat facing the whole community. Kowalski recognizes that no one else in the neighborhood can or will do anything about it. Janovich recommends talking to the gang but fails to see that the situation has escalated beyond a point where that sort of communication could bring about resolution. The authorities are content to let the gangs "kill each other" and are willing to accept civilian injury and death as collateral damage. In the wake of their inaction and a situation of "oppression" that begs for remedy, Kowalski acts in defense of his neighbors and community, "against a state of affairs . . . [and against those] responsible for this state of affairs."[52] Using violence only against "th[is] enemy" and only when it is necessary to "comba[t] another form of violence," Kowalski embodies all the traits Camus associates with the man of revolt while at the same time being inescapably ordinary.[53] An aging member of the working class, he illustrates that regular people can take a stand against serious threats and exert a significant influence.

Ultimately, as Eastwood and Camus show, security, justice, and the survival of community cannot depend exclusively on blind faith or good intentions. Instead, they rely as heavily on the decisive and courageous action of extraordinary individuals. As the main characters in *Gran Torino* and *The Plague* illustrate, these individuals are not born extraordinary; they are made so through their confrontation with desperate circumstances. Rather than surrender to adversity, Kowalski and Rieux display true integrity and conviction analogous to that shown by the ever-toiling Sisyphus in Camus's *The Myth of Sisyphus*. These extraordinary men realize that no one in heaven or on earth is going to save their communities but them. Both bear witness to ineffectual local governmental officials and religious representatives who turn the other cheek to a problem that threatens the community; however, neither character is willing to accept inaction. Instead, while these characters admit that their battles might not be won, both men fight to sustain their communities with dignity and courage. Kowalski saves his community by giving up his life. He gives his life so the next generation can take the wheel.

Notes

1. In an interview with Jeanine Delpech in *Nouvelle littéraires* (November 15, 1945), Camus stated explicitly, "Je ne suis pas existentialiste . . . et le seul livre d'idées que j'ai publié: *le Mythe de Sisyphe,* était dirigé contre les philosophes dits existentialistes." ["I am not an existentialist . . . and the only book of ideas that I published: *The Myth of Sisyphus,* is directed against existential philosophy."] Substantive portions of the original interview can be found in Camus's *Essais* (Paris: Gallimard, 1965), 1424–1428.

2. Albert Camus, "An Absurd Reasoning," in *The Myth of Sisyphus and Other Essays,* trans. Justin O'Brien (New York: Vintage Books, 1991), 21.

3. Ibid., 6, 42, 6, 50, 50, 21, 49.

4. Cecil Eubanks and Peter Petrakis, "Reconstructing the World: Albert Camus and the Symbolization of Experience," *Journal of Politics* 61, no. 2 (May 1999): 293–312, quoted on 301, http://www.jstor.org./stable/2647505 (accessed March 23, 2011).

5. Indeed, Camus's contemporary, Jean-Paul Sartre, highlights the negative impact of absurdity by associating the feeling with "nausea." See Jean-Paul Sartre, *Nausea,* trans. Lloyd Alexander (New York: New Directions Press, 1964), 18.

6. Camus, "An Absurd Reasoning," 50, 59, 6, 32, 50, 50, 55.

7. Ibid., 40, 50, 5.

8. John Cruickshank, *Albert Camus and the Literature of Revolt* (New York: Oxford Univ. Press, 1960), 60.

9. Camus, "An Absurd Reasoning," 30, 50, 31, 65.

10. Ibid., 65, 52, 8.

11. Ibid., 31, 55.

12. Albert Camus, *The Rebel: An Essay on Man in Revolt,* trans. Anthony Bower (New York: Vintage Books, 1956), 13.

13. Friedrich Nietzsche, *Beyond Good and Evil,* trans. Walter Kaufmann (New York: Random House, 1966), 68.

14. Friedrich Nietzsche, *The Gay Science,* trans. Walter Kaufmann (New York: Random House, 1974), 223.

15. Cruickshank, *Literature of Revolt,* 7, 49.

16. Camus, "An Absurd Reasoning," 55.

17. Colin Davis, "Camus's *La Peste*: Sanitation, Rats, and Messy Ethics," *Modern Language Review* 102, no. 4 (October 2007): 1008–1020, quoted on 1009, http://www.jstor.org/stable/20467547 (accessed March 25, 2011). As Davis explains, Rieux's authority derives from several factors. First, though not immediately evident at the onset of the novel, his role as the narrator of the chronicle is eventually disclosed. Thus, Rieux has a privileged perspective on the events described and a unique relationship to the reader. Moreover, Rieux has special authority within the context of the plot insofar as he is the head physician and coordinator of health services in Oran.

18. Eubanks and Petrakis, "Reconstructing the World," 310.

19. Albert Camus, *The Plague,* trans. Stuart Gilbert (New York: Random House, 1972), 3.

20. Ibid., 3, 14, 22, 169.

21. Ibid., 35, 35, 86, 15, 15, 67, 10.

22. Ibid., 161, 121, 120.

23. Importantly, this sense of the proper order of things is a sense that existentialists such as Camus argue may not actually be realistic or sensible from a rational standpoint.

24. Ibid., 279, 127, 118, 279, 169, 81, 86, 162.

25. Leo Tolstoy, *The Death of Ivan Ilych and Other Stories* (New York: Signet Classics, 1960), 130.

26. Camus, *The Plague,* 71, 39, 154, 27, 154.

27. Ibid., 104.

28. Ibid., 56, 287, 71, 69, 104, 27.

29. Camus, *The Rebel,* 13, 10, 10, 18, 16, 20, 291, 15, 16.

30. Eubanks and Petrakis, "Reconstructing the World," 293.

31. Cruickshank, *Literature of Revolt,* 130.

32. Camus, *The Plague,* 121.

33. Ibid., 87, 87, 90, 89, 92.

34. Ibid., 120, 202, 202, 201, 202.

35. Ibid., 206, 90, 207, 209, 212, 209, 194.

36. Camus, "An Absurd Reasoning," 50; Camus, *The Rebel,* 10.

37. Camus, *The Plague,* 203, 121.

38. One finds evidence of this in *Gran Torino* in the fact that Thao's family is religious and their religion is not subject to strong critique. When it comes to the target for criticism, both *The Plague* and *Gran Torino* set their sights more clearly on Christianity, particularly Roman Catholicism.

39. Camus, *The Plague,* 204.

40. Camus, "An Absurd Reasoning," 50.

41. Camus, *The Plague,* 94.

42. Camus, "An Absurd Reasoning," 53.

43. Camus, *The Plague,* 235, 237.

44. Ibid., 262, 263, 267, 268, 263, 268, 269, 269.

45. Ibid., 198, 199, 200.

46. Ibid., 262.

47. Camus, "An Absurd Reasoning," 5.

48. For a concise discussion of the principle of double effect, see the entry on this subject in the *Stanford Encyclopedia of Philosophy* at http://plato.stanford.edu/entries/double-effect/.

49. Camus, *The Rebel,* 14, 18, 15.

50. Camus, *The Plague,* 237.

51. Davis, "Camus's *La Peste*: Sanitation, Rats, and Messy Ethics," 1018.

52. Camus, *The Rebel,* 16; Cruickshank, *Literature of Revolt,* 98.

53. Camus, *The Rebel,* 161, 292.

Acknowledgments

The editors would like to acknowledge the support and helpful advice of the series editor, Mark Conard, who has encouraged us since he first entrusted this project to us in 2009. The assistance of Anne Dean Dotson and Bailey Johnson at the University Press of Kentucky has also been invaluable. Their prompt responses to our numerous queries are greatly appreciated.

We are grateful, too, for the hard work of all the contributors to this volume. In particular, we wish to acknowledge the patience and understanding they demonstrated in responding to our seemingly unending requests for clarifications or revisions. They were uniformly gracious and responsive in their dealings with us. The result is a volume of which we hope they will be proud.

One of the inspirations for this volume, apart from Eastwood himself, has been the annual Faith, Film, and Philosophy Seminar and Speaker Series, cosponsored since 2007 by Gonzaga University's Faith and Reason Institute and by Whitworth University's Weyerhaeuser Center for Christian Faith and Learning. The invited speakers and seminar participants over the years have helped us to clarify and develop our approach to thinking about philosophy and film, especially film as philosophy. We also thank the two universities for their ongoing support of the Institute and Center, respectively, as well as their support of the Institute's and Center's ongoing collaborative efforts. Gonzaga University has been particularly supportive in offering the editors freedom as philosophers to use and investigate film in their courses.

Finally, we wish to acknowledge our deepest debt to and our gratitude for our wives. They have been not only patient and supportive throughout the long process of bringing this work to completion, but have over the years been extraordinarily patient with and understanding of their husbands' love for movies and of their husbands' habit of frequently doing research by going to the movies. These remarkable women are truly the sine qua non of our work.

Contributors

David H. Calhoun is an associate professor at Gonzaga University in Spokane, Washington, where he has been since 1989. He teaches a wide range of philosophy courses, including a cross-disciplinary course, Christianity and Science. He has published articles and book reviews on philosophical theology, ethics, and philosophy of education. His current research and writing focuses on the implications of the Darwinian revolution for the traditional concept of human dignity. Calhoun also directs the Gonzaga Socratic Club, which promotes philosophical inquiry into the Christian worldview after the model of the Oxford Socratic Club.

Brian B. Clayton is an associate professor of philosophy and the director of the Faith and Reason Institute at Gonzaga University in Spokane, Washington. In addition to using films as "readings" in almost all of the courses he teaches, he also regularly presents conference papers that focus on film and literature in connection with philosophy. In his role as director, he is the founder of an annual national seminar on faith, film, and philosophy. In addition to his appreciation of the films of Clint Eastwood, he confesses to an interest in the 1998–2006 films of M. Night Shyamalan.

James R. Couch teaches philosophy at Keene State College in Keene, New Hampshire. He earned his Ph.D. at Southern Illinois University with an emphasis on Hannah Arendt and Hans-Georg Gadamer, and continues to explore themes involving hermeneutics, aesthetics, and political philosophy. He also has interests in ethics, aesthetics, and the history of philosophy, as well as film.

Erin E. Flynn is an associate professor of philosophy at Ohio Wesleyan University in Delaware, Ohio, specializing in nineteenth-century German philosophy. His recent articles include "Identity and Difference in Hegel's Model of Ethical Normativity" and "Intellectual Intuition in Emerson and the Early German Romantics." He is particularly interested in questions regarding freedom, responsibility, and the nature and justification of punishment, as well as in the intersection of philosophy and popular culture. He has published or presented papers on Led Zeppelin and Nietzsche, the ethics of intentional fouling in sport, and the Boston Red Sox and their "curse."

Richard Gilmore is a professor of philosophy at Concordia College in Moorhead, Minnesota. He is the author of *Philosophical Health: Wittgenstein's Method in Philosophical Investigations* (1999) and *Doing Philosophy at the Movies* (2005). He also contributed the chapter "Hitchcock and Philosophy" to *A Companion to Alfred Hitchcock* (2011).

Jason Grinnell is an assistant professor of philosophy at Buffalo State College, Buffalo, New York. His primary philosophical interests are in applied ethics, particularly bioethics and professional ethics, as well as ancient philosophy. This is his third foray into the world of popular culture and philosophy, after contributions to *The Philosophy of Joss Whedon* (2011) and *The Wire and Philosophy* (2013).

Karen D. Hoffman is an associate professor of philosophy at Hood College in Frederick, Maryland. Specializing in ethics (with a particular interest in Søren Kierkegaard), her research interests include the virtuousness of forgiveness and questions about the problem of evil and the possibility of the unforgivable. Her publications include several articles on these topics as well as essays in *The Philosophy of Stanley Kubrick* (2007), *The Philosophy of Martin Scorsese* (2007), *The Philosophy of the Coen Brothers* (2008), and *The Philosophy of Spike Lee* (2011).

Deborah Knight is an associate professor of philosophy at Queen's University, Kingston, Canada. She has published on topics including philosophy and literature, philosophy and cultural studies, *The Matrix, The Simpsons,* the horror film, Hitchcock, *Blade Runner* and *Dark City,* Scorsese's *The Age of Innocence,* the Western (with a focus on Altman's *McCabe and Mrs. Miller*), and *The Third Man.* Other recent publications focus on sentimentality, the genres of tragedy and comedy, and personal identity in relation to the philosophy of film.

Richard T. McClelland is a professor of philosophy at Gonzaga University in Spokane, Washington, where he has been since 1999. He previously taught philosophy at Seattle University, Seattle Pacific University, and the

University of Notre Dame. His main research interests lie at the intersection of contemporary neuroscience, anthropology, ethology, and empirical psychology with the philosophy of mind and moral psychology. He also has interests in the emerging field of neurocinematics.

Douglas McFarland is a professor of English and classical studies at Flagler College in St. Augustine, Florida. His many publications on film include recent essays on the Coen brothers, John Frankenheimer, and Steven Soderbergh. He is currently editing a collection of essays on the adaptations of John Huston.

George McKnight is an emeritus professor of film studies in the School for Studies in Art and Culture at Carleton University, Ottawa, Canada. He is the editor of *Agent of Challenge and Defiance: Films of Ken Loach.* Besides his research interests in British cinema and the film industry, he has published on Hitchcock, suspense, *CSI,* the philosophy of horror, the Western, and *Memento.*

Jennifer L. McMahon is a professor of philosophy and humanities and chair of the Department of English and Languages at East Central University in Ada, Oklahoma. McMahon has expertise in existentialism, aesthetics, and comparative philosophy. She has published numerous essays on philosophy and popular culture in volumes including *Seinfeld and Philosophy* (2000), *The Matrix and Philosophy* (2002), *The Philosophy of Martin Scorsese* (2007), *The Philosophy of Science Fiction Film* (2007), and *House and Philosophy* (2009). She coedited *The Philosophy of the Western* (2010) with B. Steve Csaki, and is currently editing *The Philosophy of Tim Burton* (forthcoming).

Index

The Philosophy of Popular Culture

The books published in the Philosophy of Popular Culture series will illuminate and explore philosophical themes and ideas that occur in popular culture. The goal of this series is to demonstrate how philosophical inquiry has been reinvigorated by increased scholarly interest in the intersection of popular culture and philosophy, as well as to explore through philosophical analysis beloved modes of entertainment, such as movies, TV shows, and music. Philosophical concepts will be made accessible to the general reader through examples in popular culture. This series seeks to publish both established and emerging scholars who will engage a major area of popular culture for philosophical interpretation and examine the philosophical underpinnings of its themes. Eschewing ephemeral trends of philosophical and cultural theory, authors will establish and elaborate on connections between traditional philosophical ideas from important thinkers and the ever-expanding world of popular culture.

Series Editor

Mark T. Conard, Marymount Manhattan College, NY

Books in the Series

The Philosophy of Stanley Kubrick, edited by Jerold J. Abrams

The Philosophy of Ang Lee, edited by Robert Arp, Adam Barkman, and James McRae

Football and Philosophy, edited by Michael W. Austin

Tennis and Philosophy, edited by David Baggett

The Philosophy of Film Noir, edited by Mark T. Conard

The Philosophy of Martin Scorsese, edited by Mark T. Conard

The Philosophy of Neo-Noir, edited by Mark T. Conard

The Philosophy of Spike Lee, edited by Mark T. Conard

The Philosophy of the Coen Brothers, edited by Mark T. Conard

The Philosophy of David Lynch, edited by William J. Devlin and Shai Biderman

The Philosophy of the Beats, edited by Sharin N. Elkholy

The Philosophy of Horror, edited by Thomas Fahy

The Philosophy of The X-Files, edited by Dean A. Kowalski

Steven Spielberg and Philosophy, edited by Dean A. Kowalski

The Philosophy of Joss Whedon, edited by Dean A. Kowalski and S. Evan Kreider

The Philosophy of Charlie Kaufman, edited by David LaRocca

The Philosophy of Clint Eastwood, edited by Richard T. McClelland and Brian B. Clayton

The Philosophy of the Western, edited by Jennifer L. McMahon and B. Steve Csaki

The Philosophy of Steven Soderbergh, edited by R. Barton Palmer and Steven M. Sanders

The Olympics and Philosophy, edited by Heather L. Reid and Michael W. Austin

The Philosophy of David Cronenberg, edited by Simon Riches

The Philosophy of Science Fiction Film, edited by Steven M. Sanders

The Philosophy of TV Noir, edited by Steven M. Sanders and Aeon J. Skoble

The Philosophy of Sherlock Holmes, edited by Philip Tallon and David Baggett

Basketball and Philosophy, edited by Jerry L. Walls and Gregory Bassham

Golf and Philosophy, edited by Andy Wible